EBURY PRESS
HIDDEN LINKS

Sangeeth Varghese is a globally acknowledged leadership thinker from Harvard and London School of Economics. He is a personal advisor to heads of states and has consulted for nations from Asia and Africa. He is the president of one of the largest European international institutions and a Young Global Leader of the World Economic Forum. Varghese is the author of *Open-Source Leader: The Future of Organizations and Leadership* (Penguin India 2010) and *Future Intelligence* (Springer Germany 2023).

Zac Sangeeth is one of the world's youngest historians. He is the author of *World History in 3 Points* (Hachette India, 2022) and *More World History in 3 Points* (Hachette India 2022), now translated into more than ten languages. He is a SCM Youth Fellow and a winner of the India Reading Olympiad. As a public speaker, he has spoken at forums such as the Global Shapers of the World Economic Forum.

Celebrating 35 Years of
Penguin Random House India

HIDDEN LINKS

How Random Historical Events
Shaped Our World

SANGEETH VARGHESE
& ZAC SANGEETH

EBURY
PRESS

An imprint of Penguin Random House

EBURY PRESS

USA | Canada | UK | Ireland | Australia
New Zealand | India | South Africa | China | Singapore

Ebury Press is part of the Penguin Random House group of companies
whose addresses can be found at global.penguinrandomhouse.com

Published by Penguin Random House India Pvt. Ltd
4th Floor, Capital Tower 1, MG Road,
Gurugram 122 002, Haryana, India

First published in Ebury Press by Penguin Random House India in 2023

Front cover photograph (bottom): Iranian women holding a banner that reads
'Women, Life, Freedom' at the historical birthplace of democracy, potesting the
killing of the twenty-two-year-old Mahsa Amini by the notorious morality
police for an alleged breach of their strict dress code for women

The views and opinions expressed in this book are the authors' own and the facts
are as reported by them which have been verified to the extent possible, and the
publishers are not in any way liable for the same.

ISBN 9780143460237

Typeset in Bembo standard by Manipal Technologies Limited, Manipal
Printed at Gopsons Papers Pvt. Ltd., Noida.

www.penguin.co.in

To Annu, our favourite

Contents

Introduction: Unknotting the Hidden Historical Connections That Built Our World

An Evening Walk Filled with Patterns

As Zac was authoring his first book, *World History in 3 Points*, a book summarizing major personalities and events of the past, he followed a unique modus operandi. First, he immersed himself in a topic that he was planning to write. Then, as we stepped out for our evening walk, he spoke about this topic threadbare. As a student of history, Zac looked at these events in silos, but being a strategy planning professional, I surveyed for patterns and trends in whatever data I was exposed to. As Zac discussed topics that had inherently no connection to one another—events separated by time, people divided by space—I innately sensed there were links running throughout. There were some uncanny connections between them—an event that happened in Bronze-age Eurasian Steppes was connected by an invisible thread to current happenings in India. It was there. But it was not obvious.

Once we started to realize these hidden patterns, we started to actively seek them out. As and when Zac brought up a topic, we tried figuring out how this was connected to topics that were discussed earlier. Did any past events have an impact on the one being discussed? Could it be the cause or effect of another, distant theme? We soon started forming our own hypotheses; then, to satisfy our intellectual curiosities, we took a path less travelled, trying to figure out ways to string these together.

Investigating the Barns of History for Clues

However, I soon realized that linking topics in history was not as simple as it was in strategy planning. Because in a corporate environment, there were a lot of givens, such as access to immense amounts of data revealing multiple perspectives, and availability of software that could help make sense of it all. In contrast, history is plagued by a scarcity of data, and at times, faced the challenge of a complete lack of it. Hence, instead of working like data scientists who had the luxury of having all the required resources, we decided to function like investigative detectives who form hypotheses, search for clues and then piece them together to arrive at a definitive conclusion. We adopted a multi-pronged strategy as we embarked on our journey to find needles in age-old barns. First, we looked for data that might prove or disprove our hypotheses. We discussed broad topics, seemingly unconnected, to figure out if there was anything at all that even remotely connected them. If there were no links emerging, we quickly abandoned them to look elsewhere. However, we often found surprising patterns in random, unexpected areas that gave us results quite different than what we expected. Then, if there was no data available at all, we wore our detective hats, and took leaps of faith into the unknown. Like Sherlock Holmes suggested in *The Sign of Four*, we eliminated the impossible, ascertained what remained and then worked towards connecting the dots.

Random but Connected

Initially, we drew up a series of topics to start with. We selected themes that were interesting but diverse, such as the Silk Road, women empowerment, the Mahabharata and the Roman Empire. Each topic was explored in such a way that we would be able to string together a series of seemingly random, unconnected events. However, as we began our writing process, we quickly realized that these connections were not limited to within topics but spread even between them. Most importantly, we stumbled across one particular era, which we referred to as the Fountainhead epoch, which connected a majority of the subjects that we covered, be it the Mahabharata or women's empowerment. Hence, in the entire book, if there is one mother link to which everything else is anchored to, it is this Fountainhead epoch. With this rationale in mind, we also decided to present that as the first chapter.

The Biggest Surprise of Recurring Climate Changes

History can sometimes be way too confusing. At least, for me, it was—with too many events, dates and nuances. So, I adopted a method from my strategy planning experience—representing things in a data centric, visual and linear fashion. Eventually, we discovered that this one step provided us with an enormous amount of clarity, especially when we dealt with topics with many linkages. It helped us simplify complexities, identify causes and effects, and separate out false causations.

However, the biggest surprise was when we discovered multiple events of climate change running across history, tying together many catastrophes that we otherwise did not attribute it to— fall of empires, spread of pandemics, decline in trade, swelling mass migrations, eruption of wars, surge in social upheavals, disruption in economies, and most importantly, a decline in levels of women's freedom. Hence we would not be surprised if our readers found this book to be a series thread linking climate change events to other major historical incidents.

Linking History into Threads

As students of history, our goal is to make the subject engaging, especially for younger people whose reading habits are different from ours. Belonging to this younger age group, Zac suggested that short text and visual content would be more appealing to them. Hence, in this book, we departed from the conventional way of non-fiction book writing. We used shorter paragraphs, simpler words and a headline for each paragraph with an overview of the storyline, in case they did not want to delve too deeply. But, most importantly, we feel the appeal of this book lies in the investigative thread that runs through the book— unravelling one layer at a time like an onion getting peeled.

Every Para Is a Stand-Alone Information Point

In a majority of books, every paragraph would have to be read in conjunction to the others for it to make any sense. Of course, in our book too this is the case, where the big picture can be arrived at only if all the paragraphs are seen in their totality. However, we have also taken immense efforts to ensure that there is a certain amount of 'stand-aloneness' built into each paragraph. Hence even if you choose to pick out a random paragraph to read, it would still make sense; it would still present before you an interesting bit of information without having to read anything else from the book. Of course, we are hoping that this in itself would pique your interest to keep reading further and finding more—on how our futures are intertwined with several seemingly random, unconnected events and lives.

Hidden Randomness in Our History: Stranger than Fiction

'History is infinitely stranger than anything which the mind of man could invent. The queer things which are going on, the strange coincidences, the cross-purposes, the wonderful chains of events, working through generations, and leading to the most outré results, it would make all fiction with its conventionalities and foreseen conclusions most stale and unprofitable.'

An adaptation from Arthur Conan Doyle's *The Complete Adventures of Sherlock Holmes.*

Hope you enjoy unravelling the hidden links.

Sangeeth Varghese

1

The Unbelievable Story of How a Climate Change Wiped Clean and Reset Our World

Keywords: Climate Change, Pandemic, Steppe Migrations, Ancient Civilization, Global Collapse, Fountainhead Epoch, Universal Religions, Geographical Transformation, Political Disruption, Modern Education, World's First Cerebral Army

Evolution of Human Society

Modern humans evolved around 3,00,000 years ago in Africa and lived as hunter-gatherers for the next tens of thousands of years. The advent of agriculture around 10,000 to 15,000 years ago led to a sea change in the way humans survived. A nomadic lifestyle soon made way for permanent settlements. Pastoralism emerged with the domestication of livestock. Around the eighth millennium BCE, civilizations started to develop across the world, such as the Sumerian, Egyptian, Indian and Chinese civilizations. Humanity progressed from an ancient Stone Age to the Bronze Age, Iron Age, Age of Empires, Classical Antiquity and then finally to the modern age.

FOUNTAINHEAD EPOCH: A TIMELINE

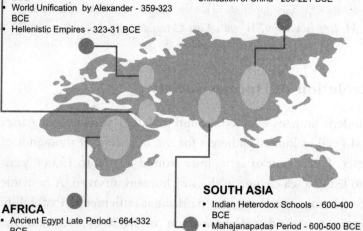

5000 BCE   -> Humans Settle Down

3300-1200 BCE   -> Bronze Age

1200-500 BCE   -> Iron Age

600-300 BCE   -> Fountainhead Epoch

NEAR EAST
- Zoroastrian Philosophy - ~600 BCE
- Babylonian Exile of Jews - 597-538 BCE
- Near East Unification by Achaemenid - 550-330 BCE
- Jews under Achaemenid - 539-332 BCE
- Hellenistic Seleucid Empire - 312-141 BCE

EUROPE
- Roman Republic - 509-27 BCE
- Greek Classical Age - 508-336 BCE
- Socrates, Plato and Aristotle - 469-322 BCE
- World Unification by Alexander - 359-323 BCE
- Hellenistic Empires - 323-31 BCE

CHINA
- Spring and Autumn Period - 770-476 BCE
- Hundred Schools of Thought - 770-221 BCE
- Warring States Period - 476-221 BCE
- Unification of China - 230-221 BCE

AFRICA
- Ancient Egypt Late Period - 664-332 BCE
- Rise Of Carthage - 600-146 BCE
- Hellenistic Egypt - 332-30 BCE

SOUTH ASIA
- Indian Heterodox Schools - 600-400 BCE
- Mahajanapadas Period - 600-500 BCE
- Indian Unification by Magadha - 500-350 BCE

A Capsule Age

From the beginning until now, we humans saw a vast change in the way we lived, interrelated with each other and interacted with the world around us. We progressed from handmade tools to sophisticated technology, developed simple thoughts into deep philosophies, while our easily manageable social structures grew into complex democratic structures. However, interestingly, the foundation of all the progress that we made as a species during the last 300,000 years was made in a short span of 300 years, i.e., in 0.1 per cent of the time that our species has lived on earth. If we observe closely, these three centuries from 600 to 300 BCE formed the Fountainhead epoch from which sprouted whatever progress we made earlier and whatever we achieved later until now.

The Fountainhead Epoch: 0.1 Per Cent Time, 100 Per Cent Progress

This Fountainhead epoch of 300 years saw great progress that was handed down to future generations, including the development of organized religions and monotheism. This period also saw the reformation of Hinduism and Judaism, giving them their current shape, and sowed the seeds for Christianity and Islam. It laid the foundations of philosophy and social equality across the world—in China, India, the Middle East and Europe. Concepts of unified China, India, Persia and Greece emerged during this time. This era also gave rise to modern education, civil service and political structures. In this short span of three centuries, subjects such as history, strategy, statecraft, science, mathematics, medicine, engineering, architecture, economics and geography were founded. Concepts that we now take for granted, like the courier system, banking system and global trade network, were established.

Fountainhead Epoch of Universal Religions

Many of the religions that have withstood the test of time—either originated or took inspiration during the Fountainhead epoch of 600 BCE to 300 BCE. The religions that were founded during this period included Zoroastrianism, Confucianism, Taoism, Buddhism and Jainism. During the same period, Hinduism and Judaism faced their defining moments and underwent transformations. The Jewish reformation then provided the fodder for the latter age religions of Christianity and Islam. This age marked such a significant transition in human cultural history that the German philosopher Karl Jaspers referred to it as the Axial Age—a period in which universalizing streams of thought appeared in Persia, India, China and the Middle East, which eventually had a profound influence on future philosophies and religions.

Sprouting of Monotheism

Zoroastrianism gained popularity by professing one God against the ancient polytheistic practices of the nomadic Persians. Once the Achaemenid Empire, which dominated the world between 600 to 300 BCE, adopted it, their philosophical thoughts rose to prominence. Meanwhile, the Jews, who followed their own form of monotheism, were in captivity in Babylon starting from 597 BCE. When the region was conquered by the Achaemenid empire in 539 BCE, Jews were released, and hence were influenced by the benevolence of Emperor Cyrus. So much so that the beliefs of an until then impermeable Judaism underwent a profound change. Judaism adopted

Zoroastrian beliefs of heaven and hell, afterlife, messianism and the final judgement. Though Christianity and Islam—rooted in monotheistic beliefs—took shape many centuries after the Fountainhead epoch, they both adopted several of these Zoroastrian philosophies from their parent Judaism. Christianity anchored themselves in the messianic redemption and universal saviour, while Islam adopted various Zoroastrian beliefs including praying five times following the Sun's movement, ritual purification, a belief in angels, heaven and hell, resurrection of the dead and a final judgement. Currently, monotheism, which counts at least six out of every ten people among their adherents, had its core beliefs shaped during the Fountainhead epoch.

The Emergence of Modern Hinduism, Buddhism and Jainism

The period between 600 BCE and 300 BCE was a defining moment for ancient Hinduism, as their Brahminic supremacy and excessive ritual reliance came under intense pressure, forcing them into a reassessment of their practices and beliefs. During this period, the prominence of Vedic gods declined, while the deities of Shiva and Vishnu rose in importance. Fire sacrifice, one of the central pillars of Vedic Hinduism, dwindled in comparison to devotional worship of the deities. The Fountainhead epoch also witnessed the composition of important religious texts like the Dharma Sutras and Shastras as well as the two epics, the Ramayana and the Mahabharata. The same period saw the rise of its two challengers—Buddhism and Jainism. Once these religions were adopted by the Mauryan Empire, one of the first to unify the Indian subcontinent, it spread across the world—primarily in South Asia, Southeast Asia, Central Asia, China, Korea and Japan—through conquests, trade routes and missionary activities. These religions laid the foundations for many important things, including the co-creation of educational institutions alongside monasteries—which at a later date was adopted by Christianity.

Confucianism and Taoism: Innovation of Diffused Religions

Between 551 BCE and 479 BCE, during a period of political upheaval in China, when the authority of the ruling Zhou dynasty was being challenged, Confucius emerged with a goal to arrest this moral decline. In China, Confucianism created an innovative religious format—referred to by sociologists as a 'Diffused Religion', where its institutions were not temples but those already existing in society, like the family, school and government. Its authorities were not priests, but parents, teachers and officials. Confucius created a religion that merged seamlessly with its social fabric, influencing not only spirituality but also administration, commerce, science, education and arts.

Meanwhile, Lao Tzu, a contemporary of Confucius, wrote the *Tao Te Ching*, which became the central theme of a new religion called Taoism. Though different from the rigidity of Confucian individual morality, Taoism had had its own great influence on our world, particularly in medicine and science. Taoists were among the first to develop the principles of macrobiotic cooking, healthy diets, systems of gymnastics and massages. The earliest surviving medical book, the *Huangdi Neijing*, composed in 300 BCE, continues to remain the fundamental doctrinal source for Chinese medicine. Formed during the Fountainhead epoch, such was the impact of Confucianism and Taoism that even after almost 2500 years they continue to have a deep influence on the Chinese culture.

Fountainhead Epoch of Philosophy

Philosophy is the process of unravelling wisdom by seeking fundamental truths of life by questioning, answering and debating. Though humanity always engaged in such a pursuit, the systematic academic branch was developed during the Fountainhead epoch of 600 BCE to 300 BCE. Interestingly, this development was not limited to any particular part of the world but spread across the globe including Greece, India, the Middle East and China. Greek philosophy which developed during this Fountainhead epoch laid the foundations of much of the Western civilization, through its influence on Hellenism, Roman philosophy, Islamic philosophy, Medieval Scholasticism, European Renaissance and the Age of Enlightenment. Meanwhile, the philosophies which took root elsewhere during the same period set into motion the wheels of change, providing humanity a bridge to transition from an ancient primitive world to the modern era.

From Ancient Mythmaking to Pre-Socratic Rational Explanations

Before 600 BCE, the Greek thinkers explained the world around them through supernatural myths, imaginary gods and heroes. Events and happenings were explained until then through the lens of emotions and senses rather than reason. However, an increase in trade and travel between Egyptian and Mesopotamian cultures enabled the imbibing and blending of new ideas. They started to ask more profound questions and looked out for more logical explanations in an era that lasted for almost 150 years until 469 BCE, known as the Pre-Socratic Age. The Ionian school was the most famous among these, where its founder Thales of Miletus attempted to find universal principles to explain questions like the origin of the world, and occurrence of natural phenomena like earthquakes. Pre-Socratic philosophers are now regarded amongst the first philosophers in the Western world, with a direct influence on Plato, Aristotle and classical antiquity.

The Socratic Age of Western Philosophical Underpinnings

Greek philosophy reached its pinnacle during the period between 450 BCE and 300 BCE. Socrates, who lived from 470 to 399 BCE, made the biggest contribution to the modern world as he reflected on important ethical questions like the meaning of virtue and justice. The Socratic method, now used as a base for teaching in even the most famous universities including Harvard and Chicago, was formulated through an active question-and-answer format, often moderated by an expert. Socrates played a role in reforming the education system, which was, until then, compartmentalized based on social function.

Plato, his disciple, introduced the idea of engaging deeply with a class of entities which he referred to as forms, which included justice, beauty and equality. Division of labour, a concept introduced by Adam Smith, the father of Economics, and which later became the cornerstone of the Industrial Revolution, was initially propounded by Plato. His book *The Republic* continues to be a master template for modern societies. Aristotle, a disciple of Plato, made significant and lasting contributions to almost every aspect of human knowledge, including philosophy, politics, psychology, metaphysics, ethics, logic, rhetoric, mathematics and even theatre. Aristotelian ethics, best known as Nicomachean ethics, outlined the social and behavioural virtues of an ideal man. Apart from these three great philosophers, the other schools of philosophy that arose during the Fountainhead epoch included Stoicism, another building block of Western philosophy, Hedonism, which enabled development of political philosophies like the social contract theory, and Scepticism, that laid the foundation for future philosophers like Michel de Montaigne, Rene Descartes and David Hume.

A Hundred Schools of Thought Bloomed in China

The Fountainhead epoch was a period of great churn in China. With the decline of the Zhou dynasty, it moved towards a land-based feudal society, resulting in several deep changes. Sensing an opportunity, several Zhou government officials who had lost their authority, strived to re-establish their legitimacy as teachers and philosophers. Some of them founded their own schools of philosophy. They included Mohism, whose central philosophy was that all are equal before heaven, hence people should practise collective love in all spheres. Meanwhile, Legalism was based on the hypothesis that people would remain selfish, and hence the state should deploy an iron hand, controlling them through strict laws and punishments to bring them to order. Legalism changed the future of China, as the Qin dynasty used their militarily strong centralized principle to unite the warring Chinese states for the first time in history. Centuries later, Legalism again made a comeback when Mao Zedong, chairman of the Chinese Communist Party, championed its ideals, thereby rejecting the more benevolent and feudal ideas of Confucianism.

Futuristic Idea of Opposing Forces from Persia

Owing to the global domination of Persia between 600 and 300 BCE, philosophical constructs of Zoroastrianism gained significant importance. Unlike the earlier concept that humanity is helplessly dependent on the fate ascribed to them by the gods, Zoroaster preached the concept of free will, where humans have the freedom to choose which side they are on, with far-reaching consequences. If people chose good and truth, they would live forever, enjoying paradise, while the choice of evil and darkness would drag them down to hell fire. Zoroaster's teachings introduced to the world the futuristic concepts of the opposing forces of good and evil, heaven and hell, and angels and demons.

Five Philosophical Schools from India

During the Fountainhead epoch, in South Asia, primarily in India, the five heterodox schools of philosophy emerged—that provided the future template for almost all thoughts that came henceforth. The Nirgrantha School of Jainism proposed ethical behaviour and extreme asceticism, as all living souls undergo the cycle of rebirth through karma—their actions and consequences. Buddhism took the middle path of moderation, where they regarded extreme austerity and indulgence as useless. The Ajivika school, founded during the same time, took an opposite stand, propounding a fatalistic philosophy that everything in life is predestined by the cosmic forces leaving nothing to free will. They rejected the principle of karma adhered to by Hinduism, Jainism and Buddhism, leaving everything to fate than to any religious or ethical practices. The Charvaka School went a step further and not only rejected karma and rebirth but all logic and reasoning, advocating pure spontaneity and hedonism. The Ajnana School, meanwhile, proposed that it was impossible to know the real truth, hence it was a useless pursuit. When inequality was the order of the day and social classifications were rigid, these schools challenged the dogmas, took exception to the privileges offered to certain classes and ensured that religion became easily accessible to the masses.

Fountainhead Epoch of Territorial Transformation

FAMILY FARMS TO UNIVERSAL MONARCH

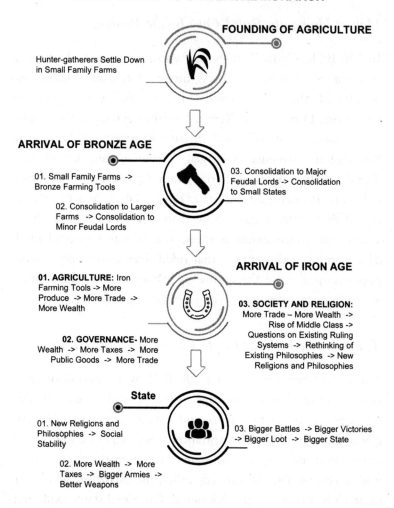

FOUNDING OF AGRICULTURE

Hunter-gatherers Settle Down in Small Family Farms

ARRIVAL OF BRONZE AGE

01. Small Family Farms -> Bronze Farming Tools

02. Consolidation to Larger Farms -> Consolidation to Minor Feudal Lords

03. Consolidation to Major Feudal Lords -> Consolidation to Small States

ARRIVAL OF IRON AGE

01. AGRICULTURE: Iron Farming Tools -> More Produce -> More Trade -> More Wealth

02. GOVERNANCE- More Wealth -> More Taxes -> More Public Goods -> More Trade

03. SOCIETY AND RELIGION: More Trade – More Wealth -> Rise of Middle Class -> Questions on Existing Ruling Systems -> Rethinking of Existing Philosophies -> New Religions and Philosophies

State

01. New Religions and Philosophies -> Social Stability

02. More Wealth -> More Taxes -> Bigger Armies -> Better Weapons

03. Bigger Battles -> Bigger Victories -> Bigger Loot -> Bigger State

Across geographies, the Fountainhead epoch was a period of great churn. From ancient nomadic societies, humans started to settle down. The earlier, smaller kingdoms expanded in scope, consolidating themselves into larger empires in the backdrop of global conquests. And this led to a larger transition in China, India, Europe and the Middle East.

Half of Humanity Ruled Over by the Persians

In 550 BCE, Cyrus II of Persia, who later came to be known as Cyrus the Great, overthrew his overlords, the Medes, and established the Achaemenid Empire. Following him, his successors, Darius I and Xerxes I further extended the empire to include most of modern-day Kyrgyzstan, Azerbaijan, Kazakhstan, Armenia, Georgia, Turkmenistan, Uzbekistan, Tajikistan, Iraq, Kuwait, Syria, Saudi Arabia, Palestine, Israel, Lebanon, Pakistan, Afghanistan, Egypt, Libya, and Greece. It is said that, at its height, more than a half of humanity lived within the Achaemenid borders, which was unprecedented. The vastness of this empire that ruled over a culturally diverse population changed the course of history in terms of politics, governance and the way people looked at geography.

Transition from Feudalism to a Unified Chinese Empire

The period between 600 and 300 BCE was a period of great change in the Chinese landscape. A few centuries preceding this was a period of relative peace and stability under the Western Zhou dynasty. Their administration was feudal in nature, with an overlord and several vassal states. However, the Zhou capital was sacked by a set of nomads called the Xianyun, who later came to be known as the Xiongnu. The vassal states exploited the resultant power vacuum and started to amass power. This period, known as the Spring and Autumn period, resulted in a change of political structure. Eventually, the smaller vassals were annexed, and the geography was dominated by a few large overlords. With the advent of the Iron age, weapons such as swords and crossbows made warfare deadlier, resulting in an era called the Warring States Period – when seven larger states rose to prominence—the Qi, the Chu, the Yan, the Han, the Zhao, the Wei and the Qin. The Qin had an advantage as they were able to produce lethal eighteen feet-long pikes. They centralized power and took over the neighbouring states, eventually uniting all of China under a single banner. Politically and geographically, this was a watershed moment for China—developing a centralized and unified mindset under the Qin dynasty.

Semi-Nomads to a Unified India

Even in the history of India, the period between 600 to 300 BCE was a major turning point, providing paving blocks for the future. This was the period of the second urbanization in the subcontinent, the first one being the Indus Valley Civilization. During the early part of this 300-year period, the semi-nomadic tribes of the late Vedic period settled down in territorial communities, owing to the growth of agriculture. Eventually, a highly organized political structure called 'Janas' started to develop, and later, through further consolidation, sixteen bigger kingdoms called the Mahajanapadas took shape. In due course, the kingdom of Magadha emerged as the predominant power. In 323 BCE a young rebel, Chandragupta Maurya, toppled the mighty Magadha, and then further consolidated his empire through the Seleucid-Mauryan War. By around 300 BCE, the Mauryan Empire emerged as the first and the biggest empire that united almost all of the Indian subcontinent. The Magadha and Mauryan Empires between 600 to 300 BCE changed the scattered political and geographical landscape of India forever.

Fountainhead Epoch of Political and Social Innovations

As territorially the world moved from smaller kingdoms to larger empires that spanned multiple continents, the world of intertwined politics underwent its own set of changes. Many of the revolutionary political tools of our modern age, including democracy, republic, bureaucracy and administrative systems, took shape during the Fountainhead epoch. Simultaneously, the societies underwent a transformation, which would then form the backbone of our modern systems.

Political Disruption through Democracy and Republic

The two biggest political innovations that have had the maximum impact on humanity's future might be the ideas of democracy and republic. Incidentally, they both developed at exactly the same period—early 500 BCE. Democracy was put into practice by Cleisthenes, an Athenian lawmaker who broke up the unlimited power of aristocracy by classifying the citizens into groups based on their demographics rather than wealth. The Athenians practised a direct form of democracy, where any citizen could stand for elections, then subjected to a voting by all eligible citizens. During the same period, the Roman kingdom, comprised of settlements around the Palatine Hill along the river Tiber, was going through its own period of churn. Under their king Servius Tullius, a new constitution that divided the population into five economic classes was drawn upon, enabling them to be part of an election process. However, as the next king Tarquinius Superbus turned out to be a violent autocrat, he was overthrown and the Roman Republic, with public representation of the Roman people, was instituted. The Greek and Roman models of governance continue to not only inspire political thinkers, but also to be imitated in spirit and form by nations across the world.

Decentralized Administrative System and Meritocratic Civil Services

The Persian Achaemenids, in order to rule over their vast empire, introduced an array of governance systems that continue to influence our modern world. The most important among them was the Satrapy, a decentralized system, where the empire was divided into small areas, with complete freedom to govern given to a set of *satraps*. This complex system of administration was then adopted by Alexander the Great as he established his empire and then by his successors, especially the Seleucid Empire. From there, it was adopted by the rulers of the Indian subcontinent, including the Sakas and Kushans. Meanwhile, in China, Confucian teachings gave them a template for creation of a civil service examination. Devoid of any favouritism, this meritocratic method of selecting the administrative officials provided continuity to the state despite regime changes. It has now been adopted as a model for civil service systems in many other Asian and Western countries.

Founding of Strategy and Statecraft

Between 544 and 496 BCE in China, Sun Tzu, wrote the *Art of War*, lessons of which was used by Qin dynasty emperor Shi

Huangdi to conquer warring states and create the first unified China. In the twentieth century, Chinese Communist Party leader Mao Zedong credited the *Art of War* for his victory over his rival. Outside China, it has influenced both West and East Asian war tactics and military thinking through the ages, so much so that it remains a recommended reading for all the United States military intelligence personnel. Meanwhile, around 350 BCE, in neighbouring India arose a master strategist and philosopher Chanakya, who authored the ancient political treatise of the *Arthashastra*, laying down the foundations of political science and economics. This seminal work helped Chandragupta Maurya consolidate his empire that united almost all of South Asia—and continues to have an influence across the world.

A Template for Human Rights and Global Diplomacy

After the invasion of Babylon 539 BCE, under the orders of Cyrus the Great, a cylinder was created on which a treatise was written in Akkadian cuneiform script. This cylinder was an embodiment of an innovative state model based on diversity and tolerance of different cultures and religions. Quite contrary to the times, which typically imposed the victor's culture on the conquered. The Cyrus Cylinder is now considered as the first bill of human rights, even gaining a great appeal among the political thinkers during the Age of Enlightenment in the eighteenth-century CE. The modern events that have been inspired by the cylinder include the Balfour Declaration, and the Universal Declaration of the Human Rights of the United Nations Organization. Meanwhile, as Zoroastrianism, Buddhism and Jainism developed as the first missionary-based religions in the world, they catalysed the development of global diplomatic ties alongside religious propagation. This strategy, which initially took root during the Fountainhead epoch, was later adopted by religions including Christianity and Islam, as well as imperial aspirants like Portugal, Spain and the British in order to establish intercontinental relations and to shape political and social structures across the world.

Global Trade Network Established the Connected World

The Achaemenid Empire has, to its credit, the advancement of the global trading systems by establishing the Persian Royal Road network. After inheriting an old trade road from Central Asia, the Achaemenids expanded this into a complex network that spanned across their empire—using a new road-building technology that they had invented. It was more than 1700 miles long, interspaced with trading posts and rest houses. The Persian Royal Road was further expanded by Alexander the Great. A few centuries later, it was connected to China by the Han Emperor Wu Ti and called it the Silk Road, making it not just an arterial trading network, but also creating a disproportionate impact on the world by spreading innovations such as paper, printing press and gunpowder. Meanwhile, the maritime trade was positively influenced, as Emperor Darius initiated a canal to connect Egypt to the Persian empire. To commemorate the opening of this waterway between the Nile and the Great Bitter Lake—a large saltwater lake, now part of the Suez Canal—he erected five monuments.

Establishment of Private Banking and Courier Systems

During the period between 600 to 482 BCE in ancient Babylon, the house of Eglibi established the first private banking system known in the world. They acted as middlemen between the producer and the consumer, where financial, storage and transport facilities were offered to the rural farmers to supply their goods like barley, dates and wool to markets, temples and palaces. The Eglibis acted as pawn brokers, accepted deposits, provided loans, serviced debts, financed trade and even founded commercial companies.

The Achaemenid Empire also laid the foundations of the modern postal and courier systems by establishing messenger posts across a wide network of roads they had built. These were meticulously placed at intervals equalling a day's ride on the Persian Royal Road. In these posts, there were restrooms, horses, caravans and messengers, so that the next one could pick it up from where it was left off, modelled like a relay. It was said that messages could travel the entire length of the road, more than 1700 miles, in one week. This led the Greek historian Herodotus to marvel, 'Nothing can travel as fast as the Persian messengers.' The Achaemenid system was then adopted and improvised to establish the modern postal and courier systems across the world.

Fountainhead Epoch of Modern Education

Foundations of modern education were simultaneously laid in different parts of the world during these 300 years. In Europe, Plato established the Academy—where a range of subjects were taught by experts, similar to the modern university system. In China, though education was until then reserved for the wealthy, Confucius overhauled it by making it a tool for maintaining harmony and unity in the society. He opened up the system to teach ethics, good behaviour and moral character to all. Meanwhile, in South Asia, great institutions of education like Nalanda and Taxila were established around Buddhist monasteries. These academic centres used the languages of the masses and new technologies like palm leaf manuscripts—enabling the democratisation of knowledge. During the Fountainhead epoch, almost every subject known to mankind today, including the sciences, social sciences and humanities, was founded.

Founding of Science, Mathematics and Medicine

The foundation of modern science was laid during the period between 600 to 300 BCE. During this time, especially in early Greece, there was a move towards understanding nature in a more logical fashion, thereby setting in motion the earliest form of rational theoretical science. Aristotle, referred to as the founder of modern science, developed his inductive-deductive methodology, leading to the modern scientific method. Aristotle studied animals while Theophrastus, his partner, researched plant life—thereby establishing the science of biology. Meanwhile, Leucippus, and then Democritus, both pre-Socratic philosophers from Greece, developed the theory of atomism—that everything in the universe is made up of fundamental indivisible and imperishable components called atoms, which centuries later was proved by the great chemist John Dalton.

Pythagoras, born in 570 BCE in ancient Greece, a great influence on scientists like Copernicus, Kepler and Isaac Newton, laid the foundation for modern mathematics, with his Pythagorean theorem and the Theory of Proportions. Euclid, who came around 300 BCE, was another Greek mathematician, now considered the father of geometry and among of the most influential of mathematicians. Hippocrates of Kos, born in 460 BCE, who is known as the father of medicine, revolutionized the medical field with his practices of prognosis, clinical observation, systematic documentation and categorisation of diseases.

Founding of Engineering and Architecture

Though the Iron age arrived much earlier in many parts of the world (except in the case of Northern Europe, when it arrived in the fifth century BCE), the real understanding of the metal's uses was realized and spread during the time period between 600 to 300 BCE. Hence, this period again emerged as foundational for engineering. Cast iron farm tools and equipment started to be made in China during the fifth century BCE, and became widespread in use from the third century onwards. As the technology spread to other parts of the world, it helped in making important breakthroughs in agriculture and warfare— as more efficient tools and weapons could now be made. This enabled further engineering innovations to improve agriculture, which included hydraulics and aqueducts. In China, in the sixth century BCE, waterwheels were employed to power the bellows of blast furnaces, while the Persians under Darius the Great commenced the construction of an irrigation network of canals and dams. These innovations were picked up by scientists at a much later date to ease our lives in the modern time. Meanwhile, the architectural and structural engineering feats achieved between 600 to 300 BCE continue to inspire us even during the modern times. The Greek temple, Parthenon on the Athenian Acropolis, completed in 432 BCE, as well as many other works from this era has inspired iconic buildings like the White House, Supreme Court of the United States, as well as many temples, churches, and palaces across the globe.

Institutionalization of Time and History

Coincidentally across the world, the counting of time was institutionalized through various calendars, all developed between 600 and 300 BCE. The Mayan calendar in Mesoamerica was developed during this period, where a year was slightly longer than 365 days. The traditional Chinese calendar, meanwhile, was developed as a combination of solar and lunar calendars. The Hindu calendar, formulated by keeping a tab on the solar, lunar and planetary cycles, were mentioned in the works of several ancient Indian astronomers. In Babylonia, from 499 BCE, they started to regulate the months based on a lunisolar cycle. Now, during the present day, it is from the Babylonian calendar that we derive the concept of the year, month and day.

Meanwhile, the foundations of the systematic study of history as a subject were laid down by Herodotus who lived between 484 and 425 BCE. Known as the Father of History, he was the first writer to undertake a systematic investigation and objective narration of historical events. He gathered his data from various sources, including his extensive travels. Herodotus is also credited with enabling the subject of archaeology, classifying objects and objectively analysing their excavation sites.

Founding of Economics and Global Trade

Though the concept of money had been around for a while, the world's first coins were minted around 600 BCE by the Lydians, located in modern-day Turkey. These coins, called the Lydian Lion coins, were made of an alloy of gold and silver with a royal lion symbol engraved on them. This technology was then quickly adopted by neighbouring states such as Athens, Corinth and Persia. In China, metal coinage developed independently during the same period. They were initially spade and knife shaped, but by around 350 BCE, round ones became popular. Coinage changed the history of humanity. It expanded trade networks, accentuated commercial activities, enabled societies to grow more complex and improved social mobility.

FOUNTAINHEAD EPOCH–FOUNDATION FOR ALL HUMAN PROGRESS

FOUNDING OF RELIGIONS

- Founding of Zoroastrianism
- Transformation of Judaism
- Inspiration for Christianity and Islam
- Transformation of Hinduism
- Founding of Buddhism And Jainism
- Founding of Confucianism
- Founding of Taoism

FOUNDATIONS OF PHILOSOPHY

- Pre-Socratic Philosophy: Explaining Natural Phenomenon
- Socrates: Socratic Method, Governance, Moral Philosophy
- Plato: Forms, Division of Labour, Justice
- Aristotle: Logical Deduction, *Nicomachean Ethics*
- Stoicism, Scepticism
- One Hundred Schools of Thought in China
- Zoroastrian Philosophy
- Five Heterodox Schools of India

TERRITORIAL TRANSFORMATION

- Spring and Autumn Period in China
- Warring States Period in China: Seven Big States
- Unification of China under Qin Empire
- Second Urbanization in India
- The Emergence of Mahajanapadas in India
- Unification of India under Magadha
- Unification of World under the Achaemenid Empire

TRANSFORMATION OF POLITICS

- Founding of Democracy
- Founding of Republic
- Global Freedom and Equality
- Decentralized Administrative System
- Meritocratic Civil Services
- War Strategy And Statecraft
- Global Diplomacy

FOUNDATIONS OF MODERN SOCIETY

- Human Rights
- Global Trade Network
- Private Banking System
- Postal and Courier System

FOUNDATION OF MODERN EDUCATION SYSTEM

- Founding of Science
- Founding of Mathematics
- Founding of Medicine
- Founding of Science
- Founding of Engineering And Architecture
- Institutionalizing Time
- Founding History
- Founding Economics
- Founding Geography and Global Trade

Among All Others, Why Do Greek Values Dominate Our World?

Now, a bigger question arises. Though the other regions had their own bit of influence, why do the Greek value systems from 600 to 300 BCE exert a disproportionate influence on every part of our world even today? In fact, during the Fountainhead epoch, though there were powerful schools of philosophy across the world—such as the Hundred Schools of Thought from China, the Vedic School of Thought from India and the Zoroastrian wisdom from Persia—it was the Socratic School that gained more importance. When it came to religions, though Persia, India and the Levant produced several formidable rivals, it was the one adopted by the Greeks—Christianity—which went on to dominate the world.

Our answer might lie in one man who set out during the fag end of the Fountainhead epoch. His exploration, though lasting for less than a decade, changed the world forever and tilted the balance towards the Greeks.

Alexander: A Philosopher Warrior

From 336 to 323 BCE, Alexander the Great created the mightiest empire the world had seen until then, stretching from the Balkans to India. While he has always been portrayed as a great conqueror, this may not do full justice to his legacy. Alexander may also have been a visionary and a philosopher. His love for philosophy was instilled in him by Aristotle, his teacher, and his interactions with other learned men like Anaximenes of Lampsacus and Diogenes. Plutarch, a historian and philosopher, mentioned that Alexander always carried a copy of the *Iliad* along with him, even sleeping with it under his pillow, demonstrating his priorities clearly. Hence, his objective while setting out might not just have been just territorial conquests, but also intellectual.

In order to facilitate these twin intentions, he doled out strong incentives like promotions and higher payout to his generals to engage them in cerebral pursuits alongside their brutal carnage.

Creation of the World's First Cerebral Army

Alexander the Great's army might have been the world's first 'cerebral' army—explained by the presence of a disproportionate number of intellectuals in his already small troop of around 32,000. These people produced an incredible amount of work in a short span of time, as they marched to unknown lands. Consider the following examples. Ptolemy I Soter, a companion of Alexander from the Kingdom of Macedon who later inherited Egypt, wrote a detailed eyewitness account of Alexander's expeditions. Androsthenes of Thasons, an admiral, who was sent by Alexander to explore the coast of the Persian Gulf, wrote *The Navigation of the Indian Sea*. Aristobulus of Cassandreia, a military engineer and a close friend of Alexander, who repaired the tomb of Cyrus the Great, wrote an ethnological and geographical account, which was then referred to by Plutarch, the great historian. Using an innovative methodology of thoroughly investigating the official papers and facts, Hieronymus of Cardia, another general, wrote the history of Diadochi covering the period after the death of Alexander.

Other philosophers and intellectuals who accompanied Alexander the Great included Callisthenes of Olynthus, a nephew of Aristotle, who wrote a eulogistic account *The Deeds of Alexander*, Onesicritus, a Cynic philosopher, student of Diogenes and helmsman of Alexander, Anaximenes of Lampsacus, a rhetorician and the author of the *Rhetoric of Alexander*, and Eumenes, a satrap, who doubled as a commander and personal secretary of Alexander the Great. Alexander's philosophical bent of mind provided a bridge from the ancient world to the modern world that we live in today.

Unification of the East and West

Before Alexander the Great, the world was divided into three parts—Europe, Asia and Africa. There was little administrative level contact between each continent. But Alexander the Great's expedition marked a turning point in history, enabling a two-way exchange of information between the victors and the vanquished, resulting in a multi-ethnic, multiracial and multicultural world. The intellectuals in his army played an important part in this symbiotic cerebral exchange—of philosophy, geography, history, the natural sciences, religion, customs and traditions. After the death of Alexander the Great, the Greek empires that ruled over Asia, Africa and Europe, including the Ptolemaic dynasty in Africa, the Seleucid Empire and Greco-Bactrians in the Middle East and South Asia, and the Macedon kingdom in Europe, accentuated this Hellenization of the world. Hellenistic concepts like democracy, humanism and scientific endeavour spread to areas far from Greece, influencing us in the most profound manner to this day.

Provision of Active Tools for Globalization and Unification

The unflinching intellectual pursuit of Alexander the Great did not stop with a natural process of symbiotic exchange. He also built an institutional framework to accelerate this process. For example, he established the great city of Alexandria in Egypt, which had the biggest library of its time, containing hundreds and thousands of books. This created an incentive for the greatest scholars and intellectuals to flock to this city, creating a multiplier effect of sorts in education and employment. As more cities were built using this template, a greater number of intellectuals converged, resulting in a faster spread of ideas and views. As Alexander's empire had brought down political barriers, it accentuated trade and commerce. At a later date, Greek emerged as a common language, Hellenism a common culture, Drachma a common currency and attic, the standard of measurement. It is this unification and breaking down of barriers, initiated by Alexander the Great, that helped pave the way for the rise of the Roman Empire and the spread of Christianity, two events that have had the greatest influence on our present world.

Why Is 600 to 300 BCE the Fountainhead Epoch and Not Any Other Age?

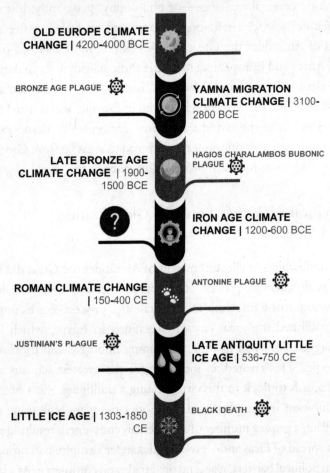

OLD EUROPE CLIMATE CHANGE | 4200-4000 BCE

BRONZE AGE PLAGUE

YAMNA MIGRATION CLIMATE CHANGE | 3100-2800 BCE

LATE BRONZE AGE CLIMATE CHANGE | 1900-1500 BCE

HAGIOS CHARALAMBOS BUBONIC PLAGUE

IRON AGE CLIMATE CHANGE | 1200-600 BCE

ROMAN CLIMATE CHANGE | 150-400 CE

ANTONINE PLAGUE

JUSTINIAN'S PLAGUE

LATE ANTIQUITY LITTLE ICE AGE | 536-750 CE

LITTLE ICE AGE | 1303-1850 CE

BLACK DEATH

Quite unfortunately, climate change is not a one-off incident. It seems to follow a recurring pattern, as if it is timed in regular intervals. Several incidents have been recorded until now from the time humans settled down, the earliest reported in 4200 BCE. Incidentally, there was one such event, the Iron Age Climate Change, between 1200 to 600 BCE, the centuries preceding the Fountainhead epoch. These six centuries of great global collapse was preceded by another period of disaster—the Late Bronze Age Climate Change—which occurred just 300 years prior to this. Together these two cataclysms brought to a grinding halt, the cultures and civilizations that had thrived earlier. The technology, architecture, culture and systems which were created until then, all ceased to exist and the world plunged into a dark age. The civilizations that collapsed during these two time periods included the Indus Valley, Sumerians, Hittites, Egyptian Middle Kingdom and New Kingdom, Assyrians, Canaanites, Cypriots, Minoans, Mycenaean Greeks, Cassites and Zhous of China.

A Perfect Storm Came Together to Destroy the Civilizations

According to Eric H Cline, a historian, this global collapse that preceded the Fountainhead epoch, cannot be just attributed to a climate change alone. Rather, it was a perfect storm with various catastrophes including famine, earthquakes, social unrest, climate change, invasions and a slump of international trade—coincidentally all happening at the same time, leading to a systemic disintegration of the world civilizations. These various disasters that struck across the world from Africa to Europe to the Middle East to South Asia, combined to produce a multiplier effect; each of these repercussions magnified several times over, spreading across the world like a domino effect. All progress made until then was wiped away. Hence the period that succeeded it—from 600 to 300 BCE—became a period of global reconstruction.

Every Perfect Storm Had a Plague at the Centre

Incidentally, at the centre of climate change almost every time was an epidemic, that accentuated the overall consequence of these disasters. For example, coinciding with the Yamna Migration Climate Change, archaeologists have now discovered several mass burial sites across China and Europe—proving several plague outbreaks. During the Late Bronze Age Climate Change, the same pattern was again noticed—evidence of bubonic plague outbreaks that brought the civilizations of Egypt, Sumer, the Indus Valley and the Minoan to their knees. Likewise, the Antonine Plague struck during the Roman Climate Change between 150 to 400 CE. During the Late Antiquity Little Ice Age, the world reeled under the Justinian's Plague and during the Little Ice Age, the Black Death provided the global death blow.

Since every climate change has an epidemic outbreak alongside, our quest now is to find clues to a plague that afflicted the world during the Iron Age Climate Change, to better understand the arrival of the Fountainhead epoch.

A Mysterious Plague Afflicted the World

Though researches point us to specific plagues at the centre of each of the recurring climate changes, in the case of the Iron Age Climate Change, somehow any such substantial evidences are missing out. John Lawrence Angel, a British-American biological anthropologist, once unearthed several skeletons from that age with malarial infections, but we need to bear in mind that even the most lethal case of this disease cannot explain the disintegration of civilizations and abandonment of settlements. However, as we look closely, we see subtle signs of a plague; for example, in many geographies, during this period, there are indications of populations quickly replacing their culturally entrenched practice of burials with cremation. Scientists now conclude that this could have been motivated by a necessity to destroy the piling and decomposing bodies due to an epidemic outbreak. So, our mystery deepens—we know there could have been a plague but don't have tangible evidence to pin it down.

Cues from the Bible on the Mystery Plague

In the absence of any substantial evidences of a plague, we turn to an unusual source—the Bible. It narrates the story of one of the Jewish forefathers, Jacob, relocating to Egypt from Canaan during the time of an intense famine that swept across the region. Though his descendants found favour and rose to high positions in the Egyptian kingdom, eventually they, being immigrants, came under systematic state oppression. During such a time, a Jewish leader arose—Moses—who approached the pharaoh with a request to let the Jews return to their homeland. As this was turned down, Moses was said to have unleashed the wrath of God through plagues that inflicted the Egyptians—including foul water, pestilence, locusts, hailstorms, darkness and death.

Much of these could be ancient myths but as we reconstruct the dates, there seems to be some truth in this narrative. Bible scholars now suggest that this event could have happened either during Ramses II or his successor Merneptah, around 1200 BCE, a period coinciding with the beginning of the Iron Age

Climate Change. To add meat to this theory, there are now records of excessive dry periods towards the end of Rameses II's rule, that resulted in the river Nile drying up. Building on this, biologist Stephan Pflugmacher, in an article, suggested that stagnant and sludgy water in the Nile was an ideal condition for the growth of the toxic *Oscillatoria rubescens*, commonly known as Burgundy Red algae, which could have then unleashed a series of calamities and diseases in humans and livestock.

Pinning Down the Identity of the Mystery Plague

However, though the Burgundy Red Algae could explain the presence of a plague, this might still not explain an epidemic of proportions that could spell the end of civilizations. Hence, we turn to another incident in the Bible. After Moses led the Jews out of Egypt into their homeland, they eventually established their own settlement in the land of Canaan. In a wooden ark they preserved the Ten Commandments tablets that Moses had given to them. Soon, this ark was captured by the Philistines, another set of ancient people who lived on the south coast of Canaan. However, as this arc was carried to their capital named Ashdod, a major port city near the Mediterranean Sea, people were stricken by a mysterious plague, symptoms of which included tumours in their secret parts. Now, this description points us clearly to the bubonic plague, the same as that of the Black Death, where swollen lymph nodes in armpits and groin are a primary symptom. Meanwhile, the Greek translation of the Hebrew Bible referred to a proliferation of rats and rodents across the land, spreading the infection like a wildfire; killing tens of thousands in a day.

In his book *Plague: An Ancient Disease in the Twentieth Century*, Charles T. Gregg traced back the Philistine's Plague to 1130 BCE, exactly the same time as the Iron Age Climate

Change. According to him, the Philistines might have contracted the epidemic from a stricken ship in the Mediterranean, but blamed it on the arc owing to ancient superstitions. Recently, large numbers of fossilised remains of *Xenopsylla cheopsis*, the flea which spreads the plague from the black rats, have been found in Egypt, providing the much required archaeological evidence of these outbreaks across the globe during that time.

This epidemic would have continued to rage on through the period, as there is yet another reference in the Bible, where Israel was struck by a plague—mostly another outbreak—during the rule of King David—estimated to be around 1000 BCE—killing 70,000 people. So, now we have three separate outbreaks—the first one in 1200 BCE, right at the beginning of the Iron Age Climate Change, the second one in 1130 BCE and the third one around 1000 BCE—pointing to a plague, which we refer to as the Philistine's Plague, persisting through the time period of the Iron Age Climate Change across regions of Africa and Asia.

Collapse of Bronze Age and Arrival of Iron Age

During the Bronze Age between 3300 to 1200 BCE, people learnt to use bronze, developed writing systems and urban settlements started to spring up. This led to the rise of civilizations like the Sumer in Mesopotamia, the Hittites in Anatolia, Early Dynastic and New Kingdoms in Egypt, Canaanites in the Levant and the Zhou in China. However, these Bronze Age civilizations collapsed like a pack of cards, as they came under the wheels of the Late Bronze Age Climate Change and the Iron Age Climate Change. According to Robert Drews, historian, these collapses were the worst disasters in ancient history, even bigger in crises compared to the Dark Ages of Europe that occurred after the fall of the Western Roman Empire. However, these civilizations might have disintegrated not only because of a climate change, but also due to the advent of a new metal and technology—iron. With the arrival of the Iron Age, bronze was quickly replaced as iron served superior purposes in warfare and agriculture. It was an age of complete disruption.

Transition from Nomads to Settlements

The advent of the Iron Age led to a sea change in agriculture. Easier production of iron tools helped people to plough tougher soil, and grow new varieties of crops and livestock. This made the process of agriculture easier and more efficient. According to Anthony Sattin, in his book *Nomads*, the Iron Age helped the previously nomadic populations across the world to settle down. This resulted in the rise of new political and social institutions, contributing to the development of states. These new states created new rules and laws to regulate their people within their four walls, unlike the earlier nomadic culture. As urban settlements grew in size, it became important for the states to erect defensive walls and towers to ensure their safety, create bigger marketplaces where they could sell their excess produce and enact new tax laws that could extract a part of this surplus. This resulted in greater interstate trade opportunities and alliances, enabling the rise of a new rich middle class, who challenged the existing hierarchies. Meanwhile, the introduction of coinage further accentuated the possibilities to acquire and store wealth. Hence, in the time period that followed the great collapse, new systems sprang up and were quickly adapted.

An Age of Deadly Wars and Greater Empires

With the Iron Age, the knowledge of iron metallurgy and tool making became widespread and on a large scale. New arms like swords and crossbows enabled a more dynamic and sophisticated battlefield, replacing the slower and less deadly bronze weapons. This also resulted in a virtuous cycle of activities. The ones who developed better weapons were able to conquer more territories, were able to build larger armies, enabled by the higher taxes they generated using the agricultural surplus of the new territories. This, then, helped them to develop even superior weapons. The existence of smaller kingdoms was challenged, territories were consolidated, and larger empires started to flourish. The period between 600 and 300 BCE saw the rise of large empires across the world like the Achaemenid, Macedonian, Qin and the Mauryan.

Development of Writing and Spread of Knowledge

While until 600 BCE most information was orally transmitted, with the rise in urban settlements and greater empires, there was significant development in writing methodologies. Writing had an overall impact across the society, enabling this age to contribute more than ever before to the development of humankind. For example, writing offered new methods to ease the administrative process, like written legal documents, devoid of any subjective interpretations. In the case of religions, it helped them to compile teachings and texts. For Alexander the Great, it helped him create a Hellenistic worlds, while in India, it helped Buddhism and Jainism to challenge the status quo.

Radical Reassessment of Thoughts

Spread of knowledge, rise of urban settlements with a new rich class that defied the existing social hierarchies, forced the intellectuals to reassess their existing thoughts about the meaning of existence, relationship between the state and religion, justification of power, and the interrelationships between people. This further enabled the period between 600 to 300 BCE to lay the foundations for the future of humanity—through religion, ethics, society, community and politics.

Bigger the Collapse, Stronger the Next Foundation

More than from a period of relative stability, we learn from a period of revival. Because the collapse that came before it, that led to this resurgence, ensures that any further progress made should be strong enough to withstand catastrophes of similar scale. Hence, any progress that comes after a period of darkness eventually turns out to be the bedrock upon which everything else is built on, a fulcrum of future progress. We see a similar pattern during the Renaissance, a period of revival after the Dark Ages, which continue to influence our modern world in many ways. However, since the intensity of the collapse before 600 BCE was much more global and mammoth-like compared to the Dark Ages, this short span of merely 300 years, between 600 to 300 BCE emerges as the Fountainhead epoch of all the progress that humanity has made since then.

2

The Epic Tale of the Silk Road through Climate Changes, Imperial Dreams and Nomadic Pursuits

Keywords: *Climate Change, Pandemic, Steppe Migrations, Silk Road, Xiongnu, Golden Age, Pax Sinica, Pax Indica, Pax Romana, Attila the Hun, Gunpowder Empire, Narcissism of Negligible Differences*

The Xiongnu Pester Power

Ruling from 1045 BCE for the next eight centuries, the Zhou dynasty was the longest regime in Chinese history. During the reign of their tenth king, Li, a nomadic barbarian group managed to infiltrate as far as its capital city, Haojing. They were a group of fierce horse-mounted warriors from the Eurasian Steppe regions, who attacked suddenly with no warning as such. Though the immediate threat was thwarted, they continued their assaults across multiple generations, until Haojing fell. The resultant power vacuum was filled once the regional feudal lords were consolidated

STORY OF THE SILK ROAD

END OF GLACIAL AGE (10,000 BCE)
Eurasian Steppes Settle Down (5000 BCE)

STABLE CLIMATE (100 BCE-150 CE)
Silk Road 1 - 114 BCE-150 CE
Roman Empire - Pax Romana - 27 BCE-180 CE
Hans Empire- 202 BCE-220 CE
Parthian Empire - 247 BCE-224 CE
Kushan Empire - 30-375 CE
ROMAN CLIMATE CHANGE - 150-400 CE
ANTONINE PLAGUE - 165-180 CE

STABLE CLIMATE (400 TO 560 CE)
Silk Road 2 - 400-700 CE
Byzantine Empire till Justinian Dynasty - 306-602 CE
Tang Empire - 618-907 CE
Khazar Khaganate - 590-969 CE
 Gupta Empire - 319-467 CE
LATE ANTIQUITY LITTLE ICE AGE - 536-660 CE
PLAGUE OF JUSTINIAN - 541-750 CE

MEDIEVAL WARM PERIOD (850-1250 CE)
Silk Road 3 - 1200-1400 CE
Mongol Empire - 1206-1368 CE
Ottoman Empire - 1299-1922 CE
LITTLE ICE AGE - 1303-1850 CE
BLACK DEATH - 1346-1352 CE

into seven states—the Chu, Han, Qin, Wei, Yan, Qi and Zhao. Called the Warring States Period, they fought among themselves to establish hegemony. But their internal wars were again disrupted by these nomads, who persistently bothered them. It became impossible to either maintain stable borders or to live peacefully. The Chinese referred to them as Xiongnu (pronounced hon-na in Old Chinese and shon-nu in Mongolian), an ethnic slur meaning 'illegitimate slaves'.

Unification of China

In 221 BCE, the Qin dynasty, under their first emperor Qin Shi Huang, ended the Warring States Period in China by conquering the rest of the six states and creating a unified empire—a watershed moment in the history of China. However, even such a large and mighty Qin empire continued to be shaken at their borders by the unending threat from the Xiongnu. These nomads would not allow Qins to settle down. Hence Emperor Qin Shi Huang asked his general Meng Tian to take them on, which he successfully did. He forced their foes flee northwards. The Qin general captured a massive swathe of land from the Xiongnu territories and stabilized the imperial borders. Meanwhile, the emperor fortified his empire to prevent any further invasions by initiating the construction of what would later become the Great Wall of China.

Consolidation of the Xiongnu

This threat and humiliation from the Qin empire united the otherwise scattered and heterogeneous nomadic tribes of Xiongnu. General Meng Tian died in 210 BCE, and during the same time a powerful leader, Modu Chanyu, took over the reins of Xiongnu after killing his own father. He militarized Xiongnu and created a centralized political structure bringing together the various diverse tribes of the Steppe grasslands. Under him, the united confederation of Xiongnu tribe was ready to take vengeance. In just under three years, the Qin dynasty fell, due to multiple reasons including internal instability and unstable borders. Though it was a period of uncertainty in China, in contrast, it was a time of growth for Xiongnu. Under Modu, they recaptured their lost territories and even conquered certain other regions including that of another ancient nomadic people—the Yuezhi.

The Insult of the Hans

Eventually, the Han dynasty founded by Gaozu, a rebel leader, replaced the Qins in China. Now, the Xiongnu, united, reinvigorated and strong, turned their attention towards the Hans. In 200 BCE, through the Battle of Baideng, they successfully laid siege of the Han fortress. In order to avoid complete humiliation of their first emperor at the hands of the nomads, Hans abandoned all military escalations and resorted to negotiations. They also came up with a strategy where common Chinese women pretending to be princesses were given in alliances to the Xiongnu leaders to keep them pacified. Though a peace settlement was eventually reached, the Han emperor was forced to concur to their enemy's unreasonable terms, including expensive tributes, status and border agreements. It was a period of utter disgrace for the Chinese.

Hans Under Emperor Wu-Ti Strategized Their Expansion Plans

Six decades later, in 141 BCE, Emperor Wu-Ti ascended the throne as the seventh emperor of the Han dynasty. His fifty-four years of reign was the golden age for China, during which it emerged as a strong centralized state with an insatiable ambition for expansion. It was the right time to repay the humiliation that the Hans had faced several generations ago. The Xiongnu were still hostile and dominated the Western regions that bordered the Han dynasty. Emperor Wu-Ti, being a strategist, would not blindly jump into a retaliation. Instead, he identified Zhang Qian, a Han military officer familiar with the terrain of the nomads, to travel on a diplomatic mission to establish an alliance with the Yuezhi tribes. Now, the Yuezhi who were also historically at war with the Xiongnu, were an equally humiliated lot. After a particular defeat they had splintered into two groups—the Greater Yuezhi, who were forced to migrate to the northwest and the Minor Yuezhi, who migrated southwards.

The Han Diplomatic Saga Led by Zhang Qian

Zhang Qian started his mission in 138 BCE. But to get to Yuezhi, Zhang Qian and his team had to pass through the regions controlled by the Xiongnu. As luck would have it, he was captured there and kept in captivity. But his mission was not a failure, as he was finally able to gain the trust of the nomadic leader by taking a Xiongnu wife. After a period of thirteen years, he escaped along with his family, and was able to reach the land of Greater Yuezhi. But after living through a period of war and turmoil, the Yuezhis were now least interested in another costly battle with the Xiongnu. Even after several months, as he was unable to convince the Yuezhi, Zhang Qian returned to the Han empire, surviving a series of adventures.

HAN–XIONGNU FRICTION

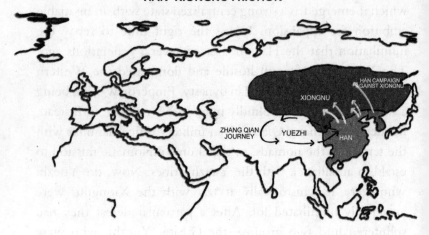

Reports of an Enticing Unknown World

As he returned in 124 BCE, Zhang Qian did not succeed in his diplomatic mission in a conventional sense. But living in the Xiongnu territories for thirteen years and spending another year in Yuezhi, he developed deep insights into their culture, lifestyle and economy, previously not known to the Chinese. He reported about the advanced civilizations that the Xiongnu maintained trade relations with the Greco–Bactrians, Ferghana, Mesopotamia and Persia. His reports included the exquisite goods that these people enjoyed, and their special breed of horses. Emperor Wu-Ti awoke to the realization that apart from the immense prospects that lay beyond the four walls of his own empire, this might also offer a solution to a unique challenge that he faced.

The Chinese Selenium Quest

Selenium is a chemical element, trace amounts of which are necessary for the wellbeing of many animals, including horses. This element is required for the muscle integrity in equines, deficiency of which could lead to their muscle disorders, degeneration, inflammation and even growth retardation. As selenium is a naturally occurring element in soil, horses get it through their grass intake. However, this element was mostly absent in China's soil and hence, their horses were much weaker, especially in warfare. Hence China was at a major disadvantage when it came to taking on arch-enemies head on, including the Xiongnu. As Zhang Qian reported on multiple things, including the powerful equine breed, what he referred to as heavenly horses, Emperor Wu-Ti realized that the prospects of connections with this outside world could be more than just commerce. If they could acquire these horses in large numbers, this could be the beginning of a Chinese regional dominance.

The Han Blueprint of the Silk Road

Narrations of these sophisticated civilizations, their richness and luxuries opened the emperor's mind to two possibilities—a commercial development and territorial expansion. The emperor realized that he could import the superior horses bred by the nomads in the Steppes for his military, while exporting the abundant grains and silk of China to them. With these objectives in mind, the emperor commissioned the construction of a road that could connect China to the outside world. Simultaneously, he sent out many trade missions to Central and Western Asia, several of them under the much experienced Zhang Qian. Soon it dawned upon them that a full-fledged trade route without interruptions would be possible only if the Xiongnu threat was eliminated. The powerful Hans started to hit the weak points of their enemy regularly, ultimately leading to the Xiongnu king's surrender. These victories enabled the Hans to establish trade posts and police guards across their new road that was getting ready by now. Almost a decade after the return of Zhang Qian, the grand strategy of a networked world of Emperor Wu-Ti unfolded. In 114 BCE, the Han emperor launched what came to be known later to the world as the Silk Road.

Expansion of the Han Silk Road

The Silk Road changed the fortunes of the Han empire, where export of silk, a prized commodity, added greatly to the emperor's exchequer, while the horses from Ferghana of Central Asia equipped his army. During this time, the Hans expanded the Great Wall of China, initially constructed by the Qins against the Xiongnu. The emperor commissioned a series of military watchtowers to safeguard their trade routes and to enable further conquests. But the Chinese domination of trade was soon challenged by the Greco-Bactrian kingdom of Dayuan because they found the Chinese import of their prized horses upsetting the terms of trade and the regional balance of power. Though the Hans tried their best to settle these through diplomatic ties, the Dayuan king refused to sell any more horses. In the resultant war, called the War of Heavenly Horses, named after the swiftness of these horses so reported by Zhang Qian, the Chinese defeated their enemies and installed a pro-Han regime. This conquest of Dayuan granted them even better control of the trade routes. The expanded Silk Road was now under the complete control of the Hans.

Pax Sinica Rose across the Silk Road

The Silk Road became the foundation upon which a time of great prosperity in China was ushered in by the Han empire, known as Pax Sinica. The trade route provided China with a steady supply of Ferghana horses, enabling them to build a reinvigorated army, projecting a new military strength across Asia. All the internal rebellions were quelled, external threats neutralized and the well protected borders were extended. The improved trade helped in proliferation of cities, burgeoning wealth, introduction to new luxuries and improved innovations. Pax Sinica was a period of economic growth, political stability and territorial hegemony of China.

DaQin: A Greater China Situated in Rome

Ban Chao was a Han general during the Pax Sinica period, in charge of their regions in Central Asia, that spread across the Silk Road, the most strategic region of the empire. The general managed to expand his territories to the borders of Parthia, a formidable empire that ruled Greater Iran and most of Central Asia. Knowing well that he could push still further, the general dispatched a diplomat, Gan Ying, to explore westwards. Though he arrived at the court of the Parthian Empire, he was discouraged from traveling further, citing the dangers that awaited such a journey. Taking heed of the advice he received, Gan Ying did not proceed beyond Mesopotamia, but managed to collect much information on a faraway great civilization that thrived during the same period—the Roman Empire. Relying on the accounts of people that he met, he narrated in detail the immense trade prospects that China could have with this new land for their luxury goods such as gold, pearls, amber and gems. In richness and culture, Gan Ying considered Rome to be comparable to China and hence called it as DaQin, or the Great China.

Pax Romana: Story of DaQin

Now, the Roman Empire or DaQin as the Chinese called it, under the Julio-Claudian and Flavian dynasties, was extending in commerce and territories across the Western world. Similar to Pax Sinica, it was Pax Romana in Rome, where a golden age was unleashed marked by economic growth and political stability. Owing to their victories in the Punic Wars, Rome controlled the entire Mediterranean trade routes, amassing large profits. Rome's arch-rival during this period was the Parthian Empire, the same power that the Han Empire fought against on the other side. Hence, though the Pax Sinica and Pax Romana happened during similar timelines, these two great empires had no direct connections as the Parthians in between kept both of them completely apart. But with the Roman conquest of Egypt by Augustus Caesar in 30 BCE, Rome was exposed to Chinese goods. Silk fabric catered by the traders who arrived from Egypt quickly became the trademark of luxury in Roman households, while the wealthy Chinese now enjoyed the superior Roman glass and silverwares. Pax Romana was now intricately connected to Pax Sinica by way of trade, though they maintained no direct contacts except through the middlemen.

Pax Khorasan: The Parthian Middlemen on the Silk Road

The Parnis were a nomadic set of Eastern Iranian tribes who initially migrated from the Central Asian Steppes. They have been part of the Achaemenid Empire, the first Persian Empire founded by Cyrus the Great in 550 BCE. After Persia was conquered by Alexander the Great, it was passed on to his general Seleucus Nicator. Sensing an opportunity, the Parnis rebelled against the Seleucid Empire and established an empire of their own—the Parthian Empire in the Khorosan region, the northeast of modern Iran. Under the Parthians, this imperial state flourished on the strength of its military and political organization, occupying most of Iran, Iraq, Turkey and Central Asia. Though a superpower in their own right, they found themselves in a unique position—sandwiched between the mighty Roman Empire and the Han Empire. The only way the greatly valued Chinese goods could reach Rome, and the Roman goods could reach China was by traversing through the Parthian territories of the Silk Road. Parthia, though constantly at war with its two formidable allies, were able to persuade themselves into the role of middlemen of the Silk Road. This control over the Silk Road propelled the territorial, economic and commercial might of the Parthian Empire, ushering in the Pax Khorasan simultaneously alongside Pax Romana and Pax Sinica.

Pax Indica: The Great Kushans on the Silk Road

The Yuezhi, like the Xiongnu and Parnis, was another set of nomadic tribes which traced their origins to the Central Asian Steppes. As the Xiognu consolidated their power due to the threat from the unification of China under the Qins and then the Hans, the Yuezhi became an incidental target. They came under the Xiongnu attack and were displaced. Splitting into two groups—Greater and Minor Yuezhi—both without their own lands, they took to their nomadic roots. The Greater Yuezhi, after almost five decades of wandering, in 128 BCE, overran the Greco-Bactrian kingdom. During the next several years they consolidated their power, advancing across Central Asia and northern India, ultimately establishing the Kushan Empire. With its borders along China and Parthia, the Kushan Empire carved out for itself a formidable role in the Silk Road trade, as suppliers of Indian goods like spices and fabrics and as worthy middlemen. Under the Kushans, their empire expanded their economic, territorial and cultural footprints, so much so that this period came to be known as the Great Kushan Era. Starting from their Emperor Kanishka the Great, the period has been described as one of the magnificent periods of world history. Pax Indica rose up alongside Pax Romana, Pax Sinica and Pax Khorasan. The Silk Road paved the way for golden ages across the paths it traversed through.

Pax Mundi. Pax Caelus

Four mighty empires—Rome, the Han, Parthia and Kushan—dominated the world over two centuries around the start of the Common Era. This was a sort of Pax Mundi, where the known world was under relative peace and prosperity. Pax Mundi, of course, was built by these empires through their long-range strategy and hard-fought victories. But there was another factor that contributed—favourable and unusually stable climate conditions that prevailed during this time—from almost 100 BCE until 150 CE.

A scientific paper, 'Climate Change during and after the Roman Empire: Reconstructing the Past from Scientific and Historical Evidence', written by Michael McCormick, suggested that Europe, especially the Roman Empire, enjoyed a steady warm period, with an even level of solar activity and exceptionally low level of volcanic activity during this period. Meanwhile, at the other end of the world, Han China progressed, riding on a similar warm period. The Mediterranean, Levant and northern African regions, including Egypt, many of which were strategic points along the Silk Road during these two centuries, went through a humid and rainy period, a time of favourable weather, resulting in better harvest and fewer crop failures.

Meanwhile, a study by Celia Sapart from Utrecht University proposed that the intense development activities undertaken by these great empires including increased use of fossil fuels, deforestation and charcoal burning, smelting of metals, paddy cultivation, livestock rearing and land refills could have resulted in a rise of greenhouse gas emissions, and hence temperatures stayed warm for almost 200 years. Whatever the reasons may be, favourable weather conditions unleashed a virtuous cycle of greater yields, greater trade, greater population growth and greater prosperity.

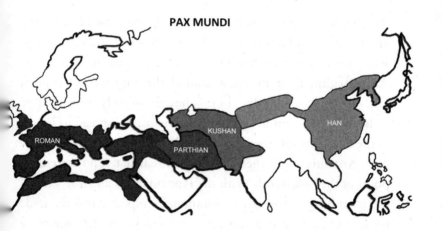

PAX MUNDI

Pax Caelus Disruption

However, the climatic bliss that the globe enjoyed for two centuries came to a halt around 150 CE. Europe suffered from deeply unstable climatic conditions, with frequent and severe droughts. According to McCormick's paper, throughout the course of the fourth century, Europe went through the severest of the drought in almost 2000 years. Their risk of volcanic winters increased multifold. Across the Middle East and Africa, the humid rainy period ended, resulting in a period of less consistent weather. Frequent floods and famines led to crop failures and disrupted food production. Central Asia suffered unpredictable weather conditions and a drought throughout the mid-third century. Meanwhile, Han China went through a similar period of climatic uncertainty with frequent temperature fluctuations, often gripped by intense cold periods. The ideal world was now disrupted by the weather gods.

Antonine Plague Struck the World

The fortunes of four mighty empires—Rome, the Han, Parthia and Kushan—riding on favourable weather and Silk Road trade, were now being challenged by adverse climatic conditions. Accentuating their miseries, around the mid-second century CE, an epidemic broke out. Though initially restricted to isolated populations in Central Asia, the plague spread to Rome as their soldiers returned from a battle with Parthia on a dispute over Armenia, until then a Roman vassal state and a strategic point of the Silk Road. With the Roman cities under its clutch, the plague raged like an all-consuming tempest across the trade routes. It rampaged across, creating cracks in the otherwise formidable empires bonded along the Silk Road. Now known as the Antonine Plague, the ancient world's worst pandemic, is thought to be a smallpox outbreak, speculated to have originated either in China or in Central Asia. Spreading through the Silk Road, it ruined economies, decimated cities and left almost ten million people dead.

Dusk Arrived in Pax Mundi

The Antonine Plague accelerated the journey towards the end, initiated by the climatic changes. In Rome, more than 2000 people succumbed to the disease daily. Their co-emperor, Lucius Verus, was one of the casualties. The surviving emperor, Marcus Aurelius, came under intense pressure as massive losses hit the economy hard, destroyed the army and weakened the empire. Sensing an opportunity, the barbarians outside Rome's borders started to attack. With the assassination of Commodus, the successor of Marcus Aurelius, the Roman Empire slid into a period of civil war as multiple contenders staked their claim to the throne.

Meanwhile, in China, the Han dynasty went through their own internal friction. It is suggested that the Yellow Turban Rebellion of 184 CE, a peasant revolt led by cult faith healer Zhang Jue, was instigated by an agrarian crisis and famine caused by the plague. During the next decade, as Vologases V took over the reins of Parthia, this empire had also weakened considerably. Its arch-rival Rome had reaffirmed its superiority on key territories including Armenia and northern Mesopotamia, and for a brief while, even their capital city. Civil wars and internal strife brewed across the Parthian Empire. Meanwhile the Kushans came under attack, as their enemies pushed towards north-western India. They lost their most important territory of Bactria, a strategic point on the Silk Road, where several trade routes intersected.

One Last Attempt to Save Pax Mundi

Four great empires had built their fortunes from the Silk Road. But now their domination was waning. Border struggles, internal strife, unstable weather conditions and the Antonine Plague extracted a heavy toll. Sensing a crisis early enough, the Roman Emperor sent out a special envoy to the Han court. In 166 CE, for the first time in over a century of trade relations, direct contact was established between Rome and the Hans in a desperate attempt to save Pax Romana. However, the Hans, who were equally struggling to retain their hold on Pax Sinica, were not in a position to take this alliance forward. Several decades later, as the reality of a waning Pax Indica loomed, the Kushan Emperor sent a similar envoy to China, with a handsome tribute. During this period of struggle, even the Parthian Empire that was otherwise constantly at war with Rome looked for opportunities to bury the hatchet. Hence a demand from Rome to send them the Parthian philosopher Antiochus was immediately acceded to. Unfortunately, none of these would save the day. As challenges compounded, it brought the curtains down on the golden ages of four greatest empires of the world.

Tale of Imperial Inheritors on the Silk Road

Once the Han dynasty declined, the fractured regimes were taken over by various warlords. Eventually, three warring states arose—Cao Wei, Shu Han and Eastern Wu. Known as the Three Kingdoms Period, it was marked by continuing internal strife and bloodshed. Plague, famines and agrarian crisis added to their woes resulting in an overall decline of trade. Rome, during this time, dealt with attacks from the barbaric kingdoms. Its rot led to an overall political instability in the region. Meanwhile,

Parthia was brought down when its emperor was assassinated by a rebelling local leader, Ardashir I, who then went ahead to establish the Sasanian Empire. The new empire was more agrarian in nature, and commerce played only a marginal part in its economy. As it let go of its most important trading routes, its role diminished in the Silk Road trade. The Kushans again went through a similar fate, where they splintered into smaller kingdoms, eventually falling into the hands of the Sasanians. Political instability across their trading geographies affected the merchants. They found it difficult to operate in uncertain circumstances, where neither their goods nor their lives were safe. It was no longer business as usual on the Silk Road.

The Xiongnu Rose Up Again as the Huns

Climatic changes and plagues are threat multipliers for imperial dreams. Without any accumulated food supplies, the nomadic populations start to look for resources by encroaching upon the borders of established empires. As Central Asia and Europe were engulfed in a severe drought starting from 338 CE, a nomadic group called the Huns was threatened by a lack of resources. Hence it started a predatory migration displacing the Goths, a Germanic people, in 370 CE. The Goths in turn fled to the Roman Empire, infiltrated it in large numbers and eventually defeated the Roman Empire, which was already reeling under the aftermath of climate change, plague, internal strife and a devastated economy.

The Huns, who catalysed the collapse of the Roman Empire, came from Eastern Europe and Central Asia, regions inherent to the Silk Road. Interestingly, modern genetic researches connect the Huns to another nomadic group intricately linked to the Silk Road—the Xiongnu (pronounced similar to Hun, as hon-na)—whose enmity with the Han Empire initiated the idea of the Silk Road itself. It seems that once they were defeated by the Han dynasty of China, the Xiongnu migrated westwards, where one of their tribes became the predecessors of the Huns. The Huns played a large part in bringing the curtains down on the Roman Empire, and on the Silk Road. At least for the time being.

Attila the Hun: The Ultimate Barbarian

Under the reign of Attila, whom Romans referred to as the 'scourge of God' and as the 'ultimate barbarian', the Huns reached the peak of their existence between 434 and 453 CE. As a military genius, Attila was able to unite the different nomadic tribes under him and move them as a single force against the biggest empires including Rome and Persia. In just a decade, with his unending thirst for blood, unmatched horsemanship and unparallel strategies, he managed a mighty land grab that stretched across central Asia and Europe, comprising large tracts of Russia, Romania, Hungary, Germany and France. Attila's winning strategy was to plunder the most profitable Roman trade centres with an utter disregard for existing peace treaties, ensuring that they lived under a shadow of constant fear. Though the Hunnic Empire quickly collapsed after the death of Attila, this Xiongnu descendent took on and destroyed the commercial and military success of one of the greatest empires of all time.

Attila: A Violent Barbarian or a Desperate, Starving Man?

However, Attila might have not been the sheer murderous barbarian that historians have projected him to be, but rather just a product of the times. The violence unleashed by Attila could be due to the same drought that earlier displaced the Huns from their homelands. A study, 'The Role of Drought during the Hunnic Incursions into Central-East Europe in the 4th and 5th c. CE', published in the Journal of Roman Archaeology, suggested that during the tail end of the Roman Climate Change, there were unusual summers. The dried pastures and famines led to intense resource scarcity, putting nomadic lives in peril. Susanne Hakenbeck and Professor Ulf Büntgen from Cambridge University, authors of this paper, after examining the climate data reconstructed from tree rings, proposed that food and fodder shortage might have triggered the aggressive invasions of Attila—who was desperately searching for resources to keep his people alive and tribes together. According to them, harsh environments that adversely affect societies lead people towards irrational and unjustifiable actions, of which Attila might have been a typical case.

The Silk Road Hibernated, Then Awoke

Political stability is a crucial factor for improving trade. As merchants traverse to unknown lands, they need protection for their lives and goods, stable tax systems and predictable diplomatic relations. When Pax Mundi disintegrated, owing to a hostile climate, plagues and civil wars, the Silk Road withered to a shadow of its earlier self. But bad things do not last long. About a century down the lane, as a premonition of things to come, the climate conditions started to improve. McCormick's paper on climate change suggested that by the fifth century, favourable wet conditions returned to parts of the world like the Levant, and another century later in western Eurasia. Meanwhile, China got out of its cold spell, and was blessed with a warm period starting 541 CE. It was again time for agriculture to flourish and for kingdoms to prosper.

Pax Indica II: Golden Age Under the Guptas

The Indian subcontinent, which had fragmented after the decline of the Kushans, was the first to revive among the various Silk Road Empires. It was united by the Gupta Empire between the fourth and sixth centuries CE, during the early phase of the Silk Road's revival. The Gupta period is considered as the Golden Age of India, where there was a great revival of religion, culture, art, architecture and literature. This era witnessed a substantial increase in the volume of trade, particularly with China along the Silk Road, which funded the region's revival. The Indian merchants traded their much valued cotton and spices for Chinese silk and other items in demand. Meanwhile, Buddhism created a great leverage as their missionaries built temples across the trade routes, reinforcing relations between geographies.

Turkic Khaganates Rose Up Alongside the Silk Road

Even centuries after the Xiongnu disturbed the Han Empire and their descendants Huns brought down the Roman Empire, their strong nomadic roots continued to sprout elsewhere. The Rouran tribe was one such. They united under a single banner called the Khaganate in 402 CE, to eventually expand and exert their control over the Silk Road. However, in 552 CE, the Rouran leadership was challenged by another offshoot of the Xiongnu tribe, the Ashina clan, nomads of Turkic descent. They established the Gokturk Khaganate under their leader Bumin Khan. Taking hold of the Silk Road, they created a huge empire that stretched from Eastern Europe to northern China. In order to facilitate smooth trade, they maintained cordial relationships with neighbouring Byzantine and Persian Sasanian empires. But with China, it was always rather bitter. Their aggressive territorial expansion also got them embroiled in the Chinese civil wars being fought between the incumbent Sui dynasty and the challenger Tang. Soon, in a twist of fate, Gokturk went through a similar fate, where a dynastic struggle fractured them into two—Eastern and Western Turkic Khaganates.

In China Rose Up the Tang Dynasty

After the fall of the Han Dynasty, it was tumultuous period for China, with infighting breaking out in a divided nation. After centuries, in 581 CE, things changed, and an able commander started the process of unifying China again under the banner of the Sui dynasty. He eliminated his rivals and rolled out wide-ranging reforms in order to consolidate his power. But Sui would not last long, and was replaced by the Tang Dynasty in a rebellion. As they established themselves, the Tangs realized the importance of the Silk Road in their long road towards prosperity. However, soon they were confronted by the Eastern and Western Turkic Khaganates, the successors of the Gokturk, who were otherwise also a threat at the Tang borders. So, through a strategic alliance that was forged with rebel Khaganate vassals, they conquered the Eastern portion first. Though the Western portion was stronger, the Chinese eventually subjugated all the regions of the Khaganate into the Tang empire.

Pax Sinica II: China Developed Alongside the Silk Road

With the conquest of the Khaganate, the Tang Empire spread as far as Afghanistan in the west and Sakhalin in the east. With their control firm on most of the strategic points, a greatly extended Silk Road was reopened for business. Many new routes were added, including the ones through the Qinghai-Tibet Plateau and Southern Xinjiang and Nepal through the Karakoram Range. Security across the route was enhanced where the four garrisons of Qiuci, Yanqi, Shule and Yutian emerged as critical crossroads. The distance between the East and West was shortened as a new route circumvented the Pamir Mountain range barrier. Luxury goods like silk, velvet, glassware and jewels were traded between Asia, the Middle East and Europe. Riding on the wave, the Tang capital city of Chang'an emerged as a major economic and cultural hub, one of the largest and wealthiest cities in the world at that time with a population of over 2 million. With the Silk Road regaining its glory, it was now a period of Pax Sinica II.

A Time of Great Chinese Innovations

As merchants, artists, artisans and intellectuals flocked to Tang China, the period emerged as a golden age for inventions and innovations. The world's first clockwork escapement mechanism was invented by an engineer named Yi-Xing. A compass which revolutionized navigation was created and used first during this time. Woodblock printing invented during the Tang dynasty enabled the democratization of reading materials. Different types of paper produced using bamboo, hemp and hide helped in easier production and circulation of the written word.

Other notable inventions during this period included the first gas cylinder, air conditioning, waterproofing and porcelain. In the field of medicine, excessive sugar levels were identified as the cause of diabetes, as well as the fact that goitre could be treated using the thyroid glands of pigs. *Materia Medica*, which compiled knowledge and usage of various substances as medicine, was done during this period. However, the most important innovation came when a Tang-era alchemist mixed saltpetre, sulphur and charcoal together, leading to the discovery of gunpowder. This single invention would then go on to change the history of the Silk Road later.

Pax Khazarica: The Xiongnu Manifested as the Gokturk

In China, initially, the Hans had curtailed the united Xiongnu front to establish the Silk Road. Centuries later, the Tangs defeated the descendants of the Xiongnu, the Gokturks, to reopen the Silk Road. In order to ensure that they do not rise up again, the Tang Empire broke up the Gokturks into ten tribes and then allocated them to two competing factions. Though this continuing pressure made them migrate all over, eventually they managed to reorganize and even conquer portions along the rivers Volga and Danube. Like a bad penny which turns up often, they then established what is called the Khazar Khaganate, a successor state of the Gokturk Khaganate, covering the Caucasus Mountains, the Pontic-Caspian Steppe and most of Eastern Europe up to the river Dnipro in Ukraine.

As their new empire covered most of the trade routes between Eastern Europe, Southwestern Asia and Byzantium, they automatically dominated the western routes of the Silk Road. Leveraging this role as the preeminent middlemen, they emerged as a major commercial power. The Khazars built one of the most dominant empires of the time, so much so that the period is now referred to as the Pax Khazarica—an age of great prosperity in the region.

Pax Romana II: A New Rome Rose Up in Glory

With all his foresight, the Roman Emperor Constantine founded Constantinople as the second capital of his empire. From a commercial perspective, the choice of Constantinople made utmost sense, since it was at a strategic position along the trade routes between the East and West, an advantage that Rome as a city had always missed. Eventually, as the Western Roman Empire fell, the Eastern part, Byzantium, with its capital in Constantinople, became the successor state.

Byzantium reached its peak during the reign of Justinian I, during a similar time as China progressed under the Tangs and the Pontic-Caspian Steppe region was united under the Khazar Khaganate. Under Justinian, his empire expanded across the regions of Africa, Italy and the Mediterranean coast. Banking on this expansion, Constantinople emerged as a hub of commerce on the Silk Road and the most important destination for merchants travelling west. Byzantium and China became the greatest trade partners, where perfume, spices, gems, gold and silver were traded aplenty between the nations. However, Justinian quickly realized that silk was still the main item that was traded. Hence he declared a state monopoly on silk in his empire, enabling it to amass a fortune. Through this booming trade revenues, he rebuilt the glory of old Rome in Byzantium. It was Pax Mundi again—Pax Byzantium alongside Pax Sinica, Pax Indica and Pax Khazarica.

PAX MUNDI II

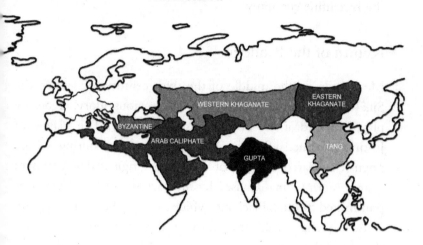

The Great Justinian Smuggle

As their trade with China burgeoned, Emperor Justinian worked on a loftier goal—if Byzantium could produce its own silk, it would greatly reduce the trade imbalance with China. However, silk was the most zealously guarded secret for over 2000 years, so much so that anyone who tried to take silkworm eggs or its secret outside China was immediately put to death. But Justinian would not give up, and had his people after it. After years of unending quest, this was made possible during the mid-sixth century CE, when two Christian monks made their way to China, and risking their lives, smuggled silkworm eggs in their bamboo canes packed with straw. Once it was presented to the emperor, he took his idea to the next level. He established silk factories across his kingdom, thus breaking the hard grip on this luxury that had lured rich Romans for years. Silk produced in their factories, though inferior in quality as compared to China, provided further impetus to the growth of the Byzantine economy.

Return of the Pandemic

Meanwhile, in the middle of the sixth century CE, when the Silk Road was reawakening to its previous glory, a deadly plague arrived at the door of Constantinople. The Plague of Justinian, named after the Byzantine Emperor during whose reign it appeared, is speculated to have originated somewhere near western China. Caused by the bacteria *Yersinia Pestis*, it is transmitted through black rats which infested the grain ships and carts. It quickly proliferated through the trade routes—the Silk Road and the maritime routes—across Asia, Africa and Europe. Spreading through the Mediterranean, Levant and Africa, once it reached Constantinople, it wreaked a havoc. Even Emperor Justinian contracted the disease, though he managed to recover. It killed nearly 10,000 people per day in this great city, wiping out almost 40 per cent and eventually killing almost half of the population in Europe. The frequent waves of the plague continued to strike from the sixth century until the end of the eighth, by which time the world was already pushed to the brink of collapse.

The Justinian Plague: The Xiongnu Connection

A team of scientists including Eske Willerslev from the University of Copenhagen, after examining DNA in human skeletons from the Eurasian Steppe, have arrived at the conclusion that the Justinian Plague might be intricately linked to the westward movement of the Huns, the descendants of the Xiongnu clan. Though the immediate results of this migration included the collapse of the Roman Empire and the decline of the Silk Road, this might have also catalysed certain second-order events, for example, the Justinian Plague. As the scientists have now detected strains of *Yersinia Pestis*, the plague bacterium, in the Hun skeletons, they point to the possibility of them being carriers of this disease from as early as 200 CE. However, some others suggest that they might not have been just passive carriers, but the Xiongnu practice of contaminating enemy water sources using dead animals could have been the real reason behind the plague itself. Whatever it was, the Huns truly might have been the 'scourge of God'.

India Went First on the Global Slide, Catalysed by the Xiongnu

Incidentally, the destruction unleashed by the Huns, the descendants of the Xiongnu, was not limited to Europe. As they migrated from the Central Asian Steppes owing to the harsh weather conditions, one section moved towards River Volga, displacing the Goths, an event that led to the downfall of Rome. Meanwhile, another section of the Huns chose to move towards the River Oxus, making inroads into Asia. They eventually set their sights on India, ruled by the Gupta Empire. Referred to as the Hunas in the subcontinent, they initially brought down several of the empire's tributary states in the northwest. But in a few decades, they launched a full-fledged attack across the heartlands. By 520 CE, they managed to reduce the mighty empire into a fringe.

This Hunnish invasion and their subsequent rule had a deep impact on the future of India. Firstly, the geography was politically fragmented into smaller kingdoms. Secondly, the acclaimed Indian urban centres including Ujjain and Mathura were left in ruins to decline. Thirdly, Buddhism that flourished until then was considerably weakened. Lastly, and most importantly, the Hunnic invasions damaged India's trade relations with Europe and Central Asia, which were, until then, carefully nurtured by the Guptas.

Another Xiongnu Avatar Enabled Byzantine Collapse

The Avars were a group of Eurasian nomads belonging to several tribes. Following their internal power struggles with the Western Turkic Khaganate, they were defeated and fled to the Carpathian Basin in southeast Central Europe in 568 CE. There they encroached upon the lands of the local Gepids and Lombards, subjugated the Steppe nomadic groups of Sabirs, Slavs, and Kutrigurs, and created an Avar Khaganate for themselves. With renewed vigour, they raided the Balkan provinces of the Byzantine Empire, leading to a collapse of the Byzantine authority in the region. In 626 CE, along with the Persians, they raided the heavily guarded Byzantine capital Constantinople. Though the attempt failed, these repeated attacks weakened an already frail empire.

However, what is interesting is that the Avars were not just another nomadic group taking advantage of a flailing empire. According to a study, 'The Genetic Origin of Huns, Avars and Conquering Hungarians' by Zoltan Maroti et al, that analysed genomes from Central Asia, Mongolia, and China, the Avars who attacked the Byzantines and the Huns, who led to the collapse of the Roman Empire, were both related, tracing their ancestry back to the Xiongnu.

Climate Change Villain Struck Again

Alongside the plague and the Xiongnu menace, a new wave of climate change, similar to the previous version that had decimated the first Pax Mundi, struck the world. Around the sixth century CE or so, there was increased volcanic activity around Europe. By the next century, these volcanic eruptions reached high levels, triggering many fierce consequences. As the volcanic ash obscured the sun, Europe slid into a cold snap leading to what is now known as the Late Antiquity Little Ice Age, dragging several geographies down to much colder temperatures for almost 150 years.

Continuing outbreaks of the Plague of Justinian intensified social disruptions like crop failures, forcing mass migrations of several bands of people including that of the Lombards and Slavs. The pandemic carried on without any mercy for a long-drawn period of 225 years, between the sixth and eighth centuries, killing anywhere between 50 to 100 million people across the globe. By the end of the eighth century, China was also gripped by climatic changes. Stronger winds resulted in shifts in the annual monsoon cycles, which then led to weaker rainfalls, intense droughts, food shortages and starvation. The empires that dominated the Silk Road trade routes—in Europe, Central Asia and China—were all severely affected.

A World on the Edge

The convergence of a climate change alongside a pandemic was a recipe for global disaster. By the time the situation eased, the world was considerably weakened. Agricultural output plummeted, resulting in famines. The economic system of Byzantium collapsed, and its trade prospects were badly dented. The vulnerable empire was under attack by the Avars and their allies, the Lombards and Slavs. Revolts broke out across the empire, leading to the collapse of the Justinian dynasty. The next emperor Maurice and his family tried to flee, but were murdered by the rebels. Byzantium continued on its downward slide even under subsequent dynasties. The Arab Caliphates captured most of its territories, leaving the empire as a mere stump of its former self. Meanwhile, during the seventh and eighth centuries, the mighty Khazars were up against the Umayyad Arab Caliphate, who were rapidly expanding into their home turf—the Caucasus—even occupying the Khazar capital in 737 CE.

The Arab peninsula was not without its own casualties. In 747 CE, there was a major uprising against the ruling Umayyad Caliphate, catalysed by merchants from the Silk Road, ultimately leading to a takeover by the Abbasid Caliphate. The Tangs were embroiled in a similar fate. The dynasty was interrupted between 690 to 705 CE, when their throne was seized by Empress Wu Zeitan to establish the Wu Zhou dynasty. In 751 CE, the Tang Empire was defeated in the Battle of Talas in Ferghana Valley by the Abbasid Caliphate along with their ally, the Tibetan Empire. The rout of the Tangs in this battle proved to be a decisive one, tipping the balance of power. In 755 CE, as the nation reeled under war, famine, starvation, migration and deaths, the An Lushan Rebellion broke out, challenging the Tang dynasty for almost a decade. The revolt shook the foundations of the region, resulting in extreme social instability.

Diplomacy to Save the World

Sensing threats like climate change, pandemics and wars, the otherwise formidable empires that thrived on friction with each other now looked out for opportunities to form an alliance. Commerce was the main source of revenue for both Khazar and Byzantium, where their trade routes passed through each other's territories. Hence, the Khaganate considered the Byzantines their close ally and fought alongside them to put down Arab and Persian threats. The scope of their relationship was even beyond the military, as Byzantine emperors Justinian II and Constantine V both took on a Khazar wife. In fact, Constantine's son Emperor Leo IV was known as Leo the Khazar.

During this time, in order to win over the Tangs to their side, the Byzantines in 667 CE sent an embassy, presenting to the Tang emperor a highly valued western medicine. Described as an effective remedy against a hundred ailments, this could have been a remedy to ease the Justinian Pandemic, the plague that engulfed both these countries during this time. Their diplomacy continued during the course of the next century as each of them took on a common enemy—the Arab Caliphate. Meanwhile, the Caliphate itself, under external threats, looked at strengthening their diplomatic ties—which they sealed by taking a Khazar bride for one of their key governors. Further, between India and China, they followed an innovative form of diplomacy—religious emissaries—whereby Huan Zhang between 602 and 645 and Yijing between 635 and 695 travelled to India from the Tang court.

Arrival of the End of Times

However, even these diplomatic relations could not withstand the pressures of the times. The Khazar bride of the Caliphate governor died unexpectedly, leading to further skirmishes between both these empires. Through the seventh and eighth centuries, the Khazars and Arabs fought against each other, inflicting heavy losses. By the ninth century, the Byzantines had turned against the Khazars as they clashed over the land of Crimea and looked at opportunities to weaken them. Hence they allied with the traditional enemies of the Khazars, the Rus, ultimately resulting in the collapse of the Khazar Khaganate.

Despite all attempts, it was the end of times for the Khazar Khaganate, the Byzantine and the Tang dynasties.

Climate Turned around Again

After more than two centuries of the Late Antiquity Little Ice Age, the weather abruptly changed. From 950 to 1250 CE, many parts of the world went through a period of warm climate called the Medieval Climate Optimum or Medieval Warm Period. This unusual rise in temperature is attributed to several reasons. Firstly, numerous glaciers, especially in southern Europe, experienced deglaciation. This melt induced warmer temperatures and prompted floods, leading to bumper harvests. Secondly, the geographies of Central Asia, South-eastern China and India, experienced wetter conditions due to favourable changes in monsoon. Thirdly, during the same period, there was an increase in solar radiation and decrease in volcanic eruptions, ushering in warmer winters across Europe, north Africa and northern Asia. Lastly, and most importantly, as many previously populated areas were abandoned with the collapse of empires, it led to an overall positive effect on the environment.

The Great Khan Arose with the Xiongnu Roots

Genghis Khan, born as Temujin, was the son of Yesugei, the chief of the Borjigin clan, a ruling class of the nomadic people with Mongol, Central Asia and Eastern Europe origins. Genghis Khan came from a Mongol tribe that took pride in keeping a meticulous account of their lineage. His great-grandfather was Khabul Khan, the founder of the Khamag Mongol confederation, one among the many tribal confederations on the Central Asian plateau. He was also a descendent of Bodonchar Munkhag, another renowned nomadic warlord. However, the genealogy of Genghis Khan takes an interesting turn when he referred to his tribe as descendants of Modu Chanyu, the legendary Xiongnu leader who created the first united nomadic confederation. In 'Unravelling the Population History of the Xiongnu to Explain Molecular and Archaeological Models of Prehistoric Mongolia', a paper written by Ryan Schmidt, this was confirmed, as he pointed to the Xiongnu biological similarity to the Mongol nomads. Diimaajav Erdenebaatar, head of the Department of Archaeology at Ulaanbaatar State University, who has undertaken extensive expeditions to find the tomb of Genghis Khan, deduced from their burial practices that the Xiongnu were indeed the ancestors of the Mongols. And if their Xiongnu genetic roots are established, then the Mongols would be intricately linked to the other nomadic tribes like the Rourans, Gokturks, Khazars, Huns and Avars, all who have been part of the Silk Road evolution.

Mongols Established the First Gunpowder Empire

Quite early in his life, Temujin was able to band together a loyal set of followers, to take on and then unite the fragmented and warring Mongol tribes. Under a united Mongol banner, during the course of a decade, he defeated their formidable rivals and hence was declared as Genghis Khan or universal ruler. His initial conquests included the Western Xia, which gave him monopoly over the Silk Road caravan routes. Immediately afterwards, Genghis Khan was ready to take on a bigger rival—the Great Jin, who offered considerable resistance to his onslaught for several years before succumbing. But during these battles, Genghis Khan was exposed to a secret weapon used by the Chinese—small packets of gunpowder attached to arrows, which were then lit with a fuse. These were probably based on the techniques suggested by the *Wujing Zongyao Military Journal*, compiled around 1040 CE, that recorded the technique of gunpowder mass production. These blazing projectiles could kill several Mongols at one go, and easily destroy wooden structures.

Genghis Khan was quick to adopt this technique, probably learnt through his Chinese captives. The Mongol army then took on this new military technology, and scaled it up as they built the formidable Mongol Empire. Hence the Mongols might have been the world's first Gunpowder Empire, quite contrary to the view of Marshall Hodgson and William McNeill from the University of Chicago, who proposed that the gunpowder empires evolved much later in time, sixteenth century onwards, through the Islamic empires of the Ottomans, Safavids and Mughals. However, according to Stephen Haw, this difference of opinion could be because 'the earliest weapons that used gunpowder were incendiary in nature, rather than conventional explosives like bombs, cannons and guns'.

Silk Road Rose to its Zenith Under the Mongols

Riding on the power of his armies and gunpowder, Genghis Khan and his successors created a vast empire that connected East, West and South Asia to the Middle East and Eastern Europe. It was the world's largest contiguous land empire, where the Silk Road routes that previously belonged to isolated imperial systems were now part of one consolidated network. Under the Mongols, the complex local taxation systems were abolished and a single system was instituted. A standardized system of weights and measures was introduced. Rest houses and refreshments for merchants were established throughout. Bottlenecks along the routes were identified and flow of trade was streamlined. New methods of doing business like bills of exchange, banking and insurance were initiated to make trading safer and trustworthy. Most importantly, the strong Mongol army, with watchtowers across the network, ensured the safety and protection of the merchants and their goods. The routes became safe from sporadic raids and loot from bandits, barbarians and aggressive tribesmen. Explorers like Marco Polo could now travel all the way from Rome to China. It was a new, revitalized Silk Road under the Mongols, which rose to its most dominant period. It became the pre-eminent medium for communication, transportation and trade, contributing to the overall growth and expansion of economies.

Pax Mongolica: Stability Brought in by the Khans

The Mongol Empire that spanned from China to the Eastern Europe ushered in a period of relative peace and stability during the thirteenth and fourteenth centuries. Though after Genghis Khan the empire split into various Khanates including the Chagatai, Ilkhanate, Yuan and Kipchak, they still followed the same administration systems and rule of law across their territories, ensuring the overall stability in the region. It was a golden age of sorts, with significant developments made in trade, economy, military, agriculture and medicine. Secrets held for centuries inside China like gunpowder, printing and paper spread to Europe, with far-reaching implications. In the meantime, the religious tolerance followed by the Mongols allowed people from different religions to coexist and prosper.

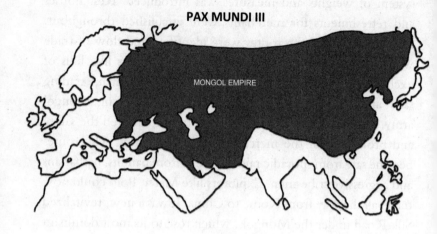

Climate Change Struck Again

By the dawn of the fourteenth century CE, the Medieval Warm Period started to give way to what is known as the Little Ice Age. Sea ice began to advance southwards from the North Atlantic and glaciers started to expand worldwide. The Baltic Sea was reported to have frozen twice between 1303 and 1307 CE and the Caspian Sea levels rose to unprecedented levels. With this abrupt ice growth, summers became colder and cold storms persisted for years together. Heavy rains led to colder than usual wet winters. The world was engulfed in a period of intense cold weather, resulting in crop failures. Meanwhile, a calamitous famine, called the Great Famine, one of the worst in history, struck Northwest Europe. Adding to these woes, a typhoid epidemic and livestock disease, speculated to be anthrax, broke out, killing several thousands and disrupting food supply. In China, the regular monsoon weakened due to the cooling of the south Eurasian landmass. The region was also struck by typhoons, droughts and famines. The geography became significantly colder and drier. The Mongols faced the heat from the intense cold weather across their sprawling empire.

Silk Road's Ultimate Fall Arrived in the Form of Black Death

Like a well-planned plot, whenever the Silk Road seemed to have stabilized it was struck by a disaster, destroying it. *Yersinia Pestis*, the same extraordinarily virulent bacteria which caused the Plague of Justinian, struck again in 1321 CE. Thought to have originated in China, it has now been classified as the deadliest plague in human history. Known as the Black Plague, it consumed over 150 million lives. With the Silk Road in its glory, it was easy for Black Death to spread from China to Central Asia to Europe. However, some reports suggest that it reached Europe in 1344 CE, when the Kipchak Khanate, one of the offshoots of the Mongol Empire, attacked the Crimean port city of Kaffa controlled by a group of Italian traders. In a bid to defeat the enemy quickly, the Mongol army resorted to biological warfare—a technique used by the ancient Xiongnu—hurling plague-infected corpses into the city.

Black Death entered Europe and went on to decimate the land. However, the agnostic plague would not differentiate between the attacked and the attacker. It also devastated the Mongol Khanates. It killed almost 50 per cent of the Chinese population and took the life of the Ilkhanate ruler along with his sons. Ilkhanate, Yuan, Kipchuk and Chagatai Khanates were destabilized, eventually leading to their fall. Once the Mongol Empire collapsed, it was now time again for the Silk Road to decline. But this time, it would be different. The Silk Road would never recover from this mighty fall.

Why the Silk Road Never Recovered after the Mongols?

The Ming Dynasty Affirmed the Han People Superiority

The final years of the Yuan Mongol Empire in China were marked by natural disasters like droughts, floods and famines which were compounded by internal unrest. Among the various civil rebellions, the one led by Zhu Yuanzhang, an insurgent commander, gathered momentum, broke the Yuan resistance and drove them to Inner Mongolia. As Zhu ascended the throne as the first Ming Emperor, the dynasty was founded on the ethnocentrism of the Han people—the majority ethnic group in China. They referred to themselves as civilized and agrarian, as opposed to the so-called barbaric, nomadic non-Hans like the Mongols. As the Ming dynasty strived to reclaim China's ancient heritage, they isolated China from everything foreign by looking inwards, erecting fortresses and building garrisons. When they found out that the Jiayuguan Pass—a critical location on the Silk Road connecting Central Asia to the Ming borders—was a weak point where the Mongolian nomads frequently attacked, they quickly closed it down and abandoned the city around it. This was the nail in the coffin for the Silk Road. This one action severed all trade between the East and West. The Silk Road was finally closed for business.

Little Ice Age Persisted Until the Nineteenth Century

Unlike the earlier periods of climate change, from which the Silk Road would quickly recover from, the Little Ice

Age was persistent. The spell is now categorized into three periods of intense cold weather. A century starting from 1458 CE, followed by another century and a half from 1600, and then the last half a century from 1840. When a recovery was just in sight another bout of bad weather struck again. This tenacious and adverse conditions affected the Silk Road more drastically compared to the other urban centres of the world. For example, as they travelled for trade mainly through the large swathes of intensely parched deserts across Central Asia, the merchants relied on occasional oases as their water source. During the Little Ice Age Period, droughts broke down water sources, and led to the expansion of deserts. These effects were even more intensely felt in the Hexi corridor, the narrow stretch of terrain that connected China and the west. The fragile ecosystem in this area, including its three independent landlocked river systems, dried up. Consumed by violent sandstorms, its grasslands became barren and vegetation perished, submerging the region in sand dunes. As the Silk Road lost its freshwater supply and the strategic points turned into deserts, there was no way merchants could continue traversing the same paths.

Islamic Domination under Pax Ottomana

During the major part of its existence, though under different empires with varied ideologies, the Silk Road was maintained as culturally and religiously agnostic, helping its expansion. But as the Mongol Empire waned, another large empire was on the rise—the Ottoman. Their transcontinental jurisdiction went on to dominate much of Southeast Europe and Western Asia for almost six centuries, allowing them to control most of the western end of the Silk Road. However, as the Ottomans imposed their religious rules and taxes, this affected the journey of merchants who came from diverse backgrounds. Trade was greatly disrupted and goods from the east became much more expensive, mostly monopolized by Muslim traders. The Ottoman blockade of trade between Europe and Ming China, and their blockage of key points after the capture of Constantinople added to the woes of the Silk Road.

Maritime Routes Disrupted Land Roads

Every great idea would be disrupted by an even better idea. For several centuries, the Silk Road land routes dominated global trade. However, with the rise of inward-looking Ming dynasty and religiously oriented Ottomans, the Europeans faced trade blockades. Hence the Europeans were forced to survey for new routes. Led by the Portuguese and the Spanish, they set out to explore new maritime trade routes. A period starting from the fifteenth century CE hence came to be known as the Age of Discovery, when naval expeditions were sent out, sponsored by the Crown. The most famous explorers of the period included Christopher Columbus, Vasco da Gama, John Cabot and Ferdinand Magellan. The world soon found out that maritime routes were quicker, safer and more economical compared to caravans attempting to cross the increasingly treacherous terrain of the Silk Road. The Spanish and the Portuguese were soon challenged by other rival trading communities from Europe—the Dutch, British and the French. Trade now shifted from land to the oceans, from Central Asia to Europe.

Disintegration of Nomadic Lifestyle

The Silk Road was facilitated by middlemen who were historically nomadic tribes from China, Mongolia and Central Asia. The time period following the collapse of the Mongols disrupted them in several ways. Firstly, the nomadic tribes were much more affected by the ecological changes compared to the others, as their economy, politics and lives depended completely on the climatic circumstances. Hence the Little Ice Age that lasted for almost six centuries had a devastating effect on them, displacing them completely. Their traditional water sources dried up and their communities were swallowed by sand. Secondly, until the time of the Mongol Empire, the nomads had an upper hand over the sedentary population. With their brute force and aggressiveness, they could strike and pillage supplies. However, with the knowledge of gunpowder, the city dwellers could now better protect their territories. Thirdly, as the European navigators found ways to trade directly with the producers from the East, the nomadic monopoly on trade was completely broken. Their economies were devastated beyond repair. The Silk Road which depended on these nomadic middlemen came to a grinding halt.

Who Created the Silk Road?

Now that we have explored the Silk Road from its beginning until its decline, let us uncover one more mystery: the creators of the Silk Road. As we have seen, the Silk Road was developed by the Hans in 114 BCE to connect the known and unknown world. A first-of-its-kind network. Through time, it expanded to become a network of trade routes connecting the East and the West. It developed into a labyrinth of roads that connected

South Asia, China, Central Asia, Persia, the Arabian Peninsula, North Africa and Europe. It was central to the economic, cultural, political and religious interactions between these regions spanning centuries and civilizations. However, was it really the Hans who created the Silk Road?

Nomads Travelled from the Steppes to Persia

Quite interestingly, Zhang Qian, who represented the Han Emperor on his diplomatic mission, reported the existence of Greco-Bactrian, Ferghana, Mesopotamian and Persian civilizations which were already trading exquisite goods with each other. If commercial ties already existed in the region, it meant that it was not really the Han Emperor who created the Silk Road. This takes us back by another 400 years to Persia. Here lived Cyrus, an ambitious young man whose grandfather was the ruler of a small tributary state of the Median, another kingdom in the same geography. The Medes as well as Cyrus descended from a set of Indo-Iranian people who migrated to the Iranian plateau around 1000 BCE from Central Asia. Historically they have been nomadic pastoralists, belonging originally to the Steppes, and ethnically related to the later Bactrian and Persian empires.

The Persian Xiongnu Connection

The Xiongnu were not really a homogenous set of nomadic pastoralists, but rather a loose alliance of multi-ethnic, multicultural and polyglot tribes. As Modu Chanyu took over the leadership of the Xiongnu and created a united confederation, it included the nomadic tribes drawn from across. Though it might have been predominantly Turkic and

Mongolic tribes, there is now evidence that a small number of Iranian tribes were also part of this. The same fact is reiterated in *The Records of the Grand Historian*, a seminal work written in 1 BCE covering 2500 years of Chinese history. It suggested that the majority of Xiongnu were of Mongoloid origin, similar in their looks to the Chinese Han ethnicity, but some of them had blue eyes, blonde hair and heavy beards.

A study by Alexander Savelyev et al., 'Early Nomads of the Eastern Steppe and Their Tentative Connections in the West' found that 18 per cent of Xiongnu ancestry had significant similarities to the individuals from Oxus Civilization, a Bronze Age Civilization genetics common to people in modern day Iran. Meanwhile, according to the *History of Civilizations of Central Asia*, published by UNESCO, the elite class and the kings of the Xiongnu could have originally been from Iran, as many of them had Iranian sounding names. Sir H.W. Bailey, who conducted comparative studies of Iranian languages, pointed to the same direction, as he proposed that almost all the earliest Xiongnu names were of Iranian type. Hence it is not a long shot to assume that the original Iranians, especially their ancient ruling class, could also have had a mix of the Xiongnu stock in them.

The First Persian Empire Brought Together Diversities

Cyrus went on to found the Achaemenid Empire, also called the first Persian Empire. Known as Cyrus the Great, he built his empire by conquering the ancient empires of Media, Lydia and Neo-Babylonian. The third Achaemenid emperor was Darius the Great, who reigned from 522 until 486 BCE, and under whom the empire was at its peak. Unlike the others, Darius faced a unique problem of having to integrate an empire with an enormous diversity of cultures, which included people from Persia, Turkey,

Mesopotamia, Egypt, the Balkans and Central Asia. In order to unify his empire, Darius resorted to several innovative strategies. He created a new imperial capital, organized his empire into smaller satrapies, introduced a new coinage, adopted a new official language and even embraced a new religion.

The Persian Royal Road Established the Fastest Communication in the World

Amongst all his unification strategies, the most important was a network of highways measuring more than 1700 miles, which came to be called the Persian Royal Road. This road would enable Darius to have a tight grip on his satrapies by facilitating communication and intelligence gathering despite adverse weather conditions. In order to ease this process, he instituted rest houses, garrisons, a spy network and a set of messengers who worked in a relay format. Darius communicated his royal decrees throughout his imperial provinces using this innovative postal system. What would have taken a normal traveller three months could be achieved by the Achaemenid courier in just nine days(!). This prompted the Greek historian Herodotus to once exclaim, 'There is nothing in the world that travels faster than these Persian couriers. Neither rain nor heat nor nights can stop them from their appointed rounds.' This road also brought in an unexpected benefit—it catered to the urge of the Persian nomadic roots who wished to travel, rather than being restricted to the four walls of an empire.

Not a Courier, but a Trade Road

However, the Persian Royal Road offers a few surprises. Firstly, some sections of the road in places like Sardis and Gordion reveal cobblestone or packed gravel surface pavements with kerbstones, while many other parts remained unpaved. Secondly, the road did not follow the easiest and shortest paths while connecting important cities in the Achaemenid Empire, a matter of common sense when it came to facilitating faster communication. And thirdly, many parts of the Persian Royal Road looked similar to other stretches that have reportedly not been a part of this project. For example, similarities in way-posting stations to some pathways that led to India and Central Asia. Hence, it can be assumed that the purpose of the Persian Royal Road might have been more than just to enable communication. It may have been a major trade route, facilitating trade in an empire that stretched from Eastern Europe to the Indus Valley and from West Asia to Egypt. When Zhang Qian reported on a road that connected Persia, Afghanistan, Central Asia and Mesopotamia, he may have been talking of the Persian Royal Road. Hence, the Han emperor on his part might have just connected the already existing Persian Royal Road built by the visionary king Darius the Great, rather than newly constructing a road spanning thousands of miles.

A Road Much Older than Persia

Is it really Darius the Great who should take credit for building the Silk Road? If so, there are several discrepancies to be sorted out before doing so. For example, though it should have taken the shortest route from Susa, the capital of the Achaemenid Empire to Babylon along the Euphrates, in reality it took a long-winded route along the Tigris, passing through another ancient trade network. Incidentally, through this road the ancient Assyrians used to trade opium, which they referred to as *hul gil* or the 'joy plant'. Hence, now the history of our road goes back to 900 BCE, when a trade route was built by the Assyrian king Adad Nirari II to exchange their merchandise, including opium. The Achaemenids, who were on an empire-building spree, found the anaesthetic properties of opium helpful for their soldiers to suppress pain during wars. However, the history of the Silk Road might not even stop at Adad Nirari II, as evidence suggests that the Assyrians may have traded with Kanes, an ancient Hittite settlement in modern-day Turkey, as early as 2000 BCE, the Bronze Age. One part of this settlement was the Karun Kanes, or the merchant town of Kanes with an exclusive trade colony set aside for the early Assyrian merchants, who arrived travelling on a mud track to trade goods, including opium. Hence, we come to the conclusion that many parts of this network go even beyond the ambit of the Assyrian kingdom or the sprawling Achaemenid Empire.

So, now the question is, whom were these ancient set of people trading with?

Glacial Changes Provided the Backdrop

The last glacial period on earth ended around 10,000 to 15,000 years ago, followed by a gradual rise in temperatures. The higher moisture content and improved soil yields enabled better plant growth and emergence of fresh grasslands. Taking advantage of these favourable conditions, a set of humans, especially in the fertile lands, started experimenting with wild crops, eventually coming up with cereals like wheat and barley. During the same time, another set started out on pastoralism—domestication of wild animals. Livestock rearing was taken up especially in those regions where climate was comparatively hostile. For example, the Eurasian Steppes of dry grassy plains with arid climate. Contrary to the sedentary agriculturists, these pastoralists followed a nomadic lifestyle, as for them staying in one place meant overgrazing of the land, ultimately rendering it unusable and unliveable.

Steppe Pastoralism with Distinct Advantages

The pastoralist communities which inhabited the Eurasian Steppes from at least 5000 BCE, have been the first ones to domesticate horses. This horse-centred pastoralism of the Steppe nomads offered them several advantages. Firstly, this allowed them to create communities focused on livestock products like milk and meat. Eventually economies emerged, revolving around secondary products like fur, hides and draft animal power. This set into motion some early technological innovations like livestock management, transportation, chariots and trade, providing them an advantage over the farming communities. Secondly, with horses on their side, the nomads of the Steppes had higher mobility compared to the sedentary cultures around the world. On the one hand, their large herds forced them to move from pasture to pasture in search of feeding grounds, while on the other hand, it helped them explore and expand their territories, even towards distant locations.

Steppe People Built the Steppe Road

The horse-riding nomads were always in search of greener pastures. Armed with an aggressive nature inherited from the hostile environment that they lived in, they migrated from the Steppes into geographies like China, Mongolia, Iran, Assyria and South Asia. It was just a matter of time before these initial pastoralist routes evolved into a chain of transport and trading links. Through these roads, ideas, goods, languages and customs were exchanged. The chariots that were developed in the

Steppes reached China, North India and Mesopotamia. The
Mesopotamian wheat and barley spread through the Steppes
to northern China. During the Bronze Age, metallurgical skills
were exchanged from the Steppes to the outside world. By the
second millennium BCE, this trade route more or less settled
down, extending to almost 10,000 km, connecting the disparate,
unkind Steppe lands. According to researchers Andre Gunder
Frank and Barry Gills, in paper 'The Five-Thousand Year World
System', 'by the second millennium BCE, the whole of Eurasia
was part of a well-established system of exchanges'. Ravi K.
Mishra echoed this point in his paper 'The Silk Road: Historical
Perspectives and Modern Constructions' that this road was fully
functional by 2000 BCE, facilitating exchanges of commodities
as diverse as jade from the Tarim Basin, silk from China, cotton
from India, turquoise from Iran, opium from Assyria, gold from
Mongolia, incense from Arabia and furs from Siberia.

Discovering the Identity of These Pastoralists

Though Frank and Gills call the ancient road network a single
global system, it was not so. It was not a continuous road that
could be covered by a single person but rather a chain consisting
of many links, operating similar to a relay system controlled by
multiple parties. It was here that the Xiongnu, along with a
few other nomadic tribes who inhabited the Eurasian Steppe,
entered the scene. They made this interlinked trade format
organized and extensive. Hence, though the initial identity of
the Steppe pastoralists might be varied and debated, it was the
Xiongnu who oiled this complex trade system. The Hittites,
Assyrians, Achaemenids, Hans and latter empires simply took
over this road, added new routes and bypassed the older ones.
But the road essentially belonged to the Xiongnu of the Steppes.

Though they have been insulted as a 'scourge of God', they still played an integral part in the rise and fall of the Silk Road—as the Hun, Rouran, Ashina, Huna, Gokturk, Khazar, Avar and Mongol—all of them with Xiongnu roots. Hence ideally, it should not be referred to as the Silk Road but rather as the Xiongnu Road.

Where Are the Xiongnu Now?

We see that the Xiongnu tribe has almost been inextinguishable. If they were to be defeated somewhere, they would emerge somewhere else in another form. Their confederation was one of the most diverse ever—with members drawn from Turkic, Mongol, Yeniseian, Iranian, Tibetan and Burmese nomadic groups. Now, the biggest question is, if the Xiongnu were able to withstand hostilities for so many millennia, how could they ever go extinct? And if they are not extinct, where could they be?

The Xiongnu Is in Europe

Descendants of the Xiongnu continue to exist amongst us as they spread out from the Eurasian Steppes to occupy various geographies. While many of these have been established by genetic and anthropological research, some of these have been mere speculations based on linguistic and cultural similarities. After the death of Attila, though, many of the Huns returned to the plains of the River Ural to live in Russia and Kazakhstan and some of them crossed the Danube and lived in Byzantium, to be called Bulgars. Bulgarians have been considered by several theories to be the descendants of the Western Huns. Hun-related ancestry has also indicated a genetic link to the modern-day Hungarians or the Magyars. Various other genetic studies link the Huns to the Turkic, Yakuts, Chuvash and Cossacks. Though some scholars disagree, there is also a hypothesis that the European branch of the Khazar ruling class, which originally descended from the Xiongnu, accepted Judaism in the ninth century CE and now constitute the Jewish diaspora of Ashkenazi.

The Xiongnu Is in Asia

According to Ryan Schmidt, author of 'Unravelling the Population History of the Xiongnu to Explain Molecular and Archaeological Models of Prehistoric Mongolia', evidence from genetic studies make these nomads 'very much a part of Mongolia's past with links to its modern peoples'. The Tiele people, a tribal configuration from Central Asia who emerged from the Xiongnu, are said to be connected to two sets of people in Asia. Firstly, the Uyghurs in the Xinjiang region according to the Chinese historical texts, and second, the Kyrgyz people through the Ashina tribe. Meanwhile, genetic studies reveal that modern day Uzbeks, Tajiks, Turkmen, Iranians and Afghans, with their significant similarities to Oxus Civilization, are ultimately linked to the Xiongnu stock. The Xiongnu lineage in Asia is, incidentally, not limited to a specific region, but can be seen even in a smaller country like Korea. The Kim royal family of Silla, an old Korean kingdom who reigned out of Gyeongju (notice the similarity to the name Xiongnu) province and credited with unifying most of the Korean peninsula, considered themselves to be of Xiongnu ancestry. Many historians point out that the Kims, who introduced several Chinese customs to Korea, might have indeed descended from Kim Iijae, a Xiongnu prince. Interestingly, according to a national census report, around 1.7 million people claiming to be Gyeongju Kims reside in South Korea now.

We Are the Xiongnu!

Now, the greatest surprise of the Xiongnu comes from South Asia. Around the fifth century CE, a section of Huns, called the Hunas, entered India through the Khyber Pass and troubled the Gupta Empire, eventually resulting in its downfall. Many historians believe that during the next few decades one of their branches—the Gurjara-Pratiharas—ascended as a significant political power in the region. As people proficient in warfare, they quickly assimilated into the Kshatriya ruling caste and assumed positions of nobility. Dominating especially the north and western India, some of them became the ancestors of the Rajputs, a renowned warrior clan. Both the Pratiharas and the Rajputs, flag-bearers of Hinduism, are credited with halting Muslim expansion into India for several centuries. Incidentally, the Indian state of Gujarat takes its name from Gurjara and the state of Rajasthan from the Rajputs—while both of them might trace their ancestry back to the Xiongnu. Prithviraj Chauhan, who had defeated an invasion bid by Muhammad Ghori in 1191 CE, belonged to one of the prominent branches of the Rajputs—the Chauhan—which according to historian Kovacs Imre Berne, shares deep-rooted cultural similarities with the Huns of Hungary. His theory is that a Mongol branch of the Xiongnu, called the Chao, are the common ancestors of Chauhan dynasty in India, and Csohan families in Hungary.

Narcissism of Negligible Differences with the Indian Backdrop

Almost 1000 years after the Hunas had entered India, a Turkic Mongol war leader, Babur, infiltrated India through the same Khyber Pass. He defeated Ibrahim Lodi, the last Sultan of the

Delhi Sultanate, in the First Battle of Panipat in 1526 CE to lay the foundation of the Mughal Empire in India. But his decisive battle would be against Maharana Sanga, the ruler of Mewar, whom Babur described as the greatest Indian king. Sanga, having put together a unified Rajput confederation, a first since his predecessor Prithviraj Chauhan, advanced to Agra to take on the fierce aggressor. In a strange twist of fate, Babur, who descended from Genghis Khan, who boasted of his Xiongnu lineage, defeated Maharana Sanga of the Rajputs, descendants of the Hunas, who could again be traced back to the Xiongnu.

It was Xiongnu vs Xiongnu fighting for the control of India, in the plains of India.

3

The Unlikely Rise and Fall of Two Global Forces amidst Random Climate and Political Disruptions

Keywords: Climate Change, Jewish Rebellions, Babylon Exile, Christianity, Pax Romana, The Great Fire of Rome, Marcus Aurelius, Emperor Constantine, Syrian Rome, Judea, Christendom, Fall of Roman Empire

A Tribe Which Constantly Rebelled

Jews who occupied the region of Judea in the Levant geography were a set of fiercely independent people who drew their identity from their ethnicity, religion and the land they lived in. However, being a small band, they were constantly under attack from the larger expanding empires of the time—the Assyrian, Babylonian, Persian, Macedonian, Ptolemaic, Seleucid and finally the Roman. Every time they were either conquered or exiled, every time their independence was meddled with, they rebelled. Being inconsequential in size compared to the mighty empires they struggled against, it is easy to presume that these rebellions might not have produced much of a result. However, each one of them, including Judea's revolts against Babylon, the Jewish-Roman Wars and the Bar Kokhba Revolt against the Romans, produced lasting effects not just across the region, but across the world—redefining the way we thought about empires, emperors and our religious beliefs.

GROWTH OF CHRISTIANITY ALONGSIDE ROME – A TIMELINE

- Emperor Augustus Caesar - 27 BCE-14 CE
- Pax Romana - 27 BCE-180 CE
- Herod's Rule of Judea - 37-4 BCE
- Jews Rebel against Herod Archelaus - 6 CE

- Apostle Paul & Saint Peter - 1-64 CE
- Great Fire of Rome - 64 CE
- Nero's Persecution - 64-68 CE
- The First Jewish-Roman War - 66-73 CE
- Emperor Vespasian - 69-79 CE
- Second Temple Destruction - 70 CE

- Emperor Hadrian - 117-138 CE
- Bar Kokhba Revolt - 132-135 CE
- Roman Climate Change - 150-400 CE
- Emperor Marcus Aurelius - 161-180 CE

- Emperor Commodus - 177 -192 CE
- Year of Five Emperors - 193 CE
- Emperor Septimius Severus - 193-211 CE
- Emperor Elagabalus - 218-222 CE
- Crisis of the Third Century - 235-284 CE

- Diocletian Tetrarchy - 293-305 CE
- Diocletianic Persecution - 303-311 CE
- Battle of the Milvian Bridge - 312 CE
- Emperor Constantine - 306-337 CE
- Council of Nicaea - 325 CE
- Fall of Roman Empire - 476 CE

Babylon Exile During the Fountainhead Epoch

With the rise of the Neo-Babylonian Empire, which eclipsed the Neo-Assyrian Empire, Babylon rose in power to dominate the region. Sensing a switch in powers, the Kingdom of Judea, a vassal of the Egyptians, quickly changed its allegiance towards Nebuchadnezzar II of Babylon. However, once they discovered that the Babylonian policies were not exactly favourable to them, Judea started to rebel, leading to Nebuchadnezzar raiding Jerusalem—the kingdom's capital city—in 599 BCE, right at the start of the Fountainhead epoch. In 587 BCE, Nebuchadnezzar again attacked the city, breaching its boundary walls. His army then burnt the city down along with their temple, the centre of Jews' social and religious lives. Subsequently, almost 10,000 upper-class Jews, consisting of the nobility, royal officials, warriors, teachers and skilled craftsmen, were deported to Babylon. Several decades later, in 539 BCE, when fortunes changed again, Babylon was defeated and was degraded to a satrapy of the Persian Achaemenid Empire under Cyrus the Great.

Persians's Benevolence Changed Judaism Forever

Jews, until then repressed in Babylonian captivity, found new shoots of hope under the benevolent Cyrus the Great. Though an impregnable monotheistic religion, Judaism started to be influenced by the Persian religion of Zoroastrianism, which was also, incidentally, the first monotheistic religion in the world. Among the several Zoroastrian beliefs that enabled the evolution of Judaism, three stood out because of their long-term implications. Firstly, belief in a universal god rather than an exclusive one reserved for a specific set of people; secondly, a yearning for a messiah, who would redeem this world and usher in a time of greater peace; and thirdly, the dualism of heaven and hell, and an afterlife based on their worldly choices. And as Cyrus allowed the Jewish exiles to return to their homeland and reconstruct their temple, they took back an evolved Judaism, shaped by these new beliefs. Back in Jerusalem, this new Judaism would come to dominate their existing belief systems.

As Jerusalem Revolted, the Roman Military Revealed an Iron Hand

Judea passed through the hands of the Macedonians, Ptolemaics and Seleucids, and then finally was raided by General Pompey of Rome in 63 BCE. He attached Judea to their strategic province of Syria. Years later, Herod, the son of a prominent Roman governor, rose in the ranks to be designated as the King of Judea. In 4 BCE, once Herod died, the kingdom was divided and his third son Herod Archelaus inherited Judea. However, the new ruler turned out rather short-sighted and meddled with the Jewish religious practices including the appointment of the High Priest. A rebellion erupted, which filled the streets and toppled an eagle statue—a symbol of Roman supremacy—from the gates. Archelaus reached out to Rome for help, for which they responded by sending legions who brutally crushed the revolt and crucified almost 2000 rebels. Judea lost what little they already had and was then placed under Roman military occupation.

End Time Messiahs and the Arrival of Christianity

Through centuries, as Jews continued to live in a state of constant rebellion and discontent under several regimes, there arose several prophetic figures, uniting them and giving them a hope of better times. For example, Babylonian exile was the period of prophets like Jeremiah, Ezekiel and Daniel. However, once the exiles returned to Jerusalem, instead of prophets, people longed for someone even greater—a messiah, a belief borrowed from Zoroastrianism. This messiah, according to Jews, would have a divine mission to unite their tribes in order to usher in an age of universal peace. The fourth century BCE was one such period, and though their rebellion was quelled by the Romans, Jews continued to hold on to their desire of defeating their enemies and winning back their independence.

Jesus arrived in Judea at this decisive moment, with a messianic mission of preparing the people towards a greater glory. Christianity, founded on the teachings of Jesus, focused on a redeemer and the redemption he offered. As their core values remained Judaistic, Christianity's early adopters came from the synagogue communities of Jews. However, two events became the watershed moments for this new religion; the first one was when Saul, a conservative Jew and an intense persecutor of Christians, converted after receiving a vision. He later came to be known as Paul, the apostle to the gentiles, one of the principal figures, who laid the foundations of Christianity. The second one was the conversion of Cornelius, a Roman commander from the Cornelia gens family, a greatly respected ruling clan from ancient Rome. He became the first influential gentile to adopt the faith, facilitated by Jesus's disciple Simon Peter. These events enabled non-Jews also to come into the fold, allowing Christianity to develop characteristics distinct from Judaism.

Christianity Adopted and Adapted to Thrive

But Rome continued to consider Christianity as a sect of Judaism, and hence greatly persecuted its adherents. But compared to other Jewish sects, the greatest advantage of Christianity was their adaptability. As they took root in the eastern provinces, dominated by Roman law and Greek culture, they were influenced by the Greco-Roman values. They adopted the Greek system of political assemblies, and the Roman system of administration. Though against Jewish values, they even took on elements from Hellenistic mystery cults like Demeter and Dionysus.

Christianity also built its early teachings on popular philosophies of the time. For example, Stoic philosophy, in demand among Romans during that period, was used extensively by Apostle Paul to explain Christian ideas, while philosophies of Cynicism were used by Christian preachers to justify denunciation of the world around them. This ability of Christianity to work with two contrasting sets of ideals—Greco-Roman systems alongside Jewish values—enabled the religion to spread easily compared to others. According to his book, *The Rise of Christianity* by sociologist Rodney Stark, 'while in 30 CE, Christianity had just a few dozen followers, it grew to around 7500 members by the end of the first century'.

GRECO-ROMAN INFLUENCE IN THE ROMAN EMPIRE

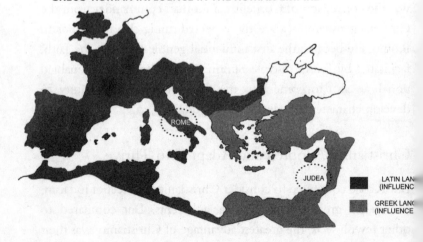

Nero Played the Fiddle While Rome Burned

During this period, back in Rome, after Augustus Caesar, Tiberius, Caligula and Claudius, in 54 CE, Nero took over the throne as the final emperor of the Julio-Claudian dynasty. The image that comes into our mind when we think about Nero is of him playing the fiddle while Rome burned. While this might not be entirely true, the Great Fire of Rome broke out in 64 CE and it continued for about nine days, engulfing almost two-thirds of Rome. According to the Roman historian Tacitus, many believed that this might have been the doing of Nero himself, to clear land and rebuild Rome. But as several hundreds of people died and the economy was devastated, Nero came under immense pressure. To enable reconstruction efforts, he increased the taxes and devalued the Roman currency, further adding to the woes of the citizens.

Nero Scapegoated the Minorities

Nero, burdened with an economic and social wreck, desperately needed a scapegoat to deflect the allegation that he was personally responsible for the disaster. In polytheistic Rome, they believed that calamities were unleashed when their gods were angered by the misdeeds of humans. Monotheistic Jews and Christians were easy targets—as they refused to bow down to the Roman gods. Nero hoped that by blaming the minorities for the mishap and taking strong action against them, he could win back public support. So, he unleashed one of the worst persecutions on Jews and Christians from 64 to 68 CE. Many were arrested, and subjected to the most horrifying forms of punishments—execution in gruesome ways, such as burning them alive, feeding them to the wild animals and crucifying them publicly. However, these Neronian persecutions would result in diametrically opposite defining moments for both Judaism and Christianity.

Jews Rebelled Against the Persecution

As Jews were systematically persecuted, their properties confiscated and their temple breached, they revolted. The result was a major rebellion that erupted in 66 CE, called the First Jewish–Roman War. As tensions brimmed over, Roman legions were quickly deployed. But the Jewish insurgents managed to defeat them, capture their garrisons and kill several thousands of soldiers. As war escalated, Nero entrusted his ablest general—Vespasian— with the task of crushing the rebellion. The general managed to secure the support of Mucianus, the governor of Syria, the province that managed Judea. Though he made great advances across the Jewish strongholds, Vespasian was soon called back to Rome, as Emperor Nero committed suicide following a bout of mental instability. In his absence, the responsibility of Judea passed over to another general, Titus, son of Vespasian. Following several months of brutal siege, in 70 CE Jerusalem was set on fire, its wealth was plundered and almost 100,000 Jews were either killed or sold to slavery. Titus's army then pillaged the Jewish temple and burnt it to the ground, the spoils of which would then be used by the new emperor, Vespasian, to build the Colosseum.

As Jews Rebelled, Christians Submitted

Jews rose in rebellion against the Neronian persecutions and lost it all—their life, their freedom and, most importantly, their temple. The plight of Christians was not in any way better. Their properties were confiscated, their churches destroyed and many of them were either arrested, expelled or executed. The worst blow came immediately after the Great Fire of Rome—in 64 CE—two stalwarts who had laid the foundations of Christianity were executed by the orders of Emperor Nero. Apostle Paul was beheaded and Sant Peter was crucified upside-down. However, compared to the Jews, who revolted against authority, Christians chose an alternate path—they perfected a template of 'persecution glorification'. They started to willingly embrace their suffering as an act of imitation of Jesus, with a view towards an eternal life. Christianity started to celebrate their humiliation. They used this as a witness of their faith. And they leveraged their courageous faith to attract even more believers into their fold. So, in a way, the Neronian persecution achieved the opposite in the case of Christianity. Instead of extinguishing this faith, it enflamed it.

Bar Kokhba Revolt Destroyed Jerusalem

The pattern of revolts and repressions continued in Judea. In 130 CE, Emperor Hadrian visited the ruins of the Jerusalem temple and ordered it to be replaced with one dedicated to the Roman god Jupiter. He also banned circumcision, a practice most important to the Jews. In 132 CE, enraged by Hadrian's acts, the Jews united under a charismatic leader, Bar Kokhba, who created guerrilla warfare to take on the might of their oppressors. As the war spread, leading to heavy Roman casualties, Hadrian dispatched a general along with reinforcements from Egypt and Syria, who brutally crushed the rebels. Eventually, Bar Kokhba, whom many Jews regarded as a messiah—one who would establish the glory of independent Judea—was also killed, along with thousands of Jews. Their villages and fortresses were destroyed, and Jewish communities were devastated. Jerusalem was then converted to a pagan city which forbade Jews from entering. Hadrian then changed the name of Judea to Syria-Palestina, as if to permanently erase this region from the Jewish memory.

Christianity Decoupled from Judaism

Every Jewish revolt produced its own significant results. The Bar Kokhba revolt had its own notable impact. It managed to unite all the splintered groups of Judaism. The Christians decided not to join, as for them, Jesus was their road to salvation and not Bar Kokhba whom many Jews considered a messiah. However, Christians were still subjected to persecution as Romans considered them to be a part of Judaism. But as Emperor Hadrian banned Judea to be the centre of Jewish religious and cultural lives, Christianity came across a hidden opportunity. It found its moment to expand beyond Judea to the other parts of the Roman empire, predominantly the Greek-speaking eastern provinces which easily related to its Greco-Roman-Judaistic values. Over there, firstly the Jews—who had suffered a humiliating defeat, hence yearned for a true messiah—and then the Gentiles— who were hungry for a new spiritual experience—started to embrace the new way offered by Christianity. The Bar Kokhba crisis enabled Christianity to take shape as a separate religion as opposed to being splinter sect of Judaism.

Bar Kokhba Breached Pax Romana

The Bar Kokhba revolt not only changed the fortunes of the Jews and Christians, but also had lasting repercussions on the mighty Roman Empire. Though historians suggest that Pax Romana, a period of unprecedented peace and prosperity for Rome, extended from Augustus Caesar until 180 CE, in reality it would have tapered down with the Bar Kokhba revolt in 132 CE, which exacted a massive toll on the empire. Though Hadrian moved half of his imperial army to crush the rebellion, the losses were so heavy that he had to disband two of the most important legions immediately thereafter. Rome also lost hundreds and thousands of its most competent soldiers, that it engaged in unprecedented levels of conscription across geographies. Historian Sir Ronald Syme suggested that the Bar Kokhba revolt not only inflicted heavy causalities upon an until then invincible Rome, but also dealt a death blow to Hadrian's aspirations of a united and cosmopolitan empire. As his political and religious policies bit the dust, Hadrian is said to have attempted suicide several times. He finally died in 138 CE due to a heart attack, merely two years since the rebellion was put down.

Antonius Pius Held the Fort for a While Longer

Hadrian's first choice to succeed him was an ordinary consul. But as this person was found to be of ill health, he nominated another man—Antonius Pius. Though a mere second choice, this new emperor might have been just the remedy that Rome required at that point of time to arrest its slide. Unlike his predecessors, Pius withdrew from all military acts, never left Italy, but promoted a diplomacy-led foreign policy, which was even recognized by the far away Kushan Empire of the Indian subcontinent. His reign is noted as the most peaceful, with no reports of any major rebellions or incursions. He exercised financial prudence and focused on the overall wellbeing of his subjects, offering generous financial assistance to the economically distressed provinces. Further worsening the situation, from 150 CE onwards, the world came under what is now known as the Roman Climate Change, when stable weather that prevailed from 100 BCE onwards turned around for the worst. As Roman provinces were affected by fires, earthquakes and natural disasters, Emperor Pius opened up his treasuries and suspended tax collections to help overcome the crisis.

Roman Climate Change Halted Pax Romana

Succeeding Antonius Pius was Marcus Aurelius, a well-known Stoic philosopher and author of *Meditations*, who acceded the throne in 161 CE. By then the world was already in the throes of the Roman Climate Change, resulting in several geopolitical changes, including a wave of migrations from Central Europe, sparking nomadic attacks across Rome's northern borders. Meanwhile, the strain on the commercial fortunes of the Silk Road triggered a war with the neighbouring Parthian Empire, as their occupation of the strategic Kingdom of Armenia disturbed the regional stability. Though Rome succeeded eventually, the returning troops came back with a plague, now known as the Antonine Plague. This plague, that had an accentuating effect on the climate change, is estimated to have wiped out almost 10 million people, and up to 25 per cent of the population in some areas. This demographic decline weakened the empire's military, economic and social structure, making it even more vulnerable to external threats and internal unrest. The subsequent decline in labour caused a significant decrease in agricultural output, leading to food shortage and rising prices, inflation and reduced tax revenue. The plague is said to have even contributed to the decline of the traditional Roman family structure, as many of them were destroyed by the disease.

To Counter Climate Change, Marcus Instituted Two Revolutionary Reforms

Being a philosopher, Marcus Aurelius could have had foresight of the tumultuous times ahead, and hence refused to take office unless he was allowed a co-ruler, Lucius Verus, alongside. A co-emperor would allow Marcus to be stationed in Rome, while a younger and stronger Lucius could defend the borders. As the Roman Senate accepted, the empire was ruled by two emperors for the first time. However, this did not go as planned, as Lucius became one of the casualties of the Antonine Plague.

Another interesting act of Marcus Aurelius immediately after his confirmation was to visit the camp of the Praetorian Guard—an important legion in the imperial Roman army. The Praetorian Guards were designated personal bodyguards of the emperor, and also their intelligence agents. Though initially constituted by Augustus Caesar, with time, they became so important in the system that they exerted a disproportionate amount of influence even on matters of imperial succession. As Marcus addressed these guards, though the empire was reeling under internal and external distresses, he declared a large monetary gift to each one of them. This act of the new emperor was rather strange from two perspectives: firstly, Marcus's claim to the throne was unopposed and peaceful hence he did not need to take extra efforts to appease the troops, and secondly, the Roman emperor was considered, until then, as a god, hence the complete allegiance of the people and army belonged to the throne without even asking.

Pax Romana Held Together by Imperial Divinity

In order to understand why Marcus Aurelius might have declared a large gift to the troops, we need to look at the socio-politics of Rome during that period. From the first century BCE, there was a wave of intense and growing interest towards religion across the Roman Empire. All gods were welcome—even new ones from their conquered lands were adopted alongside their old ones. The Romans attributed the resounding success of their empire—

Pax Romana—to their good relations with all these gods—their collective piety. Hence, in this deeply devout society of Rome, with many religions, many gods, many rituals and many more temples, religion and political office often went hand in hand. Leveraging this social sentiment, Julius Caesar nurtured an imperial cult, deifying the emperor himself as a god. Augustus built on this by commissioning several imperial temples that honoured Caesar and the imperial family. As this practice continued through the Julio-Claudian, Flavian and the Nerva-Antonine dynasties, the various families that ruled Rome, this imperial veneration became the glue that held together the vastly diverse Roman Empire, which stretched as far as Africa and the Middle East.

Imperial Divinity Unglued During Marcus Aurelius

Max Weber, a pioneer of sociology and political science, was the first one to define three sources that legitimized a ruler's authority. In the first form, the traditional authority, the command of the leader, emanated from existing social beliefs, values and cultural patterns. Charismatic authority, the second one, relied on the extraordinary personal qualities of the leader to demand obedience. In the third case, the legal rational authority, the power of the ruler was authorized by rules and regulations, which then would be implemented by the bureaucracy and the military. As the Caesars built an imperial personality cult, it formed the backbone of a traditional-charismatic authority template. This worked well until its real foundations were challenged almost a century and a half later.

The Bar Kokhba Revolution, a small, obscure band of guerrilla attackers followed by the climate change, Antonine Plague and nomadic menace, dented this claim of divinity. The Roman emperor was no longer considered invincible. Marcus

Aurelius, being a thinker, might have been able to sense this trend reversal. In order to protect the imperial claims, he then would have attempted to fall back on a legal, rational route by appealing to the key stakeholders—the Praetorian Guards.

PAX ROMANA VS MARCUS AURELIUS

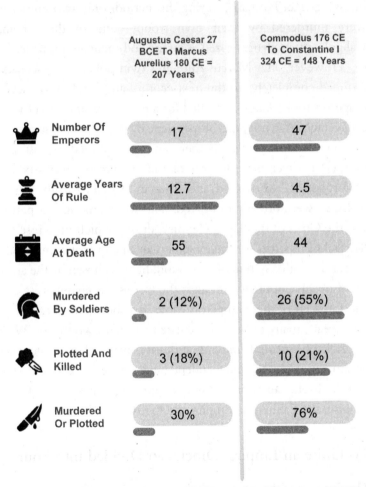

	Augustus Caesar 27 BCE To Marcus Aurelius 180 CE = 207 Years	Commodus 176 CE To Constantine I 324 CE = 148 Years
Number Of Emperors	17	47
Average Years Of Rule	12.7	4.5
Average Age At Death	55	44
Murdered By Soldiers	2 (12%)	26 (55%)
Plotted And Killed	3 (18%)	10 (21%)
Murdered Or Plotted	30%	76%

Ref: Causes of Death Among The Caesars (27 BC-AD 476), Acta Theologica Supplementum 7, 2005

Though the intentions were different, the two strategies of Marcus Aurelius—appointing a co-emperor and the appeasement of the army troops—both led to the weakening of the imperial command, something that was opposite to the desired result. During the first two centuries of the Roman Empire, it had just seventeen emperors, ruling for an average of thirteen years. Also known as Pax Romana, during this period, only two emperors were murdered by their own troops—one of them being Caligula, often characterized as insane and mentally unstable.

However, after Marcus Aurelius's twin policies, the scenario changed completely. In the next century and a half, forty-seven emperors took charge and ruled for a mere four-and-a-half years on average. A whopping 55 per cent of them were assassinated by their troops, while another ten were plotted against and murdered. Over three-fourths of the emperors—thirty-six out of forty-seven who ruled after Marcus Aurelius, from 176 to 324 CE, were brutally murdered. The worst among this period was the Crisis of the Third Century, during which time rose the 'Barracks Emperors'—where rather than an emperor coming into power through a system of succession, he was chosen by the army based on his popularity amongst the troops. As favours rose and fell, fourteen of these emperors came in a short period of thirty-three years, many of them assassinated by their own troops. With the lack of a central unifying authority, many Roman generals became increasingly independent, and hence in 268 CE, the empire broke apart into three competing states—The Gallic Empire, the Palmyrene Empire and the Roman Empire.

To Unite an Empire, Diocletian Divided into Four

The fortunes of the sagging empire appeared to turn around, when the Crisis of the Third Century came to an end with Emperor

Aurelian ascending the throne in 270 CE. Aurelian finally managed to subdue the broken-away Palmyrene Empire and then the Gallic Empire. He even tried his best to bring back the divine status of the emperor by initiating the cult of Sol Invictus, the Sun god, which propagated the ideal of 'one god, one empire'. However, the empire continued to be in a state of churn until the accession of Diocletian in 284 CE.

A year after taking over, Diocletian, realizing that the empire had grown too large to be managed by a single ruler, named a trusted comrade, Maximian, as his co-ruler. Unlike Marcus Aurelius, in this case the empire itself was divided into two and made diarchic—while Diocletian chose the city of Necomedia as the capital of the Eastern Roman Empire, Maximian ruled out of Milan, the Western Roman Empire. In a few years, the co-rulers picked two more emperors, Galerius for the East and Constantius for the West, thereby dividing the empire into four, creating the system called the tetrarchy. According to this system, four chosen leaders commanded multiple geographies as its emperors. In addition to allowing for checks and balances, tetrarchy also ensured continuity of administration in case one of the tetrarchs passed away.

The Warring Princes of Rome

Though the tetrarchy enabled some control over the vast empire, it further compromised the authority of the emperors, just as it had done during Marcus Aurelius's reign. With the retirement of Diocletian and Maximian, the empire drowned in a series of civil wars between the crown aspirants. As Constantius died in 306 CE, though Diocletian's tetrarchy did not provide for hereditary succession, Constantine, his son, based in York, supported by his troops, quickly staked his claim to the throne. At the same time, in Rome, Maxentius, the son of Maximian, incidentally also the brother-in-law of Constantine, challenged his authority with the support of the Praetorian Guards. After six years of strife and continuing civil wars, in 312 CE, Constantine gathered his army and marched to Rome to take on Maxentius.

The Decisive Battle of the Milvian Bridge

Instead of taking on Constantine in his stronghold of Rome, Maxentius marched outside and chose to meet his adversary on the side of the River Tiber. With a plan to corner Constantine in a territory unknown to him, Maxentius cut off all the bridges across Tiber, except for the Milvian Bridge, a stone bridge that crossed over to Rome. However, when the two armies clashed, it did not go according to Maxentius's plan. His army of Praetorian Guards was pushed back towards the Tiber. Unable to withstand the onslaught, Maxentius ordered a hasty retreat back to Rome. Ironically, now his escape route was limited to one—the Milvian Bridge. Unfortunately, the bridge, which was already weakened by the siege, collapsed under the weight of the army and Maxentius drowned. On October 29, 312 CE, Constantine entered Rome and took total control of the empire for himself.

Rome Rebuilt on a Miracle from the Sky

Maxentius clearly had an edge—because Rome was home turf for him, where he had successfully endured the earlier sieges with the support of Praetorian Guards. He even stockpiled large amounts of food and arms inside the fortress in preparation for any eventuality. So, what tipped the balance? According to popular accounts, as Constantine was marching towards Rome, he looked up to the sun and saw a cross of light shining with the Greek inscription 'In this sign, you shall conquer'. That night, Constantine had a dream in which Jesus Christ appeared and asked him to emboss the sign of the cross on the shields of his soldiers. With the confidence given to him by the vision and the inscription on their shields, Constantine's army won the decisive battle. Upon the throne, one of Emperor Constantine's first acts was issuing the Edict of Milan, which accorded to Christianity, until then a minority religion with several hard restrictions, a legal status and reprieve from persecution. According to historians, this conversion of Constantine to Christianity was a major turning point in the history of the Roman Empire and in the history of the Christian church.

But why would Constantine really decide to adopt Jesus as the god of Rome when the emperor himself was, at some point of time, counted among their gods? Could it just be faith—the substance of things hoped for and evidence of things unseen—as defined by Apostle Paul or was there something else hidden in plain sight?

Arrival of the Syrian Stock in Rome

The Syrian province was always a region of great importance for Rome—economically, commercially and strategically—from the time it was annexed to the Roman Republic by General Pompey the Great. Commercially, it had some of the most prosperous and largest cities in the eastern part, including Damascus, Palmyra and Aleppo. Commercially, the ports and trade routes of Syria provided important connections globally, enabling exchange of items including silk, wool, linen, spices, grain and resin. From a military perspective, Syria was such a strategic part of the empire that they permanently stationed four of their legions against their biggest adversary—the mighty Parthian Empire. The Syrians also contributed majorly towards the Roman military recruitments owing to their valour and courage.

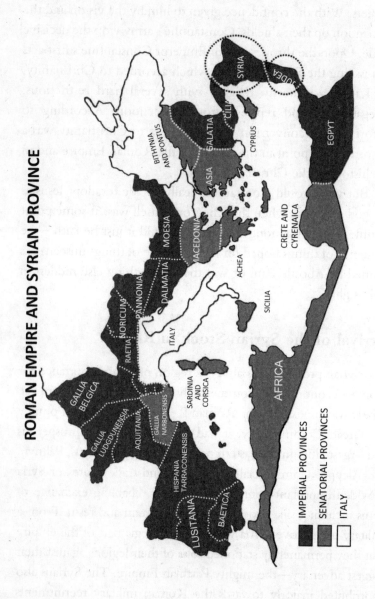

ROMAN EMPIRE AND SYRIAN PROVINCE

IMPERIAL PROVINCES
SENATORIAL PROVINCES
ITALY

Syria Rose to Power Alongside Vespasian

The First Jewish Roman War of 66 CE was a thorn in the flesh for the Roman Empire, but for Syria, it proved to be a lucky charm. Though General Vespasian was deployed to contain the revolt, he had to leave his campaign in the middle, as Rome plunged into a time of crisis after the suicide of Emperor Nero. What followed was a challenging time of internal strife, and a succession of short-lived rulers, known as the Year of the Four Emperors. Though initially not the most preferred candidate, Vespasian found a formidable ally in Mucianus, the Governor of Syria, with whom he collaborated to put down the Jewish rebellion. As the Syrian legion was among the first to swear its allegiance to Vespasian, its governor quickly rose in favour. A prophecy during the time that the future emperor would arise from Judea reiterated his candidacy. Vespasian proclaimed himself the emperor, and deployed Mucianus to be in charge of Rome until his return from Egypt. As Macianus proved his loyalty, a long relationship with Syria began. The region came to be of great importance for the empire. Syrians became preferred members of the Roman army, and an increasing number were awarded Roman citizenship.

A Crisis Founded the Severan Dynasty

During the same time when Vespasian took the help of the Syrian legions to quell the Jewish rebellion, he struck a friendship with a Syrian prince called Gaius Julius Alexion, who was also the high priest of their Sun God Elagabal. Alexion boasted of a high pedigree—from the lineage of Alexander the Great, Seleucid and Ptolemaic dynasties. More than a century down the lane, the high priest position was taken over by his descendent Julius Bassianus. During this time, Rome was going through a period of crisis with a civil war looming after the assassination of Emperor Commodus. Called the Year of the Five Emperors, multiple rulers came in but were murdered by the Praetorian Guards. Upheaval in Rome continued until Septimius Severus, a Libyan-born Roman governor, defeated all his rivals and ascended the throne as its first non-European emperor. Along with his wife Julia Domna, he then founded the Severan dynasty in 193 CE.

Syrians Introduced Rome to the Cult of Sun God

Incidentally, Julia Domna, now the empress of Rome, was the youngest daughter of Julius Bassianus, the Syrian high priest, and a descendent of Gaius Julius Alexion. Her name Domna came from the Arabic root word for their sun god Elagabal, often depicted as a black phallic meteorite. Domna, unlike most other empresses, wielded high influence in her husband's political and social life and even accompanied him in his military campaigns. On her advice, the emperor trimmed the authority of the Praetorian Guards and executed many who posed a risk to his throne, which might have been a reason why his reign lasted for eighteen years, at an age and time when the average rule lasted for a mere four-and-a-half years. Influenced by the powerful religious viewpoints of Domna, Severus initiated solar worship in Rome and took charge of the entire pantheon. He then constructed a building called Septizodium, where the sun god was worshipped and the emperor was the judge.

Syrians Took Over and Established Themselves as Severan

Once Severus died of ill health, he was succeeded by his sons Caracalla and Geta. Domna, their mother, continued to wield her authority behind the throne, and was declared as the first empress dowager and Augusta. The new rulers continued their mother's focus on sun worship, trying to overshadow all other gods and religions of Rome. But once Caracalla was assassinated in a rebellion, Domna was dejected and committed suicide. However, the Severan dynasty, which in reality was Syrian than Roman, refused to die down. Her sister Julia Maesa quickly took advantage of the unrest across the empire to instigate a revolt. She spread the rumour that her grandchild, the fourteen-year-old Elagabalus, was the illegitimate son of the slain emperor Caracalla. She gained the support of the army, who then replaced Caracalla's short-lived successor with Elagabalus as the new emperor in 218 CE.

If I Cannot Be a God, I Would Be His High Priest

Emperor Elagabalus, though just a fourteen-year-old child, had an interesting past. Just like many of his forefathers, he was the high priest of the Syrian sun god Elagabal. Elagabalus took his priesthood seriously. He underwent circumcision and followed the dietary restrictions imposed on him by his religion. Once he was installed as emperor, he started on an almost impossible mission of goading a polytheistic Rome towards monotheism, where his foreign god would be honoured. He replaced the head of the Roman pantheon, Jupiter, and instated Elagabal as the chief deity, proclaiming its birthday festival on the date of the winter solstice—December 25. He then went a step further and adorned the temple of Elagabal with the most sacred relics and symbols confiscated from the shrines of the other Roman gods.

Now, with the presence of all these relics in the temple, it came to such a situation that, in Rome, no other god could be worshipped unless alongside Elagabal. Of course, he ensured that the emperor himself had a special place in this scheme of things. He named himself Pontifex Maximus—the high priest. So, by promoting monotheism around Elagabal, Emperor Elagabalus attempted to address a significant challenge faced by his predecessors—diminishing imperial divinity. He chose to be the high priest of the one and only preferred god, which was the next best option.

Syrians Introduced Christianity to Rome

However, Elagabalus's religious practices were so radical, and probably ahead of their time, that the Praetorian Guards found them divisive. He was assassinated and the throne passed over to his cousin, Severus Alexander, another fourteen-year-old. His mother, Julia Mamaea, unlike the rest of her family, was positively disposed towards Christianity, a popular faith at that time back in Syria. Hence, as Alexander returned from a battlefield, she asked a Christian priest to spend time with him. Alexander held on to these beliefs and even built a church, which could have been the first instance of imperial endorsement of Christianity. Unfortunately, Alexander was also murdered by his troops, leading the empire into a period of chaos called the Crisis of the Third Century, during which time several emperors were swiftly deposed.

In 244 CE, Philip the Arab, from Syria and a member of the Praetorian Guards, assumed the throne. Though he was not related by blood, he considered himself to be part of the Severan dynasty and adopted the Severus surname for his wife and children. Incidentally, what Alexander started, Philip took to the next level. He continued his tolerance towards Christians and according to some historical narratives, he was the first Christian Roman emperor. So, the Syrian emperors not only introduced Rome to monotheism but also to Christianity itself, a legacy that would be further built on by Emperor Constantine.

Constantine's Mission of Building a United Rome

Constantine faced immense challenges due to his predecessor Diocletian's idea of tetrarchy. This model undermined the authority of the rulers, reduced each one into a minor king, opened up a constant threat of civil wars and put the emperor's life at the mercy of his troops. Once Constantine took over the throne in 312 CE, he quickly turned his attention towards reuniting the Roman Empire under one emperor. In order to achieve this, the first step he had to take was to release himself from the clutches of the Praetorian Guards, who were wielding a disproportionate influence in the administration of the country. They had, until then, either murdered or plotted against three-fourths of the emperors since Marcus Aurelius. Constantine quickly disbanded them, and dispatched them to remote corners of the empire. With the threat of the Praetorian Guards gone, he turned his attention to restoring the traditional–charismatic authority by attributing a sense of divinity to the emperor. However, he was also aware that regaining godly status in its entirety might not be a possibility since the character of the empire had changed.

When in Rome, Be a Syrian

As Constantine went about his mission of building a united Rome, he quickly realized that the empire he had inherited was significantly different in character from what his predecessors had built. Firstly, Constantine's empire was no longer Greco-Roman, but rather Syrian in character and culture due to the presence of Syrian-lineage emperors, soldiers and citizens. Secondly, due to this Syrian influence, their gods and religions had gained popularity. However, quite unlike the inclusive Roman cults, these religions had unique initiation rituals that made their members feel exclusive. For example, you could not become a member without going through a public initiation ceremony like baptism or an act of allegiance like circumcision. At the same time, these religions also had a sense of adaptability to them. They easily absorbed the customs of the existing Roman cults to even come up with a modified Roman version. For example, Elagabal was the Latin name given to the Arabic god Ilah-al-Jabal, meaning God of the Mountain. Thirdly, the Roman pantheon was historically adorned with a myriad of gods but during Constantine's time, worship of a main god was gaining momentum. The sun god, depicted as Elagabal or Sol Invictus, was the most popular amongst many, owing to the efforts of emperors like Elagabalus and Aurelian.

The Great Constantine Strategy: Adoption of Christianity

In order to reunite a splintered empire in territories and in spirit, the best step would have been to regain the divinity of the emperor. As that was not possible in the changed circumstances, the alternative would be to associate with a religion that could imbue the emperor with its divinity. For this, Constantine realized he would need a religion with several special qualities. For example, it would be a great advantage if this religion was from the Syrian province, owing to its increasing popularity in the empire. It had to be monotheistic so as to unite the empire behind one god and one emperor. Also, this religion should neither be old nor conservative, so that it could be moulded and adapted to Constantine's special requirements. Incidentally, Christianity fit the bill on all counts. This monotheistic religion from the Syrian province had grown from 0.02 per cent in the first century to 10 per cent of the Roman population. It was the religion with the highest growth rate. It also had evolved from a religion of poor, lower-class outcasts to be the preferred religion of the rich in positions of power.

The Syrianisation of Christianity

Meanwhile, there was an added advantage that Christianity offered to Constantine. As the Roman Empire increasingly became influenced by Syria, Christianity itself was getting Syrianised. Though the religion was born in Judea in the Syrian province, Judea itself was only a small part. There were other great cultural and commercial centres like Antioch, Aleppo, Damascus, Emesa and Palmyra. Christianity, during its initial stages, as a sub-sect of Judaism, was restricted to Judea and to Jews. However, conversion of two important Roman citizens helped it to break out and expand across the Syrian province. The first was Apostle Paul—from Tarsus, an important commercial destination—who adopted Christianity while he was on the road to Damascus. According to many scholars, it was Paul who created Christianity by synthesizing Judaism with other Syrian belief systems, undertaking missionary journeys from Antioch, the capital of the Syrian province, as a base, and establishing churches across the region. Out of the twenty-seven books of the Christian *New Testament*, he authored thirteen, making him the philosophical backbone of Christianity. The second was Cornelius, a Roman centurion stationed in the Syrian province who converted to Christianity. As he was a non-Jew and a prominent official of the Roman Empire, his conversion played a pivotal role in the spread of Christianity. He eventually became the bishop of Caesarea. These two incidents ensured that Christianity no longer remained an obscure Judean sect, but rather an important religion that anyone in Syria could easily relate to.

Diocletianic Persecution of Christians

How was Constantine introduced to Christianity? Was it really the vision of a cross in the sky, as he professed? While his claim remains a matter of debate among historians, it is important to revisit the time of Emperor Diocletian, who reigned until 305 CE, to better understand the sequence of events. As a religious conservative, he did not introduce any new cult like his predecessor Aurelian who reunited the splintered empire. Instead, Diocletian focused his energy on reviving the cults of older gods like Jupiter and Hercules. However, his insistence that all his subjects adhere to these traditional values put him at loggerheads with Judaism and Christianity. Both these religions were monotheistic and refused to bow down to the Roman gods. Judaism had the advantage of antiquity and hence had imperial protection. But Christianity, whose faith was relatively new and unfamiliar, had no such excuse. So, it came under the most severe persecution through the Diocletianic Persecution that was signed off by all the four emperors of the tetrarchy—Diocletian, Maximian, Galerius and Constantius. Out of these, while Galerius and Diocletian were the most aggressive in their persecutions, Constantius generally remained unenthusiastic.

The Galerius Effect on Diocletian

However, Christians had mostly lived in harmony for most of Diocletian's reign. Though Diocletian's reign started in 284 CE, there are no records of him being an anti-Christian for almost two decades. In fact, for most parts, Diocletian has generally been regarded as a religiously tolerant ruler. So, what could have resulted in this change of character? Enter Galerius—Diocletian's son-in-law—who, despite being part of the tetrarchy, was the lowest-ranked of the four emperors. Galerius yearned to be in favour with the senior-most emperor—Diocletian. Hence, as a devoted pagan, he realized that a campaign against Christianity would get him the attention he desired. Meanwhile, he was egged on by his mother Romula, a priestess in the region of Dacia (now in Romania) who nursed bitter resentment towards Christians for not respecting her gods. After almost a year of relentless effort, Galerius finally managed to persuade Diocletian to get his law enacted against the Christians in 303 CE.

Overcoming the Galerius Effect

How did this Great Persecution of Christians affect the standing of Constantine in the Roman empire? Constantine, son of Constantius, owing to his distinguished career and military support, believed that he would be chosen as Diocletian's successor. But with the unfolding of Diocletianic Persecution, the power balance shifted. Galerius rose in favour and was selected to succeed. When Diocletian's health deteriorated after a campaign that he undertook alongside Galerius, it was rumored that he had a role to play. In fact, it is said that Galerius manipulated and weakened Diocletian so much so that he was forced to retire— the first Roman emperor to voluntarily step down.

However, even after being named Diocletian's successor, Galerius still considered Constantine as his main adversary and hence continued his acts to derail his career. He even held Constantine as a captive in his court, though in 305 CE, he managed to escape. After his father's death, who was a part of the tetrarchy, as Constantine sought recognition as the legal heir to the throne, Galerius was reportedly so furious that he almost set the emissary on fire. For Constantine, Galerius was his archnemesis who was constantly pulling him down. Hence, it made logical sense for him to reverse any policy, especially those made with an intent to give Galerius an advantage. And the most important among them would be his act of Christian persecution.

Helena: The Effect of an Unmarried Mother

For Constantine, adopting Christianity had a dual advantage. On the one hand, this monotheistic religion from the Syrian province enabled him to rebuild an empire severed by conflicting interests. On the other hand, it allowed him to be seen as a tolerant restorer, unlike Galerius, who was perceived as an intolerant persecutor. However, there might be just another factor as to why Constantine zeroed in on Christianity as the central element of his rule. Constantine's mother Helena was from a family based in the eastern part of the Roman empire. Unlike Galerius's mother, who harboured strong anti-Christian sentiments, being from the Greek provinces of the Roman empire, Helena had a strong

Christian background. She met Constantius, Constantine's father, during one of his campaigns while he served under Emperor Aurelian. Though in 272 CE Helena gave birth to his child—Constantine—she still could not be married to Constantius, as according to Roman law, nobles were not allowed to marry women of lower origins.

The Disappearing Queen

When Diocletian assumed power, Constantius was chosen as a part of the tetrarchy. One of the strategies devised by Diocletian to keep the system intact was to forge alliances between the families of the four different emperors. Hence Constantius, though he was in an unofficial relationship with Helena, chose to marry Theodora, daughter of Maximian, another emperor in the tetrarchy. Meanwhile, in 295 CE, influenced by Galerius, Diocletian issued two proclamations—first, an edict from Damascus forbidding all incestuous marriages and second, in 303 CE, the Diocletianic Persecution of Christians. Both these proclamations put Helena on a negative footing because of her religious beliefs and her relationship with Constantius. So, Helena, probably by choice, disappeared from the pages of history for a few years.

Helena: The True Heroine Behind the Scenes

Though for several years Helena lived a life of obscurity, she reappeared in history from 306 CE when her son Constantine assumed power. Constantine was fond of his mother and she lived with the emperor in his palace. Considering the relationship and the influence that his mother had on Constantine, it is reasonable to assume that he might have already had a positive view of Christianity, long before the Battle of the Milvian Bridge itself. Helena was soon elevated to the position of Augusta Imperatrix, an empress with an important mission to accomplish. She was given unlimited access to the imperial treasury to locate valuable Christian relics. She travelled to Judea, where she discovered the birthplace of Jesus Christ, and built the Church of Nativity in Bethlehem. In Jerusalem, she tore down the Temple of Venus and discovered in the ruins a cross that she claimed to be that of Jesus Christ, along with several other relics such as Christ's tunic. All of these helped in increasing the credibility of Christianity in the empire. Helena died in 330 CE with Constantine by her side.

Constantine: Truly Faithful or a Master Strategist?

In 313 CE, Emperor Constantine issued the Edict of Milan, granting Christianity all legal rights and a protection against persecution, as well as several imperial favours including tax exemptions and access to treasury funds. Though this was one of his first important decisions made after ascending the throne, another equally salient early act stands out. Constantine built a triumphal arch to celebrate his victory in the Battle of the Milvian Bridge. Quite contrarily, it was decorated with images of Roman gods rather than any Christian symbols. Though Constantine claimed to have won this battle due to the favour accorded to him by Jesus Christ, sacrifices were made to the pagan gods. Hence a question still lingers on as to whether Constantine was truly committed to faith, or was he using Christianity to gain an advantage over his rival Galerius and rebuild a fragmented empire.

Constantine: A Master of Many Dreams

Interestingly, the Battle of Milvian Bridge was not the first time Constantine had a divine vision. In 310 CE, while he was struggling to gain legitimacy, in one of his speeches in Gaul, Constantine spoke about another divine vision that he had received. However, this time around, the vision came from the Roman gods Apollo and Victory, who, according to the dream, granted him the right to rule the world. They bestowed upon him three laurel wreaths of health, longevity and the throne. Constantine declared that though tetrarchy propagated imperial equality, he was above the others, due to this divine right accorded to him.

Hence it is not difficult to assume that Constantine built on this experience later in 312 CE to effectively get rid of the tetrarchy and stamp his sole right over the throne. But this time around, he evoked the divine rights accorded to him by Christianity rather than the Roman gods. Strikingly similar to the three laurel wreaths he received from the pagan gods, once Constantine completed thirty years as the emperor in 336 CE, he referred to the tricennial crowns bestowed upon him by Jesus Christ. Constantine, after all, might have been a master of divination.

Running with the Hare and Hunting with the Hounds

Though Constantine embraced Christianity as an important tool to aid his reign, he did not completely renounce his pagan roots. He remained an active member of the cult of Sol Invictus, the sun god, until much later during his rule. His official coinage, even several years after taking the throne, continued to depict images of Roman gods like Mars and Sol Invictus, rather than any Christian symbols. Strangely, Constantine himself got baptized only on his death bed by his distant relative, the bishop of Nicomedia. Considering all these, it is highly possible that Constantine may have used Christianity to his advantage rather than being an ardent believer.

A Solution to the Climate Change Adversity

Rome was different until 150 CE, when a massively prosperous Empire was able to fund its citizens' decadent lifestyle. Bounty and slaves from the regions they conquered, supported their selfish, pleasure-centred pursuits. However, with the advent of the Roman Climate Change and Antonine Plague, the situation overturned. Egypt, often referred to as the 'breadbasket of Rome', went through a period of extreme drought, resulting in the degradation and desertification of agricultural lands. As standing armies could no longer be supported, conquests dwindled, wealth reduced and the slave supply diminished. This in turn put stress on the Romans, who found it difficult to adjust to this adversity. Constantine innately understood that the existing paganism might not be able to explain nor withstand the economic and social distress. He could have then found his remedy in the form of Christianity. Jesus exhorted poverty, and asserted that it was almost impossible for the rich to enter the kingdom of God. Christianity encouraged charity and urged its followers to sell their goods and give to the poor. With the adoption of Christianity, the Roman Empire was able to push these messages of abstinence and denial in a subtle but effective manner. Hence, for Constantine, Christianity might have also been an practical strategy to tide over the crisis period.

A Road Map to Provide Social Desirability to Christianity

Enabled by Christianity, Constantine emerged as the sole emperor, a great feat accomplished after several decades of civil wars, uncertainty and co-rulership. However, Constantine's relationship with Christianity was not selfishly one-sided. While he took what he wanted from the religion, he also enhanced it and enabled it to grow to the next level. His most important step after taking over the throne was to provide legitimacy to Christianity through the Edict of Milan. Through this, he returned all the previously confiscated church property and granted to Christians the right to organize churches. With this significant act, he demonstrated the importance the empire gave to Christianity, thereby increasing the religion's social desirability.

Forced Diffusion into Roman Society

Constantine, being an active member of the sun worshipping Sol Invictus cult, was aware of the importance of religious symbolism in the daily lives of the Roman citizens. He embarked on a process of diffusion, where Roman values would be imbibed by Christianity and vice versa. In a show of respect to Jesus Christ, Constantine abolished death by crucifixion and replaced it with hanging. A sense of tolerance was shown towards the prisoners and convicts, and cruel games like the gladiatorial games were abolished. He promoted the cross as a superior religious symbol above many of the existing pagan symbols. Sunday, the day of the Sun, was made the official Roman day of rest, and was declared sacred for Christians. Markets and offices were closed on this day. December 25, a day of winter festival in Rome, was celebrated as the birthday of Jesus Christ.

Incorporation of Symbols and Relics

Constantine went about addressing the lack of relics and symbols in Christianity by constructing many of them from scratch. Helena, his mother, was sent to Judea with funds to discover and institutionalize these relics. There, she discovered the birthplace of Jesus, his tunic, his cross and a rope which tied him to it. This was followed up with the construction of the Church of Nativity, Church of the Holy Sepulchre, Church of Eleona and several other basilicas. Starting from 324 CE, the emperor set out on a mission to build a new capital city at Byzantium in Istanbul. This new city, which would later be named Constantinople, employed an overtly Christian architectural style, besotted with churches and devoid of all pagan religious associations. In 331 CE, Constantine also commissioned an order to deliver several volumes of scriptures to churches across his empire.

Establishment of Vatican Over a Cult Temple

The ancient city of Rome, the capital of the Roman Empire, was built on seven hills, the central one being Palantine Hill. Outside the city boundaries was another one, the Mons Vaticanus or Vatican Hill, upon which Emperor Caligula built a racing circus and erected an imposing Egyptian obelisk. Subsequent rulers transformed this circus to a place of worship for various prophetic cults, including that of the sun god. However, when calamities like the Great Fire of 64 CE struck, it was thought that the gods had unleashed their fury in retaliation to Christians refusing to offer sacrifices to them. This hill then became the focal point for persecuting early Christians, including Peter, an apostle of Jesus Christ, who was allegedly crucified upside down by Emperor Nero. Hence this spot became popular with Christians, who wished to be interred alongside Apostle Peter. Now, in 320 CE, noticing the importance of this site to Christianity, Emperor Constantine started the construction of his new Basilica of Saint Peter, directly over the ruins of the cult worship.

Unification of the Church

For a unified empire, Constantine recognized the need for a monotheistic religion that was devoid of religious dispute and controversy. However, the early church was rife with divisions and diverse opinions, even on the fundamental question of who and what the true god was. Hence Constantine assumed the role of Pontifex Maximus, the high priest, who would be responsible not just for the material well-being of his citizens as the emperor, but also their spiritual health. He adopted the solar Julian Calendar as the official one of the Church, compared to the earlier Hebrew Calendar. Through the First Council of Nicaea that he convened in 325 CE, Constantine exhorted the church, with all its various divisions, to take a unitary view towards maintaining orthodoxy, rooting out heresy and enforcing the doctrines.

Carrots to Christians; Sticks to Non-Christians

Unlike Galerius and Diocletian, who resorted to persecution against the religions that they disliked, Constantine was careful to avoid using brute force. Instead, he resorted to softer measures. For example, withdrawal of state support for Roman temples, confiscation of all valuables from pagan temples and melting them into coins, and public insult of pagan priests. All these eventually led to the closure of temples. New taxes were imposed on non-Christians, where they were asked to fund his territorial expansions, and the construction of his new city in Constantinople. It was made illegal for Jews to attack Christians, convert to Judaism, own Christian slaves and circumcise their slaves. All these measures forced pagans and Jews to desert their ancestral religions and flock to Christianity in hordes and masses.

Roman Empire Transitioned to Christendom

Until the time of Constantine, the Christians played from a position of weakness. They were constantly persecuted, their wealth was often confiscated and they were almost always overlooked when it came to positions of high power in the empire. In what is referred to as the Constantine Shift, the emperor created an intricate alliance between the state and the Church. As more Christians filled social and political seats of authority, it led to a form of Caesaropapism, where there was no longer any demarcation between the Church and the state. Meanwhile, the foundation of Christendom was laid where the Roman government stood on the pillars of Christian values, and the state machinery spent its forces and funds on protecting and spreading the ideology of Christianity. The relationship between faith and governance was so intricate that many a time, the voice of the clergy reigned supreme in matters of statecraft. The church became the defining institution, or in a way, the state itself.

Expansion of Christianity Out of Roman Borders

As Christianity became the most important religion in the Roman Empire, where the emperor was both Pontifex

Maximus and Caesar, it became a prerogative of Constantine to support Christians not just in his empire, but also elsewhere. For Constantine, it was as if he was the protector of Christians across the world. Hence, though Rome was constantly at war with the Sassanian Empire of Persia, Constantine still wrote to Shapur the Great, the longest reigning Sassanid monarch, with a request to safeguard the Christians under his rule. With imperial support, Christianity now took wings even outside the Roman Empire—across Europe, Africa and Asia.

Growth of Christianity Burst at the Seams

With Constantine driving the growth through innovative initiatives like state funding, building of new churches and basilicas, incorporation of new symbols and relics, unification of the divided church, and putting Christians in positions of power, Christianity started to see exponential growth. According to sociologist Rodney Stark, from a minority religion in 250 CE, in just under a century, Christianity grew to a position of clear majority in the empire. From 6 million members in 300 CE, it grew to 34 million in just fifty years. An unprecedented growth for a new religion by any standards was achieved by Christianity under Constantine.

The Legacy of Constantine the Great

Emperor Constantine ruled the Roman Empire from 306 to 337 CE. Leveraging his innovation called Christendom, he secured his power and reunited the empire under one emperor, a feat that has been elusive for more than a century under several of his predecessors. He won major victories against the enemies of Rome, including the Franks and the

Germanic tribes, and reoccupied the long-lost province of Dacia, and founded the city of Byzantium, later renaming it as Constantinople, on the eastern part of the empire in Istanbul. Though there are contradicting accounts which portray him as a scheming, self-serving secularist, Constantine is generally regarded as a revered ruler and a religious revolutionary. The church hails him as one of their greatest heroes. The Christian Orthodox Church venerates Constantine as a saint, and an equal to the apostles of Christ.

The Great Fall of Rome after Constantine

However, Rome started to decline during the latter period of Constantine. An empire which was once considered to be infallible started to show deep foundational cracks. During the next few decades, these fissures widened, leading to the ultimate collapse of the colossus. Now, there are different reasons attributed for the fall for the Western Roman Empire. Firstly, after Byzantium was founded, when the administration of the empire was divided into East and West, the Eastern part inherited the richer regions like Egypt, Syria and Asia Minor, while the West was left with the poorer portions like Africa, Spain, Gaul and Britain. Secondly, in the military, the West was at a disadvantage, as the bigger portion was assigned to the East. And thirdly, the West constantly came under barbaric occupations and invasions, eventually leading to the fall of the Empire in 476 CE.

Role of Christianity in Accentuating the Fall of the Empire

While it might seem that political, economic and military fissures caused the downfall of the Roman Empire, the adoption of Christianity may have unleashed a chain of events that accentuated its implosion. Constantine embraced Christianity in order to reunite his empire. He adopted it to enable him regain imperial authority. However, the results turned out to be just the opposite, especially in the longer run. Preference of Christianity over the entrenched cultural and value systems resulted in a set of psychological, economic, political and even racism effects, weakening the already flailing Roman Empire.

Psychological Weakening of the Empire

For the last several centuries, even before the beginning of imperialism, Rome had adhered to a pagan form of polytheistic worship. They followed a more or less secular philosophy when it came to their devotion—where all gods, including even external ones, were accepted and respected. However, monotheistic Christianity demanded allegiance to only one god and rejection of all the others. Christianity altered the overall spiritual fabric of Roman society. Many could not come to terms with the glorification of crucifixion, a humiliating punishment reserved for miscreants. Christian beliefs in physical resurrection, and ascension, violated Roman religious taboos. Christianity weakened the power structure, social hierarchy and the value systems of the traditional Roman society.

Moral Weakening of the Army

Valour was one of the most respected values in Roman society— which had helped them win wars and conquer regions across the globe. However, Christianity was a religion that professed passive values—turn-the-other-cheek virtue. Christianity did not glorify military achievements, rather propagated sobriety. There were even internal church debates to refuse army men the Christian communion on the grounds that they had committed murders during the war. This weakened the military machinery considerably and dampened the martial spirit of the Romans, especially at a time when the barbaric kings were knocking at their doors. Eventually, this led to the collapse of the internal security and external defence of the empire.

The Roman Economy in a Free Fall

The Christian value system took a toll on the Roman economy in several ways. First of all, the Church emphasis on values like poverty, afterlife and salvation weakened the traditional Roman values such as state service. Christianity also valued prayer and idleness, which undermined the value of hard work. As a result, a majority of the Roman working class slid into poverty. As the army was demoralized, conquests dwindled and the empire faced a shortage of slaves who carried on them the load of grunt work. An increase in unemployment rates put pressure on government distributions. Stress on the treasury resulted in the neglect of infrastructure, including roads, waterways and temples. Increasing corruption further eroded the existing system. As the rich and the Christian churches managed to evade paying their dues, the burden of the taxes fell on the lower and the middle classes and the pagans. Overall, the Roman economy was under duress.

Change in the Political Landscape

Religion was deeply embedded in the political structure of the Roman Empire, where Romans believed gods to be the reason for their empire's prosperity. Their state institutions were expressed in an elaborate system of religious rituals. Gods were many, and they followed a system where the emperor was also considered a part and worshipped. Hence people rarely disagreed with their emperor, and the armies did not think twice before laying down their lives for their emperor. Under Christianity, the empire faced a deadly double blow to these belief systems—firstly, shifting from polytheistic beliefs to monotheism and secondly, where their emperor, instead of being revered, now served and bowed down to another god.

Moral Fabric Destroyed through Rampant Racism

Throughout its history, the Roman Empire was known for being a tolerant society. They respected diverse religions, cultures, viewpoints and races. This ability to adapt without prejudice helped Rome to flourish across regions as one of the most ethnically varied empires in history. However, as Christianity took over, there were several instances of religious radicalism where Christian mobs destroyed and desecrated synagogues and pagan temples. Many Romans were now being targeted and persecuted for not believing in one single Christian God. The enormous political power wielded by the Christian clergy further helped in justifying many of these instances of persecutions, destroying the secular moral fabric embedded in Rome.

Church Monopoly on Wealth and Power

Under the emperor's patronage, Christianity utilized valuable public resources for building churches and for propagating their religion. The Church's wealth rose significantly as a result and it acquired large tracts of land, often at the expense of the state. Bishops emerged as the new centres of authority, who led a decadent lifestyle—hosting lavish banquets and entertainment. Eventually, the number of clergy and nuns increased to half the size of the Roman army, leading to a decline in internal security and increased pressure on the state treasury. All these factors negatively impacted an already ailing Roman economy.

Internal Church Conflicts

On one hand, the Church was spending significant state resources to suppress paganism, while on the other, it was also busy sorting out internal rivalries. Different sects in Christianity engaged in bitter political struggles, striving to prove that their belief was the correct one. Several conflicts erupted over dogmas and orthodoxy. For example, even though the emperor himself adhered to a sect called Arianism, which asserted that Jesus's character was distinct from and subordinate to God, the Ecumenical Council of Nicaea denounced many of these views as heretical, leading to an overall confusion. This division within the Church, by then a pre-eminent institution, had a negative effect that further weakened the empire.

The Journey Continued after the Host Was Subsumed

Even before Constantine took over the throne, policies pursued by previous emperors, combined with uncontrollable external factors like the Roman Climate Change, plagues and rebellions had weakened the Roman Empire considerably. Constantine might not have had any antidote as such, except for the actions which he presumed might work. He chose to adopt Christianity over paganism with the hope of uniting the empire under one emperor. While he did achieve some success, unfortunately it proved to be short-lived. Fault lines soon emerged and his remedy itself became the cause, where the religion ended up playing a significant part in the decline of the Roman Empire. But Christianity, which enticed Constantine with its unique characteristics and offerings for him, had already achieved its purpose. With the collapse of the empire, it was now larger than its host. It was now ready to take on the other parts of the world.

From the Roman Empire to the World

The fall of the Roman Empire was the right moment for Christianity to spread its wings. In the absence of an emperor, it was the bishop of Rome, the Pope, who filled the vacuum. The Italian scholar Petrarch referred to this age as the Dark Ages, a period of cultural and intellectual decline. It was a period when the Church dominated all affairs, and opposed all else that came in its way. Political institutions were taken over and run by the Church. And with this legitimacy acquired from Rome, the church imposed their beliefs even on other parts of the world. For example, though the Barbarian kingdoms conquered Roman territories during its fall, they underwent a gradual Christianization than the other way around. The church quickly consolidated its power by setting up a vast network of institutions—controlling not just the religious, but also the intellectual and political thoughts of the rulers and the commoners alike. It established empires across Europe, instated and legitimized emperors. In about two centuries after the Fall of Rome, the situation came to be such that there was no other political authority in Europe that could rival the power wielded by the Church.

Light at the End of the Dark Ages

The Church remained at the pinnacle of its power despite the Dark Ages. Though it had grown to immense proportions, it still retained the agility and adaptability it had exhibited during its initial years. Just as it had absorbed Greco-Roman characteristics alongside Judaistic values, it now reinvented itself during a time of crisis. It reformed during the Renaissance, after the Eastern Roman Empire's fall which marked Europe's transition from the Middle Ages to modernity. It soon became a catalyst in that quest for modernity, by offering a reason for countries like Spain and Portugal to initiate the Age of Exploration. The religion reached out to lands as far as the Americas and to the farthest corners of the world. Currently, one in three people across the world are Christians, with a followership of over 2.4 billion.

A religion that was once just an obscure apocalyptic messianic Jewish sect, born out of a rebellion in Judea, a miniscule territory in itself, thus conquered the world, while the Roman Empire, that once held this world in its palm, faded away into the oblivion.

4

Unravelling the Hidden Links between Three Starkly Different Religious Forces

Keywords: *Climate Change, Narcissism of Negligible Differences, Universal Religions, Social Disruption, Geo-political Disruption, Roman Empire, Caliphate, Maurya Empire, Fountainhead Epoch*

How the Closely Connected Exaggerate Their Differences

Sigmund Freud commented in one of his essays that communities which were closely related to each other had a higher probability of engaging in bitter feuds. The more a group was indistinguishable from another, the more they were prone to attacking each other. Hostility between brothers was hence a much higher probability compared to hatred between strangers. Anton Blok, a Dutch anthropologist, further built on this premise to arrive at the conclusion that in the absence of noticeable differences, communities connected to each other would be forced to

133

emphasize and reinforce their subtle dissimilarities, as they are the only available means for them to defend and prove their superiority over one another. Hence relationships between the Rwandan Hutus and Tutsis, Indian Hindus and Muslims and Israelis and Palestinians—closely related in their ethnicities—would constantly be marred by conflicts, as each of them seek to ascertain their primacy. This is the narcissism of negligible differences.

Chalk and Cheese and Cucumber: Three Totally Different Religions

Three religions, which went on to dominate the world, have so far convinced their followers that they are unique in their origins, philosophies and paths, propagating the idea that they hold a monopoly on the truth. To protect this idea, some of their followers would even die or kill. The origins of these religions are separated by time—a gap of at least 500 years between each faith. Buddhism originated in the late sixth century BCE, Christianity in the first century CE and Islam in 610 CE. These religions are also separated by space—Buddhism born in India spread initially across South Asia, China and Southeast Asia, Christianity developed in Judea and grew initially across the Roman Empire, while Islam emerged in Saudi Arabia and proliferated across the Middle East. Eventually, each of these religions went on to compete not only for followers but also for geographical subjugation in a world where religious ideologies diffused into political ideals.

Different, Yet So Similar

On the face of it, these religions seem to be vastly different from one another. But a deeper analysis reveals that they are quite similar in many ways—the myths surrounding their founders' births and lives, the early development of these religions, the times the founders lived in and the strategic advantages they created. The fierce conflicts and violence that have marred our history can be explained by this narcissism of negligible differences and a desire of each religion to prove its worth by emphasizing on subtle differences. Now, let us look at the various similarities of the so-called vastly different religions.

The Social Context That Gave Birth to These Religions

Rituals Dictated Pre-Buddhist Indian Society

South Asia was undergoing a period of churn in the era leading up to the sixth century BCE. The Indus Valley Civilization had declined and the nomadic Aryans had moved in. Compared to the urbane civilization they displaced, the new settlers were pastoral in nature, with their society organized into villages and tribes. The foundation of their society was a system of rigid impermeable castes that divided their citizens into four compartments. This caste system provided an opportunity for the upper-class priests, which comprised the Brahmins, to dominate, creating deep fissures and inequalities. The complex rituals and sacrifices performed by them assumed high importance, even as morality and ethical behaviour took a back seat. Eventually, these priests came to be venerated more than the gods themselves, leading to a moral decline and in turn to a widespread resentment in society. South Asia was ready for an idea that would challenge existing values that centred on rituals, orthodoxy and exclusion.

Exiles Dominated the Pre-Christian Judea

In 587 BCE, Jerusalem was attacked again and the Judean elite were taken as captives to Babylonia. After fifty years, when Babylon fell to the Persian Empire, the descendants of these elite Jews obtained a favour from Cyrus the Great and returned to their homeland. Back in Jerusalem, they were literally like nomads, having lived in Babylon for several generations. However, these minority returnees could still exert control over religious matters owing to their upper-class background and Persian connections. They emerged as the chief priests and the rabbis, the social aristocrats, while the native population were relegated being farmers, carpenters and artisans. Due to its intermingling with Persian culture and religion, the Jewish religion that they brought back from their exile was significantly different from what originally existed in the region. Leveraging their religious control, this minority revised, edited and assembled much of the Hebrew Bible that now forms the foundation of Judaism. They defined the laws and the traditions that the rest of the citizens were forced to follow. They ensured rigid laws around everything that regulated common citizens' daily lives—their interactions, diet, work and even holidays. To add to the confusion, there also emerged three small but significant religious factions—the Pharisees, Sadducees and Essenes, who held conflicting theological opinions on important matters. Later this period, Judea was taken over by the Roman Empire, who started to persecute the Jews for their religious beliefs. Jews yearned for redemption and relief from the yoke of their sufferings.

Nomadic Superiority in Pre-Islamic Arabia

Arabia was again undergoing a period of churn during the sixth century CE. The region had two distinct sets of populations—the first set was sedentary, who settled in tribes around towns such as Mecca, while the second was the nomadic floating population of the Bedouins. The unrestrained and individualistic Bedouins made a living by plundering and taxing the trade caravans in the Arabian deserts. The Bedouins considered others as inferior and created a constant source of anxiety and fear for those who lived in the urban settlements. Their religious beliefs, though both believed in polytheism, also differed. While the settled inhabitants developed a more complex belief system that revolved around a pantheon of deities which they worshipped in permanent shrines, the nomads' beliefs were more attuned to their lifestyle. They never bothered with questions like the meaning of life or afterlife, nor believed in rituals, but were rather fatalistic, picking up several practices from the places that they frequented. They worshipped objects such as trees, stones, caves and even their dead. There were also religious divisions and distrust between every other tribe, leading to a period of constant conflict. Hence, there was a yearning for a more spiritual form of religion that could act as a uniting force.

Striking Similarities

Before the advent of all these three religions, their respective regions went through a period of churn—between the settlers and a set of nomads who tried to displace them. The native population was eventually subjugated, primarily using religious control exerted by the nomads.

Buddhism Broke Hierarchical Commands

The Vedic religion during the times of Buddhism was centred on the authority of the priestly class and the rigid caste system. This system underlined ritualistic domination and the privileges attributed to them who derived their authority from their bloodline rather than any meritocracy. In a way, the religion itself existed for their sake, emphasizing their ritualistic command, with no role for the individual as such. Buddhism emerged as a challenge to this hierarchical authority, rejecting the inequalities imposed by the caste system. Buddhism believed that social position and gender were not barriers to attaining enlightenment. It de-emphasized the centralized authority and the traditions enforced upon the laypeople. By presenting the Four Noble Truths as their guiding principle, Buddhism played up the individualistic component— that people were responsible for their own happiness—as opposed to the rituals and the caste system propagated by the Vedic religion. Buddhism went against the grain by suggesting that one's caste was not a punishment for the deeds committed in the past life, thereby rejecting the idea of fixed caste duties based on one's bloodline. Buddhism espoused one universal moral law based on which anyone could attain salvation.

Christianity Introduced a Humane God

During the time of Jesus Christ, Judaism was a rigid religion controlled by a small set of priestly classes. It had developed a transactional side, where the relationship between man and God was defined by a covenant, as God was seen as an inaccessible being in heaven. Hence, the overarching focus of Judaism was on the practice of a set of laws called the *mitzvot*, that regulated not only the religious practices but also each and every aspect of one's daily life. These inflexible laws, which numbered in the hundreds, were focused on orthodoxy, rituals, prayers and actions. However, Christianity broke this centralized orthodoxy and brought God and religion within reach for the common people. Through Jesus Christ, Christianity made God a human being in flesh and blood. By focusing on a new agreement mediated by Jesus Christ, they rendered all the inflexible, stiff laws of Judaism null and void, and in that place they highlighted attributes like faith, love and hope. According to Christianity, human beings were redeemed from the generational curse of Adam's original sin by the sacrifice of Jesus on the cross, and hence it was now possible for each individual to attain salvation devoid of all orthodoxy and rituals.

Islam Empowered the Deprived

Islam brought several sweeping changes to the Arab society. It created a new religious and social system by adopting the best of both the nomadic Bedouin and the sedentary populations. While the earlier tribal society was built on aristocratic privileges and hierarchy, the monotheism introduced by Prophet Mohammad opened up opportunities for people of all socio-economic classes. The Quran propagated a new system of moral guidance that replaced the earlier entrenched practices like blood feuds, female infanticide, loose morality, unethical practices and exploitation of the poor. Many historians suggest that the social status of the two deprived classes in pre-Islamic Arabia—women and slaves, improved multifold—as Islam reformed unlimited polygyny, patrilineal marriage and slavery, by assigning quasi-legal rights for both. Dale Eickelman, an American anthropologist suggested that the most important reform that Islam brought about was the value it placed on individuals, that each person was personally accountable to divine law, replacing a collective community-wide responsibility prescribed by the tribal law.

Striking Similarities

All these three new religions challenged the existing hierarchical and ritualistic religions, where power was concentrated in the hands of a few. They established novel, democratic structures where the earlier unrepresented lower classes also had a go. While previously the accountability was borne in a collective fashion across the tribe, the new religions ushered in an era where individuals were at the centre.

Good Artists Copy, But Great Ones Steal

Buddhism Built on Hinduism

Though Buddhism developed by rejecting the core concepts of the Vedic religion like the authority of the Vedas, the priestly class and caste system, it also borrowed heavily and built upon several of the existing ideas from its predecessor. For example, the core theme of both the religions is that living beings are constantly wading through a process of birth and rebirth called samsara with the hope of a spiritual liberation. The Hindus refer to this as moksha while Buddhists call it nirvana. Likewise, the ideas of karma and dharma. Karma is applied in both the religions in the realm of cause and effect, having clear consequences and a determining factor in the cycle of rebirths. Meanwhile, dharma, referring to the universal order or the natural laws, again is a concept that Buddhism has built on taking cues from Hinduism. Apart from the core concepts, Buddhism has even integrated various Hindu deities into its system including Vishnu, Shiva, Brahma and Saraswati.

A Renewed Judaism through Christianity

As Christianity was initially just one of the splinter groups of Judaism, almost all of its theological concepts have been borrowed. The foundational basis for both these religions is the belief in a special covenant that God entered with their forefathers—Abraham, Isaac and Jacob. Though Christians came up with a new interpretation that this covenant was renewed by Jesus Christ through a New Testament, they still retained the Old Testament, the same as the Hebrew Bible. Hence for Christians, the creation story starting with Adam and Eve, the long line of prophets and the belief in a God who judged according to one's deeds yet forgave their sins remained the same as the Jews. Christianity was established on the foundation of Judaism, borrowing their ideas on universe, sin, worship, redemption, prayer and rituals.

Islamic Foundations on Pre-Historic Arab Traditions

Islam, being the last of the major religions in the world, had the privilege of co-opting from several religions that originated before it. Islam borrowed heavily from Judaism and Christianity, which were also prevalent in the same geography during that time. Islam is again an Abrahamic religion, descended from Judaism, which worshipped the god of Abraham. While Judaism and Christianity traced their roots to Isaac, the second son of Abraham, Islam traced its roots to his eldest son named Ismail. Islam also borrowed heavily from Arabic tribal systems that flourished in the region for several centuries, including the practice of a pilgrimage to central Mecca during specific months of the year, which the nomadic Bedouin people undertook as an act to free themselves from otherwise common tribal feuds.

Striking Similarities

Though the new religions were formed to mitigate the shortcomings of the earlier ones, each one of them borrowed heavily from their predecessor. In fact, their foundation itself is based on the religion that they tried to replace.

Strategies That Drove Initial Adoptions

Buddhism Democratized Religious Thinking

With a keen awareness of the social and political challenges that plagued Vedic society, Buddhism tried to mitigate them. Their focus on non-violence, peace and abstinence enabled them to gain popularity among the masses. In order to boost its immediate appeal, the new religion consciously adopted several practices that were diametrically opposite to that of the incumbent religion. First of all, as Buddhism was founded on democratic values, people from the lower castes could easily embrace it. Everyone including the Vysyas, Shudras and outcastes, who were earlier looked down upon by the small percentage of upper-class Brahmins, found these values liberating. Buddhism communicated its message in Pali, the language of the masses, unlike elite Sanskrit. However, its most important innovation was the Jataka tales, one of the oldest Buddhist collection of fables illustrating the many lives of Buddha and the path to enlightenment. The Jataka tales, comprising around 550 fables, conveyed the most profound lessons in the simplest fashion. In contrast to the Vedic texts which could be understood only by the learned priests, the Jataka tales were easily enjoyed by anyone, making it a creative way to spread Buddhism.

Christianity Appealed to the Gentiles

Judaism was an exclusive religion, reserved for a specific set of people traced meticulously through their bloodline. However, Paul, along with Peter, two important and early apostles of Christianity, opened up their religion to everyone, including the Gentiles, and declared their religion to be universal. This relaxation of requirements democratized the new religion and paved the way for Christianity to extend much beyond the niche Jewish community. Christianity welcomed with open arms people like fishermen and tax collectors, who were marginalized by Judaism. Unlike Judaism, which primarily used Hebrew as its religious language, Christianity was flexible in adopting other local languages like Aramaic and Greek, helping it to gain immense popularity. But the real game changer was the innovative Christian style of teaching in parables, where complex theologies were made approachable through allegorical stories. Compared to the Jewish philosophies, which were mostly abstract and impractical, parables took the Christian message straight to the people in a way it resonated deeply.

Universality of Islam

Compared to the tribal religions that were exclusively based on clan membership, Islam was based on the principle of universality. It did not discriminate or look down upon any of the ethnic groups—which until then were engaged in constant feuds with each other. Islam professed that all were equal as long as they were righteous. The common man found Islam to be highly attractive as it brought the conflicting people together under one umbrella, minimizing bloodshed. Unlike the deeply unequal and unjust tribal societies, where the poor were trampled upon, the Islamic tenet of charity, one of its central pillars, helped in empowering the underprivileged. Meanwhile, compared to many other tribal religions, Islam made their philosophy less complicated by resting it on five pillars—faith, prayer, charity. fasting and pilgrimage—making it easier to follow. As the Arabs were already exposed to the other Abrahamic religions, their holy book the Quran contains several narratives of biblical persons like Adam, Abraham, Moses and Jesus, which made it relatable. Quran's extensive use of parables and shorter narratives, compared to the Hebrew Bible and New Testament, again helped their cause significantly.

Striking Similarities

The predecessor religions which these new ones challenged, like Judaism, Brahmanism and nomadic systems, were reserved for an exclusive set of communities. But the new religions took an inclusive stand, which immediately made them popular. Their use of the common man's language, use of parables, allegories and fables again added to their charm.

Buddhist Diet of Vegetarianism

As the Vedic texts prescribed ritual sacrifice, their religion had a high prevalence of animal slaughter, especially the cow. During functions like Ashvamedha and Rajasuya, cattle were sacrificed in hundreds and thousands. However, since the society was primarily agrarian, with cattle as their lifeline, people came to resent this practice. Hence when Buddhism took a stand against the killing of cows and propagated vegetarianism, this had an immediate appeal. For the Kshatriyas, the ruling caste, lesser sacrifices meant higher agricultural produce and hence higher taxes, while for the Vysyas, the traders, this meant better trade prospects and for the Shudras, the working class, higher income. Hence the Buddhist stand on vegetarianism and non-violence, though it took an opposite stand to the dietary habits of the period, helped building its attractiveness and growth.

Christians Broke Free from Kosher Restrictions

Jews followed strict dietary rules—called kosher—where animals were classified as clean and unclean and would have to be slaughtered and cooked in accordance to the Jewish law. They were forbidden from eating, touching and interacting with substances that were outside the purview of the law. However, since Christianity was promoted as a universal religion with mostly Gentiles in its fold, this became an impediment, as different people had their own dietary habits which were not easy to give up. Christianity found an innovative solution to this challenge—that the grace of Jesus Christ made everything clean, including the Gentiles and their food habits, hence the laws regarding Kosher were now redundant. Absence of strict dietary laws and openness towards all food habits immediately made Christianity more appealing to people from various classes and regions.

Islam Emphasized the Halal Diet

Arabia before the advent of Islam was a debauched society. Historians say that alcohol was consumed widely, where the nomadic Bedouins drank even five times a day. This resulted in widespread acts of violence such as robbery, pillage and murder. Society was in a state of constant feud and bloodshed. Since there were no dietary restrictions, even animals that died of illness, injury or poisoning were consumed, leading to diseases and outbreaks. Animal sacrifice was practised widely, especially that of camels, a highly valuable and culturally important creature in the desert. There were even human sacrifices, the victims usually being prisoners of war. As Islam came up with halal dietary laws, forbidding certain types of meat and alcohol in totality, the common people who were otherwise in a state of suffering found it as a redemption.

Striking Similarities

The dietary stand taken by these three religions formed an important stimulant in their growth process. All of them took a starkly opposite stand towards the dietary habits of the day, thereby correcting some of the prevalent vices in the society.

Founders' Lives and Times

Buddha Suffered Early Losses in Life

Buddha was born as Siddhartha, in the royal family of the Shakya Republic that belonged to the powerful Kosala kingdom. According to the legend, his mother, Queen Maya, had a dream on a full moon night. She was carried away by the gods to anoint her. Then a divine white elephant with six tusks appeared, holding a white lotus flower in its trunk, and entered her womb through her right side. As the queen awoke and narrated her dream, it was interpreted that she was selected by the gods as the purest one for a miraculous conception of a child who would go on to be a great being. However, rather than at the royal palace, she gave birth while visiting a mangrove at a place called Lumbini. Her child was born from her right side, as was prophesied. But an early tragedy struck the life of the newborn when Queen Maya sadly passed away seven days after his birth. Prince Siddhartha was then left in the care of the queen's sister and his stepmother.

Jesus's Birth Was Prophesized

Mary, the mother of Jesus, was betrothed to Joseph, a Jewish carpenter, who traced his lineage back to King David, an important figure in the Bible. Both Mary and Joseph were from a small hill town on the caravan route called Nazareth in Israel, which was then under Roman rule. According to the Bible, Mary, while she was still a virgin, was visited by an angel, Gabriel, who informed her about being chosen by God to miraculously conceive a child—the son of God. This child would be holy, would inherit the throne of their ancestor David and would rule over an everlasting kingdom. Joseph then had another dream, where the angel confirmed this miraculous conception, and hence chose to wed Mary and raise Jesus as his own son. When the birth of Jesus was nearing, Augustus Caesar decreed a census, and Joseph travelled along with his fully pregnant wife to his native town of Bethlehem, almost 80 miles away. As all the inns were overcrowded, Mary gave birth in a stable and placed her baby in a manger. However, tragedy struck when Herod, the king of Judea, shortly after Jesus's birth ordered for the slaughter of all male children aged two or younger, who were born in the vicinity of Bethlehem. Hence the parents, along with their newborn, trekked hundreds of miles to Egypt, mainly on foot, surviving biting cold and fierce summers. Until Jesus was three years old, they lived in a state of absolute affliction, fear and deprivation.

Early Tragedies Struck Muhammad's Life

Tragedy marked Muhammad's life even before his birth. His father, Abdullah, died six months before he was born. Muhammad's mother Aminah, during her pregnancy, reported a vision of a bright light emanating from her that lit even faraway places. She said she experienced no pain during childbirth, and that her house was aglow with lights and stars. When Muhammad was still an infant, he was given away to a wet nurse who belonged to the nomadic Bedouin tribe, with whom he spent the first four years of his life in the desert. It was only in his fifth year that he met his mother again. But any happiness was short-lived, as he lost her to illness within a year. As an orphan, Muhammad was then raised by his paternal grandfather, who again died in two years, leaving him in the care of his uncle.

Striking Similarities

The founders of all the three religions, though separated by time, space and ideology, reported of strikingly similar visions received by their mothers before their birth. Each one of them went through early personal tragedies, which could have had a deep influence on their future life and mission.

Buddha Came Face to Face with Real-life Miseries

As a young prince, Siddhartha lived a sheltered life within his royal palace. Having lost his mother as an infant, his father was highly protective and surrounded him with all kinds of joys and pleasures. He was not allowed to leave the palace, as his father wanted no more sorrow to come his son's way. He was married at the age of sixteen to his cousin, from another royal family. However, his defining moment came when he once got a chance to leave the palace with his chariot driver. He was then exposed to four things that he had never seen before: an old man, an ill person, a dead person and a holy man. Until then restricted and confined to the castle walls, these scenes shook the foundations of his being. An intrigued Siddhartha wanted to find out the reasons for this suffering and a path to end it.

Jesus Exposed to Temple Life

As a young boy, Jesus, after returning from Egypt, spent his life in the town of Nazareth. He was raised like any other Jewish boy, observing religious traditions and studying the holy book of Torah. He also began helping his father Joseph in his carpentry. When Jesus was twelve years old, his parents decided to take him along with them to Jerusalem for the Jewish festival of Passover. Having led a secluded life in a small town, this might have been the first time Jesus travelled to a big city, which was several days away. Jesus would have been amazed by the marvels, particularly the glorious temple, the high point in any Jew's life. But during their return journey, Joseph and Mary realized that Jesus was missing. They searched for him for three days until they traced him back in the temple, listening keenly to the Jewish rabbis and asking them questions. This was likely a defining moment for Jesus—until then he had led a protected life but now was exposed to theologians and experts. It must have dawned upon him that this was his true calling, which he expressed while comforting his mother saying they need not have searched for him, because he was in the place where he truly belonged to.

A Self-fulfilling Prophecy in Muhammad's Life

Muhammad had a disrupted childhood. He lost his father before he was born, his mother at the age of six and his grandfather at the age of eight, after which the care of this young boy passed on to his uncle Abu Talib. Initially, Muhammad worked as a shepherd, but then he started to accompany his uncle on his trade journeys. At the age of twelve, he had his first long journey—to Syria for a few months. As they reached the city of Busra, they took a break at a monastery, where they met a Christian monk named Bahira—a wise old man with deep knowledge of ancient sacred texts. Though Muhammad was guarding the camels, Bahira took a special interest in him and engaged with him in a discussion. The monk was impressed by the boy's wisdom and curiosity, and became convinced that Muhammad was not meant to be just a trader but a great soul. Hence he advised Abu Talib to take the boy back to Mecca, where no harm would befall him.

Striking Similarities

In their early youth Buddha, Jesus and Muhammad underwent life-changing experiences which changed their understanding of themselves and the world. They were exposed to a realm vastly different from their earlier perceptions.

Buddha Attained Enlightenment

As Prince Siddhartha was exposed to suffering, poverty and death for the first time, he was transformed and spent his time in contemplation. In due course, at the age of twenty-nine, he took the tough decision to renounce all luxuries and leave his palace. Knowing that he would be stopped, he secretly left in the middle of the night, and as he crossed his kingdom, he gave up all his clothes and ornaments and shaved his head to become an ascetic. He wandered through the forest, seated himself under a pipal tree and then meditated. According to a Buddhist legend, a demon named Mara appeared during this time and started to tempt Siddhartha. Firstly, the demon tried to evoke anger about his family losing the throne. Next, he tried to strike fear by unleashing rain, darkness and thunderstorms. Finally, he tried to seduce the prince with women. But the prince successfully overcame all these to achieve enlightenment, which some say happened in three days while others say it took forty-five days. He became the Buddha, or the awakened one, at the age of thirty-five. This was a moment of private awakening, where he attained deep insights into the meaning of life and suffering.

Jesus Overcame Satan

Little is known about Jesus's life from the age of twelve for the next several years. But at the age of thirty, he left his home and travelled beyond Jordan to Bethany, several miles from his hometown of Nazareth. There, Jesus's relative John the Baptist, a revolutionary prophet, preached in the wilderness, exhorting people to repent. Jesus went up to him to be baptized—an initiation ritual in some sects of Judaism during that period. This was another defining moment, a self-fulfilling prophecy, as John then publicly proclaimed Jesus to be greater than him, a messiah. After this, Jesus wandered into the wilderness, where he spent time alone with the spirit of God, for the next forty days. During this period, he was tempted by Satan. Firstly, since Jesus was weak and hungry, Satan used the temptation of gratification, asking him to turn stones into bread. Next, he used the allure of pride by asking Jesus to jump from heights, to prove that he was indeed the son of God. Finally, he used the enticement of power, asking him to bow down to him in return for authority over the earth. Once Jesus overcame Satan successfully, he travelled to the town of Galilee to start his ministry.

Muhammad Confronted an Angel

In his late thirties, for about three years, Muhammad had the habit of retiring to a small cave named Hira, around 2 miles from Mecca. He would sit there and meditate in solitude. Once, when he was around forty, in the month of Ramadan, he was unexpectedly sought by an angel in this cave. When this angel asked him to recite the words in front of him, Muhammad confessed that he did not know how to read or write. But as the angel insisted and pressed down on him physically, Muhammad repeated the verses. When he came outside the cave, Muhammad was stricken with fear. He feared that he might have become a soothsayer, or worse, even possessed by a djinn. He was so confused that he wanted to kill himself by jumping off a cliff. Soon, however, his wife took him to a scholar, who told him that he had been chosen as a prophet. Muhammad then came to the conclusion that these visions were indeed from God and a great responsibility had been conferred upon him.

Striking Similarities

Coincidentally, all these three founders spent several days in solitude, either in the wilderness or in a cave, away from their homes when they were between thirty to forty years of age. After a life of near obscurity, during this meditative time, each one of them had a divine experience which transformed their life. Incidentally, each of these experiences were completely private ones, with no one else around, and hence solely based on their own recounts.

Buddha Preached at Sarnath

After attaining enlightenment, Buddha was eager to share the revelation he had received. He set out on foot and reached out to five monks, who had been his companions on his journey towards asceticism. Though these monks initially doubted Buddha, as he had given up on the conventional path of self-mortification, they were drawn towards his newly acquired charisma. These five became his first disciples. Buddha gave his first sermon at Sarnath, where he spoke of the 'middle way' philosophy, that lay between the extremes of self-indulgence and self-denial. This was a marked departure from the previously understood philosophies. He then preached the fundamental principles of the Four Noble Truths—life is suffering, the cause of suffering, end of suffering and the way to end suffering through the eight-fold path.

Jesus Declared the Good News

After his experience in the wilderness, Jesus was eager to start his ministry. He set out, and while walking beside the Sea of

Galilee, he saw two brothers, Peter and Andrew, who were fishermen. He urged them to follow him and told them he would teach them how to fish for people. He met a few more, who became his initial disciples—a band of twelve members. As his popularity grew, with people crowding around him, Jesus went up on a mountainside and from there preached a new gospel previously unheard of. He proclaimed that the kingdom of God was near, and it was reserved for those who were suffering, who were mourning, who were humble, peaceful and merciful. Unlike the Jewish law which stated an 'eye for an eye and tooth for tooth', he taught that they should be merciful and love their enemies, and that they should pray for those who persecute them.

Muhammad Proclaimed the Oneness of God

After receiving the revelation, the first one to believe and convert was Muhammad's wife Khadija. A few of his other relatives like Ali Ibn Abi Talib and close friends like Abu Bakr were the next set of converts, followed by a group of merchants and foreigners. However, Muhammad's first public sermon would take three more years, which he delivered to a gathering on a hill near Mecca. Here, he preached his message of oneness of God, quite contrary to the practices of the time. He exhorted a life of monotheism rooted in faith, love, truth and purity.

Striking Similarities

After revelations were received, the first task of all the founders was to gather together an initial set of disciples who believed in their message. All started with a small set—Buddha five,

Jesus twelve and Muhammad three. Their next mission was an initiation speech, which each of them delivered in a public place such as a park or on a mountain, where people could see and listen to them easily. From there, they delivered a message that was contrary to the practices of the time.

Buddha Showed His Supernatural Side

Following the sermon in Sarnath, Buddha is said to have performed several supernatural feats through the powers he attained by meditation. Once when he was visiting his kingdom, he performed what came to be known as the twin miracle—where he emitted water and fire from his body while levitating, and once he returned to the ground, even as it started to rain heavily, he remained dry. He performed other notable miracles such as walking on water, walking on walls, becoming invisible, extinguishing forest fires and healing the diseased.

Jesus Established Himself through His Miracles

Jesus performed his first miracle immediately after he started his public ministry by turning water into wine during a wedding function. The Bible counts thirty-seven major miracles that Jesus performed, which included feeding thousands of people, healing the blind, deaf and injured, and raising dead people. He walked on water and calmed a storm with a word. Demons trembled at his sight and fled from those they had possessed. One of the significant incidents included the transfiguration of Jesus, when he shone brightly while on a mountain. When Jesus was crucified, it was said that darkness fell on earth for several hours during the daytime.

Miracles Reaffirmed Muhammad's Status

During his public ministry, Muhammad performed a broad range of miracles. During one of the feasts, food just enough for one person was multiplied to feed 300 guests until they were all full. In another major feat, he stood on a mountain and split the moon into two. Once, when water for ablutions fell short, he manifested it from his own body. Other miracles included healing the sick, restoring sight to the blind and punishing the wicked. He is said to have ascended to the heavens to hold a communion with God. The day he died, darkness fell over the city of Medina.

Striking Similarities

All three founders are credited with performing supernatural miracles. Coincidentally, many of them similar in scope.

Buddha Was Plotted Against by His Own

Devadutta was Buddha's cousin and a brother to Buddha's wife. Being an early entrant to the order of the monks and from a royal family, he quickly gained favour among others. Driven by excessive ambition, he once approached Buddha and suggested he be made the head of the order immediately. However, when this proposal was rejected, Devadutta became hostile and started to scheme. Firstly, he sent several men to assassinate Buddha but soon he took the job upon himself by dropping a rock and unleashing a furious elephant. As all his schemes proved to be unsuccessful, Devadutta persuaded 500 monks to defect and become his disciples. Though they later returned to Buddha's fold, after

Devadutta fell mortally ill, Buddha still went through a time of extreme tribulations.

Jesus Betrayed by His Disciple

Out of his twelve disciples, Judas Iscariot was the treasurer and among the ones whom Jesus trusted deeply. But in between the last supper of Jesus, Judas hurriedly left. After the meal, as Jesus retired for a time of prayer in the garden of Gethsemane, outside the city of Jerusalem, Judas, knowing well that he would be in the garden, arrived with a gang of Jewish priests. Armed with swords and sticks, they wanted Jesus to be taken into custody for treason. In order to help them identify the person, Judas greeted Jesus with a kiss. He was then grabbed by the crowd and taken away for a trial and impending crucifixion. Following the arrest, his favourite disciple, Peter, denied knowing or being associated with him three times, which again would have caused Jesus a great deal of sorrow.

Muhammad Insulted and Afflicted by His Tribesmen

Muhammad suffered betrayal several times during his public ministry. Umayr Ibn Wahb and Safwan ibn Umayya, who later became Muhammad's companions, initially opposed him in Mecca and even plotted to get him killed. Many of his early disciples were insulted and beaten up publicly in the streets of Mecca. During several instances, tribal believers abused and demonized Muhammad. They showered insults on him by calling him a soothsayer, a magician and even a madman. They boycotted all interactions and trade and refused to marry the relatives of those who followed him. Once, when Muhammad prayed in public, his adversaries attempted to strangle him from behind. He was spat upon, beaten unconscious and even had camel intestines dumped on him in public. Muhammad was afflicted by his own tribesmen.

Striking Similarities

All three founders suffered several public humiliations. They were betrayed by people whom they trusted, loved and thought were by their side.

Expansion Strategies and Geopolitical Ambitions

Magadha, and then Maurya, Reoriented Their Systems with Buddhism

During the emergence of Buddhism, the Vedic society, monopolized by the Brahminical caste system, was being replaced by the monarchical system. This monarchical rise was funded by the economic surplus generated by the newly wealthy agrarian and merchant class. However, this resulted in two challenges. Firstly, the farmers and traders expected integration of economic and trade structures and protection against thefts, robbery and instability. However, the smaller kingdoms, which were constantly threatened by their enemies, were unable to guarantee these. Secondly, since large tracts of land and resources were held by Brahmins with immunity from taxes, the state was deprived of revenue. Hence, the existing political systems were an obstacle to the ambitious rulers who wanted to consolidate these smaller kingdoms. So, with each conquest, they started to replace the prevailing structures with the ones they preferred. Meanwhile, Buddhism supported the theory of a universal monarch. According to them, it could put an end to petty conflicts between the smaller kingdoms and would be able to establish peace and harmony. This made Buddhism, as a religious order, highly attractive to the new consolidators. The first great empire to emerge was Magadha. Bimbisara, one of their earlier kings, realized the potential in this new religion and hence was a great patron and protector. Ajatashatru, son of Bimbisara, was an early follower of Buddhism, a patron credited with erecting a great shrine, renovating several monasteries and sponsoring the first Buddhist Council. However, the real turning point arrived when Ashoka the Great of the Mauryan Empire, that replaced the Magadha Empire, adopted Buddhism. Legend has it that Emperor Ashoka went through a change of heart after witnessing the violence, slaughter and immeasurable suffering caused by his conquest of the kingdom of Kalinga, and hence decided to embrace Buddhism and the non-violence that it propagated.

Roman Empire Wanted to Rebuild Its Glory Leveraging Christianity

Christianity originated when Judea was under the Roman rule. Though it initially began as a sect of Judaism, it soon developed its own unique ideologies and branched out. Its early members included those Jews who were tired of the strict ritualistic attitudes. But soon it spread to several other areas, especially the Greek-speaking regions of the Roman Empire, to be embraced equally by the Gentiles. During this time it went through several bouts of persecutions from the Roman emperors, who alleged the Christian refusal to bow down to Roman gods as a reason for several natural calamities, including the Antonine Plague. However, the real turning point of Christianity came about when Emperor Constantine adopted it as the official religion, following a victory in the Battle of the Milvian Bridge which enabled him to consolidate the Roman Empire. According to Constantine, a vision of the cross helped him win the war. This event changed the fortunes of Christianity, a religion which until then was a minority.

Rashidun Caliphate Built on Islamic Foundations

Muhammad founded Islam when the entire Arabian Peninsula was fragmented among several small idol-worshipping nomadic tribes. His journey was probably the most difficult among all the three founders since he faced enormous challenges towards attracting early converts. Most of the initial adoptees were either women, children, slaves or foreigners, all who were low-standing members of the hierarchical Arabic tribes. But this changed when Abu Bakr—a prominent person from the Quraysh tribe that controlled the city of Mecca and Kaaba— converted to Islam. It was a watershed moment for Islam, granting it the credibility that it had lacked. Abu Bakr then persuaded many of his friends and slaves to convert, and even contributed his wealth and resources to the work of propagating the religion. He gave public speeches and presented Islam in such a way that it was easier for people to convert. He stood alongside Muhammad in his migration to Medina and in his military conflicts. Overcoming the initial inertia from the Quraysh tribe, they eventually won widespread support. A complete conversion was in order by 630 CE. After the death of Prophet Muhammad, Abu Bakr took over and established the Rashidun Caliphate, claiming supreme political and religious authority over the Islamic world. A religion that was earlier restricted to certain tribes of Arabia now spread across West Asia under the Caliphate.

Striking Similarities

Three mighty universal empires—Magadha, Rome and Rashidun—separated by time and space, were going through a period of churn. Their rulers figured out that co-opting a new religion that had been obscure until then, accorded them special advantages that was not present in the older religions.

Mahadevi Introduced Ashoka to Buddhism

Before Ashoka ascended the throne, he was appointed as a viceroy to Ujjain by his father, Emperor Bindusara. While there, he met a merchant who belonged to the Shakya clan, the same as that of Buddha. Ashoka fell in love with the daughter of this merchant, Mahadevi Shakyakumari, whom he later married and who bore him his first two children. Mahadevi's Buddhist influence would have certainly exposed Ashoka to her religion. In fact, legend has it that Mahadevi even tried to convert Ashoka to Buddhism but failed. After his father's death, Ashoka returned to Pataliputra and captured the throne. As an emperor he married another woman, this time from a royal family, unlike Mahadevi. Though Mahadevi disappeared from the narrative for some time, her beliefs could have had a deep impact on Ashoka's life, leading him to embrace her religion after the Kalinga War. Meanwhile, Mahadevi herself went on to have a great influence on Buddhism at a later date—her children Mahinda and Sangamitra led the first missionary to Sri Lanka, which was then converted completely to Buddhism. Mahadevi also had an important role to play in the construction of the first Buddhist monuments in Sanchi and Bhilasa and the great monastery of Vedisagiri.

Helena Influenced Constantine on Christianity

While Constantius, father of Emperor Constantine, served Emperor Aurelian in Asia Minor, he met Helena, a Greek Christian lady, with whom he fell in love. Helena, though he could not officially marry due to her lower-class origins, gave birth to his first son—Constantine. Later, once Constantius married another lady from a royal lineage, Helena chose to live a life of obscurity. She reappeared in the pages of history once her son Constantine took over as emperor, when she received the title of Augusta. Though Constantine's conversion to Christianity was said to have occurred after he received the vision of the cross, the seeds could have been sown by his mother—a practising Christian. Helena continued to exert immense influence on the future of Christianity; she was given unlimited access to the state treasury to locate the sacred relics, including the true cross of Jesus Christ. She commissioned churches including the Church of Nativity in the birthplace of Jesus and Church of Eleona in the place of ascension of Jesus.

Aisha Provided Islam a Pillar of Strength

The adoption of Islam by Abu Bakr, a prominent tribesman, changed the course of Islam. After the death of Muhammad's first wife, Abu Bakr's daughter Aisha was proposed to marry Muhammad, as they felt that this relationship could strengthen their ties. Aisha, once married to Muhammad, became a pillar of strength behind the prophet, along with whom he received several of his revelations. According to a legend, when asked whom he loved most in the world, Muhammad said it was Aisha. He valued Aisha's intellectual prowess and even advised his companions to learn from her. She delivered speeches and helped the followers of Islam to understand the right practices. It is believed that though there were other strong contenders to succeed Muhammad, Abu Bakr was chosen because of the strong ideological and political influence that his daughter wielded. As the daughter of the first Caliph of the Rashidun Caliphate, Aisha was given the title of al-Siddiq, and she continued to play a strategic role in the affairs of the empire and Islam.

Striking Similarities

Though initially it seemed like the imperial adoption of these three religions was driven by a divine vision or a relationship, a woman played a strong role behind the scenes.

Ashoka Spread Buddhism through Education and Missionaries

Ashoka's embrace of Buddhism changed its fortunes. He funded missionaries to travel throughout his kingdom and neighbouring countries to propagate the religion. He even put his children to the task so that they led a successful mission to Sri Lanka, converting their king and subjects. Ashoka issued edicts and commissioned artists and authors, all in the local languages, so that Buddhist philosophies could be made palatable even to the uneducated. Pillars were erected across borders, visible to neighbouring nations, in their languages. He opened up his state treasuries to develop Buddhist educational hubs, monasteries and temples. He personally undertook several pilgrimages to Buddhist sacred places, exempted religious sites from taxes and proclaimed his undeterred support for the religion at every forum. From one of the minority religions, Buddhism became the predominant one.

Rome Gave Christianity Credibility and Universality

Early Christianity faced several challenges. First, as a growing religion in Rome, it faced imperial persecution, which drove it underground and turned many potential converts away. Second, it suffered from several internal conflicts, where factions argued over beliefs, teachings, worship and even the nature of Jesus Christ. Constantine's adoption of Christianity transformed it. From a religion running for cover it was now the official one, with complete immunity from all persecution. The Christian bishops and clergy gained power and exerted an upper hand in many state administrative affairs and appointments. Constantine then presided over a meeting of over 300 bishops at the Council of Nicaea, creating a uniformity on many of the contentious issues. He also liberally supported the church with finances and resources. His mother Helena undertook a pilgrimage to Israel where she claimed to have discovered several sacred sites, giving the religion immense credibility and popularity. Constantine then commissioned the Church of Nativity in Bethlehem, Church of Holy Sepulchre in Jerusalem, and Church of Holy Apostles in Constantinople. Christianity spread not just throughout the Roman Empire but also to every other region it had trade and diplomatic relations with. Soon, it emerged as the dominant religion across the globe.

Islam Provided Imperial Backbone

The Rashidun Caliphate, which was founded on the tenets of Islam, expanded its religion alongside their empire. The Caliphate relied on three main strategies—military expansion, increased trade and missionary expeditions. Though Muhammad's military conquests had integrated most of the warring tribes of Arabia, with the Rashidun Caliphate it grew to mammoth proportions. It expanded outside towards the neighbouring Byzantine and

Sasanian empires, and territories to the east and west. The swift military victories of the Caliphate created a massive empire spanning across continents in a short span of time. The brute force was then complemented by softer measures such as trade and missionaries, enabling the Islamic ideas to be adopted by large numbers of the native population.

Striking Similarities

Initially these religions were small and limited in their scope, as they were officially adopted by their patron empires. But soon, with the staunch support and resources accorded to them by their rulers, they spread their wings and expanded across the globe.

Buddhist Pacifism Weakened the Mauryan Empire

The Mauryan Empire started to decline after the death of Ashoka in 232 BCE, and in under five decades, completely collapsed. Ironically, the very religion that the empire adopted and promoted globally by spending much of its resources— Buddhism—may have been one of the main reasons behind its downfall. Firstly, since Buddhism opposed animal sacrifice on account of its adherence to non-violence, it put them at loggerheads with the priestly class of the Brahmins, who derived most of their income and authority from such practices. Hence, Brahmins actively started to support other rebel factions which weakened the empire. In fact, the last ruler of the Mauryan Empire, Brihadratha, was murdered by his general Pushyamitra Shunga, a Brahmin, who went on to establish the Shunga dynasty. Secondly, Ashoka spent heavily to promote Buddhism. He sent missionaries on state-funded trips to faraway lands and established and supported large monasteries across his empire. He also constructed temples and donated gold images throughout his empire; all this put high pressure on his already stretched treasury. Thirdly, Ashoka diverted his most efficient children from administrative matters and tasked them with religious propagation. His first son—Mahinda—became a Buddhist monk and went on a missionary trip to Sri Lanka, eventually settling there. This affected the plan of succession, resulting in the throne passing on to weak rulers. Inefficient administration further destabilized the empire. And lastly, the policy of non-violence and pacifism pursued by Ashoka in his later years proved to be the nail in the coffin for the empire. The state treasuries and the armies that depended on new conquests for their wealth and resources were either depleted, or demotivated. The formidable Mauryan Empire was weakened by its adoption of Buddhism.

Monotheism Challenged Polytheistic Rome

Christianity was adopted by Emperor Constantine not only because it appealed to him, but also because he felt that 'one empire under one god' could reinvigorate the sagging fortunes of an empire riddled with multiple problems. However, Christianity, which worshipped only one God and rejected idolatry, pagan rituals and polytheism, ran contrary to the traditional Roman way of life. Hence, ironically, the adoption of Christianity could have resulted in the downfall of Rome. Firstly, many Roman citizens loathed and persecuted Christians, but when it was made the official religion, it led to much internal confusion and discontent. Secondly, Romans considered their emperor as a god. They took pride in bowing down to him, fighting for him and laying their lives down in battles to uphold his honour. However, as Christianity prohibited bowing down to anyone else but Jesus, this undermined the authority and credibility of the emperor, and in turn the empire. And thirdly, the Christian philosophies of pacifism, sobriety and poverty weakened the

Roman economy and military considerably, especially at a time when the empire was being threatened by its enemies.

Islamic Chism Led to Rashidun Collapse

The Rashidun Caliphate expansions continued under the first two Caliphs—Abu Bakr and Umar. To decide on the next caliph, a committee was appointed, which shortlisted two people—Uthman from the Umayyad clan and Ali, Muhammad's cousin and son-in-law. Ultimately, when Uthman was selected, there was an uprising with a demand to correct the injustice done to Ali. The protests soon turned into a siege, which Uthman refused to quell in order to maintain peace between the different factions. Uthman was eventually murdered by the rebels and Ali took charge as caliph. But trouble was still brewing. To avenge the assassination of Uthman, an army was put together by a few companions of Muhammad along with Aisha, his widow. In the battle that followed, the companions of Muhammad were killed and Ali emerged victorious. Aisha was escorted back to Medina. But civil wars across the caliphate continued, now led by Muawiya, the kinsman of Uthman. It eventually ended in the murder of Ali. The unified Islamic religion upon which the Rashidun Caliphate was founded was divided forever into Sunni and Shia factions. The first caliphate collapsed and gave way to the new Umayyad under Muawiya.

Striking Similarities

Religions were co-opted by empires not just because of any special affiliations, but as they foresaw definite political benefits. However, the same religions eventually undermined the existing systems and resulted in the collapse of these mighty empires.

STRIKING SIMILARITIES BETWEEN BUDDHISM, CHRISTIANITY AND ISLAM

	BUDDHISM	CHRISTIANITY	ISLAM
ORIGINS	~600 BCE	~30 CE	610 CE
SOCIAL CONTEXT	Ultra-conservativism of Vedic civilization	Domination of Judea by elite and ultra-religious Jews	Friction between nomadic Bedouins and urban settlers
PHILOSOPHICAL UNDERPINNINGS	Borrowed from Hinduism	Borrowed from Judaism	Borrowed from Judaism, Christianity and prehistoric Arabia
MEMBERSHIP AND HIERARCHY	Flat compared to caste hierarchy of Vedic Brahminism	Inclusive of and equality to gentiles compared to exclusive Judaism	Universality compared to clan-based tribal polytheism
DIET MODIFICATIONS	Vegetarianism vs animal sacrifices	Open food habits vs Kosher	Halal vs open food habits
FOUNDERS' BIRTH PROPHESIES AND EARLY TRAGEDIES	Miraculous dream about birth, mother's early death	Prophecies on birth, Herodian decree on child slaughter	Miraculous vision about birth, given away to a wet nurse
DEFINING MOMENTS	First-time exposure to life's miseries	First-time visit to the Jewish temple	First long journey and discussion with a monk
SOLITUDE AND TEMPTATION	Meditation under pipal tree and temptation by Mara the Devil	Solitary time in the wilderness followed by Satan's temptation	Solitary meditation in Hira Cave. Confusion about being possessed by a djinn
FIRST SERMON	First sermon at Sarnath	Sermon on the Mount	Sermon on Mount Safa
ALTERNATE PATH	Middle way as opposed to self-indulgence and self-denial	New gospel of love as opposed to an eye for an eye and a tooth for a tooth	Oneness of God as opposed to polytheism
MIRACLES	Ascending to heaven, walking on water, extinguishing forest fires and healing the diseased	Transfiguration on the Mount, walking on water, calming the storm, healing the sick and blind	Ascension to heavens in Mi'raj, manifesting water from the body, splitting of the moon, healing the sick and blind
BETRAYAL	Murder plot by Devadutta, Buddha's cousin	Betrayed to crucifixion by Judas Iscariot, a trusted disciple	Afflictions and attempts on life by own tribesmen
IMPERIAL ADOPTION AND CHANGE OF FORTUNES	Adoption By Mauryan Empire, the first Buddhist empire	Adoption by Roman Empire, the first Christian empire	Adoption by Rashidun Caliphate, the first Islamic empire
REASON FOR EMPIRE'S DECLINE	Non-violence and pacifism weakened the empire	Monotheism and pacifism weakened the empire	Division and factions within Islam weakened the first caliphate

Why Are These Three Starkly Different Religions So Similar?

Ancient Origin of Religious Beliefs

Religious beliefs originated in human societies as they tried to make sense of their environment and their place in the universe. Complex questions regarding the creation of the world, purpose of life, life after death, changing weather patterns and even personal questions like survival and fertility led the early humans to start believing in supernatural forces. Soon, they realized the power of religion in unifying a population which otherwise were divergent. Common beliefs and behaviours helped people find common ground, and trust. Rulers and leaders soon discovered two greater advantages—to justify and authorize their power over people and to maintain social hierarchies. Though separated by time and space, various civilizations in different parts of the world learnt the same lessons as far as religions and beliefs in them were concerned. And as new social orders, civilizations and religions developed on the ruins of earlier ones, these collective lessons were not forgotten, but carried as cultural memories and were passed down to future generations.

Trade Routes, Conquests and Myth Propagation

As the footprints of humanity expanded through conquests and trade routes, it was not just the territories that expanded and commodities that were exchanged, but also culture, ideas and knowledge, including religious beliefs. The Silk Road, which connected China, India, Central Asia and the Roman Empire, the Incense Route which connected the Arabian

Peninsula to the Mediterranean, and the Tin Route which provided a vital link across Europe, were some of the major trade routes that enabled the spread of religions and their myths from the ancient world to the modern world, defying time and space. Adapting, adopting and borrowing the best practices shared through commerce and conquests, religions grew everywhere. Hence we see similar rituals and beliefs across different parts of the world, which to onlookers might seem nothing less than surprising.

Impact of the Fountainhead Epoch

As we saw in the first chapter, the foundation of all progress made by human beings was achieved in a short span of three centuries between 600 and 300 BCE, making it the Fountainhead epoch. During the millennium before 600 BCE, our entire world, including the Indus Valley Civilization, the Hittite, the Egyptian New Kingdom, the Assyrian, the Canaanite, the Cypriot, the Minoan, the Mycenaean Greek, the Cassite and the Zhou of China, collapsed, literally wiping away all the progress achieved until then. The later period of transition formed the bedrock of our future, from which everything else emanated. During this Fountainhead epoch, many religions that have withstood the test of time either originated, like Buddhism, or took their inspiration from, like Christianity and Islam. Hence, as these world religions trace their origins back to this age, we see uncanny similarities between them.

A Long Tail of Climate Change Impact

The Fountainhead Epoch was a result of two closely packed climate changes—the Late Bronze Age Climate Change, which lasted for 400 years until 1500 BCE, quickly succeeded by the Iron Age Climate Change, which lasted for another 600 years. These cataclysms more closely and directly shaped and spread Buddhism, a religion that emerged from this rubble. Though Christianity and Islam took indirect, passive inspiration from this era, their adoption and growth were actively influenced by two other climate changes. Firstly, the Roman Climate Change that halted Pax Romana from 150 CE, prompting the visionary Emperor Constantine to adopt Christianity resulting in the religion's unprecedented growth and globalization. Secondly, the Late Antiquity Little Ice Age, which began in 536 CE, increased the strain on the Eastern Roman Empire, leading to its eventual decline. In the Arabian Peninsula, this climate change resulted in extreme dry weather—a period of crop failures, famines, declining trade, and hence, economic, political and social unrest. The desperation of the population added to their aggressiveness—enabling the Rashidun Caliphate to take over regions of Levant, Egypt, Mesopotamia and Persia—ushering in a global Islam. Hence, in more ways than one, these three religions could have been physically and psychologically shaped by the long invisible tail of climate changes.

So Different, Yet So Same

More than half of the world's population belongs to one of the three religions of Buddhism, Christianity and Islam. Each one of them considers themselves unique; in philosophy, value and path, propagating the idea that they have a monopoly over the sole truth. However, no religion emerged out of a vacuum. No religion is so unique that it is completely different from everything else. Some of their beliefs were built on the collective memories from ancient times, some were unwillingly thrust during territorial conquests, while some others were borrowed through the trade routes. But now we have come to a stage where these religions are propagated as starkly different. However, this might just be the narcissism of negligible differences because they might, after all, be strikingly similar to each other.

5

Hidden Triggers, Plot Twists and Global Geopolitical Undercurrents in the Mahabharata

Keywords: Climate Change, Steppe Migration, Narcissism of Negligible Differences, Kurukshetra, Mahajanapadas, Indus Valley Civilization, Vedic Civilization, Universal Religions, Universal Monarchy, Social Disruption, Geo-political Disruption, Fountainhead Epoch, United India

Mahabharata: Real History of India than an Imaginary Tale

The Mahabharata war was a great dynastic succession battle for the throne of Hastinapura of the Kuru kingdom, presently located in the Indo-Gangetic basin of Delhi, Haryana and parts of Uttar Pradesh. It unravelled the rivalry between two sets of cousins—the Kauravas and Pandavas—from the lineage of a great king named Puru, who belonged to the Kshatriya caste, the ruling aristocracy of ancient India. The war took place on the battlefield of Kurukshetra and spanned eighteen days, after which the Pandavas emerged victorious. The saga of Mahabharata written in Sanskrit is the longest poem ever, several times longer than the likes of the *Iliad* or the *Odyssey*. Though often mentioned to as an epic and a great poem, it is much more than a subjective imaginary chronicle. According to historian Romila Thapar, the Mahabharata calls itself Itihasa—'the way it was in the past'—which means it is a retelling of history rather than just a mere fable. As such, it provides important clues to the times that the nation of India has traversed through.

Beginnings of Pandavas and Kauravas

The great Kuru king Shantanu's first born—Bhishma—was a lifelong celibate, and had relinquished all his claims to the throne. Hence his two step-relatives—Dhritarashtra, the eldest, and Pandu—both the grandsons of Shantanu, were left to compete for the throne of Hastinapura. Dhritarashtra married Gandhari of the Gandhara kingdom, presently in north-west Pakistan and Afghanistan, and begot a hundred sons, called the Kauravas. The eldest of them was Duryodhana. Pandu had two wives: Kunti from the kingdom of Kunti, a smaller kingdom from central India, and Madri, from the kingdom of Madra, near present-day Punjab. From his two wives, Pandu begot five sons—Yudhishtira, Bhima, Arjuna, Nakula and Sahadeva. They came to be known as the Pandavas.

A Feud between the Cousins

Since Dhritarashtra was blind, Pandu, though younger and weaker in health, was initially chosen to be the king. But through a twist of fate, Pandu had to prematurely retire to the forest with his wife and children. The crown then passed back to Dhritarashtra. However, after the death of Pandu and his second wife Madri, the Pandava boys along with Kunti decided to return to their palace in Hastinapura. As Pandu was originally the king, and Yudhishtira, the eldest Pandava, was also the oldest among all the cousins, Dhritarashtra came under pressure from his courtiers to declare him as the crown prince. This sparked a bitter family feud—a typical case of narcissism of negligible differences, where close blood relatives struggled amongst themselves to establish their superiority over the other.

Enraged Kauravas Plotted to Kill Their Cousins

Though Yudhishtira was made the first in line to the throne, King Dhritarashtra wanted his own eldest son Duryodhana to inherit the kingdom. Duryodhana, on his part, came up with a devious plot: an eminent architect was hired to build a beautiful palace. But this palace was constructed out of lacquer—a highly flammable material. This palace was gifted to the Pandavas, with the secret plan of later setting it on fire so that the unwitting Pandavas would be burnt to death. It would be convenient as the deaths could be passed off as an accident. However, Vidura, the prime minister of the kingdom and the uncle of the cousins, happened to be a well-wisher of the Pandavas and hence warned them in advance of the plot. Vidura then arranged for a miner who dug a secret tunnel, which enabled the Pandavas to escape to safety after the palace was set on fire. With the Kauravas presuming them dead, the Pandavas went into exile to avoid any further mishap.

Kauravas Exiled Pandavas through a Game of Deceit

While the Pandavas stayed in exile, their third brother, Arjuna, got married to Draupadi, the daughter of the king of Panchala, a powerful neighbouring kingdom, now encompassing the regions of Uttar Pradesh and Uttarakhand. After this wedding, the Pandavas were invited back to Hastinapura, and a peace brokered according to which the kingdom was divided between the rival cousins. Pandavas inherited a small, thickly forested portion, which eventually prospered under them. However, Duryodhana, the crown prince of the bigger portion of the Kuru kingdom, was enraged by the success of his rivals. Hence, through a well-planned game of deceit, he sent the Pandavas into another exile. After almost thirteen years of living in the wilderness, when the Pandavas tried to reclaim their part of the kingdom, the great Mahabharata war erupted between the cousins.

This is the story that we have heard until now. However, is this the entire truth? Let us find out.

A Great War That Drew Every Kingdom In

During the time of the Mahabharata war, the Indo-Gangetic basin was going through a period of urbanization, dominated by sixteen oligarchic republics called the Mahajanapadas. Among these, the real powerful ones were concentrated in the Western and Central Ganga region, including the Kurus. Hence the Mahabharata war was a defining moment, where all of them aligned with one family or the other. The allies of each party included Panchala, Kasi, Magadha, Matsya, Chedi, Vatsa, Malla and Asmaka with the Pandavas and Anga, Avanti, Gandhara, Kamboja, Kosala, Vriji and Surasena with the Kurus.

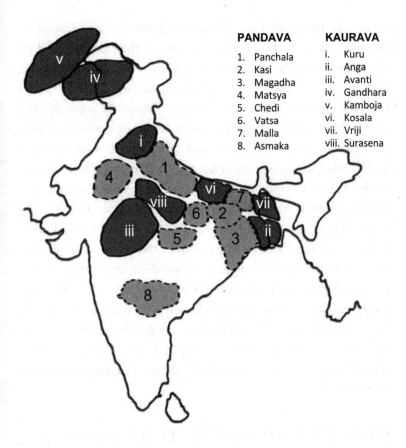

PANDAVA	KAURAVA
1. Panchala	i. Kuru
2. Kasi	ii. Anga
3. Magadha	iii. Avanti
4. Matsya	iv. Gandhara
5. Chedi	v. Kamboja
6. Vatsa	vi. Kosala
7. Malla	vii. Vriji
8. Asmaka	viii. Surasena

The War Puzzle: A Less Competent Non-Pandava-Appointed Supreme Commander

In any war, the Supreme Commander is the most demanding job, in-charge of the entire armed forces hence reserved for the highest-ranked warrior. In cases where the war is fought alongside allies, the chief ensures that the combined military is deployed effectively to carry out its mission in unison. As protecting the kingdom at war's interest is paramount, the chief is almost always drawn from the lead army rather than from an ally. In the case of the Kurus, this position was adorned by Bhishma, their most powerful warrior, and the protector of their kingdom. In the case of the Pandavas, without any question this position should have gone to Arjuna, the most valiant and a part of the core Pandava army. On excellence, Arjuna was rated as the 'Maharathi'—a warrior above all other warriors. Oddly enough, he was overlooked and the position was accorded to Drishtadyumna, the twin brother of Draupadi and the son of the Panchala king, an ally. It is an intriguing case, because Drishtadyumna was just an 'Atirathi', rated several notches below Arjuna in his military prowess. Surprisingly, in addition to the Supreme Commander position, two more commanders were drawn from the Panchala army—their king Drupada, the father of Draupadi, and Shikhandi, another brother of Draupadi. Further adding to this mystery, though typical allies commit just a part of their army, King Drupada pledged his entire forces to this war. This army was then commanded by Satyajit, another son of Drupada. It was as if he had put his entire kingdom at risk for this war.

Panchala Held a Higher Stake, Even Compared to the Pandavas

In the Mahabharata war, the Pandavas were fighting for their own cause—to reclaim a kingdom what justly was theirs. Oddly, we see a larger role played by Panchala kingdom, even compared to the Pandavas. The Supreme Commander should have ideally been a Pandava but was handled by Drishtadyumna. Two key commanders of the combined forces and the personal army of Panchala kingdom were led by Panchala warriors. In addition, all sons of Drupada were on the battle front—Yudhamanyu and Uttamaujas were assigned as protectors of Arjuna and Kumara was a protector for Yudhishtira. Even the grandchildren were not spared. Kshatradharman, Kshatravarman and Kshatranjaya, the sons of Drishtadyumna and Khsatradeva, the son of Shikhandi, all of them tender in age, were put right out there in the forefront. Addionally, Panchala even convinced their vassals to be part of this war: these were Srinjayas, Somakas and Prabhadrakas, their tribal allies. In short, the Panchala kingdom put their king's and heirs' lives at risk and devoted a much higher proportion of valuable resources. It is indeed surprising that an ally was contributing much more in this war than the key player itself. This does not make sense, unless the Panchala kingdom had a bigger stake in the war than even Pandavas.

So now the question arises, what was this personal cause that the Panchala kingdom was fighting for, committing higher stakes to a war where all other allies were considered equal?

Draupadi Wedding Contest: Panchalas' Track and Trace for Pandavas?

The wedding of Draupadi to Arjuna provides us with certain interesting cues. The Pandavas were on the run to escape the wrath of the Kauravas. As they were in disguise, there was no way anyone could track them down. Around this time, Drupada, the king of Panchala, organized a *swayamvara*—a function where his daughter Draupadi's groom would be chosen based on a contest. Coincidentally, this competition happened to be the one which Arjuna aced—hitting the target with an arrow. Arjun's mastery of the bow and arrow was already legendary. In fact, when they were students under their teacher Drona, a game was played once where the target, a bird, was identified atop a distant tree. As the students gathered with their bows and arrows, Drona asked each of them to describe the target to him.

While everyone began narrating the features of the bird and the tree on which it was resting, Arjuna replied that he was unable to see anything other than the eye of the bird. Unsurprisingly, his arrow pierced the tiny eye of the faraway bird with stunning precision. Having displayed such mastery at a young age, it is reasonable to believe that the swayamvara contest was framed not by any coincidence, but instead was carefully planned by Drupada as a masquerade to track down the Pandavas.

Only Arjuna Would be Chosen as Groom, Even if Others Were Better

There might still be more to this swayamvara than what meets the eye. If the contest was indeed fair, Draupadi would have had to marry anyone who won, whoever that might be. But it was not to be so. As Karna, king of the Anga kingdom, an ally of the Kauravas and an ace archer Maharathi who even surpassed the prowess of Arjuna, walked up to the stage, Draupadi was quick to insult him, mocking him for being a 'charioteer's son'. In fact, as the real motive might have been to track down the Pandavas, if anyone else other than Arjuna emerged as an able contestant, he would have been insulted and eliminated by Draupadi. So much so that even if Ashwatthama, the son of Drona, another able contender, someone described as a very handsome man born with all the auspicious marks, counted among the eight 'Chiranjivis' or immortals, and a Maharathi himself, was to volunteer, Draupadi would have found some reason to reject him.

But Arjuna, disguised as a poor Brahman, without a hint of royal heritage, was gladly accepted, in stark contrast to the hostile treatment the others received. Karna and the rest of the kings who had gathered out there tried to dissuade Draupadi, exhorting that she being a Kshatriya should not be marrying outside her caste. Despite all disapprovals, Draupadi's resolve to marry Arjuna seemed as if it were a pre-decided affair.

Draupadi as Pandava Wife—to Keep Them United for an Imminent War?

After Draupadi's swayamvara, when the Pandavas announced Arjuna's grand win to their mother Kunti, she asked them to 'share the spoils', thinking it was another prize that they had won. Considering the fact that Draupadi was a strong-willed princess who chose her husband despite all objections, it is not too hard to imagine that this suggestion of sharing her as a wife between the five Pandava brothers could not be possible unless she herself was in agreement. Taking a leap of faith, would this have been a strategic move by Draupadi herself, shooting from the shoulders of Kunti, to be wedded to all the Pandavas? Her premonition might have been that only a woman could keep these five independent-minded warriors together in case there was a war scenario.

Draupadi Triggered a Future War through a Well-planned Insult of Duryodhana

From the beginning, Draupadi behaved as if she was expecting a war to break out in the near future. In fact, an important trigger for the Mahabharata war itself could be traced back to her. As the Pandavas returned to Hastinapura after Arjuna's wedding to Draupadi, a truce was agreed upon with the Kurus and a portion of the kingdom was given to them. Duryodhana was invited as a guest of honour to the Pandava palace to further seal the peace between the cousins. However, as he fell prey to certain illusions in the palace, like mistaking the glossy floor for water and a pool for a polished hard surface, Draupadi, along with her maid servants, ridiculed the king, publicly insulting him as 'a blind man's blind son'. This seemed strange and out of order as Duryodhana was her guest, and courtesy demanded that he be treated with respect and honour. However, with this single incident, Draupadi, as if deliberately, eliminated all chances of reconciliation and reignited a bitter feud.

Duryodhana Repaid His Insult in Double Measure

To avenge his humiliation at the Pandava palace, Duryodhana hatched a master plan. He invited Yudhishtira to a game of dice, where he gambled away his wealth, kingdom and eventually Daraupadi's honour. The Kauravas dragged Draupadi by her hair and subjected her to public humiliation—way more than what Duryodhana was subjected to at the Pandava palace. As the losers, the Pandavas were expelled for almost thirteen years to a forest, during which time they prepared themselves for any future confrontation. At the end of their exile, as the Pandavas returned to their kingdom, their claim was rejected, and prospects of a war brewed between the Kaurava and Pandava cousins.

Draupadi Wanted No Peace, Only War

Even as war looked imminent, most Pandavas wanted to avoid it, and Krishna, their close ally and strategist, agreed to go as a peace emissary. However, Draupadi was adamant that there should be a battle to avenge the insult she was subjected to. While any other wife would be more upset with her husband for gambling away her dignity, Draupadi focused her anger on the Kauravas. She would not be satisfied with anything less than an utterly vanquished Duryodhana with a broken thigh. Krishna tried his best to bring her to her senses, even reminding her about the tens of thousands of lives that would be lost and the miseries that women and children would be subjected to if a war broke out. However, Draupadi remained insistent, which leads us to the question whether there could be any other reason for this unquenched thirst for revenge. Also, given the facts that she was the one who set in motion these events by insulting Duryodhana first, and then it was Yudhishtira, her husband, who put at stake her modesty—this doubt seems to be a highly justified one.

Panchalas Let Others Steal Their Thunder

To reveal this puzzle, let us look at the behaviour of the Panchala royals on the battlefield. The war was fought for eighteen days, and during this time, the Kurus saw their Supreme Commander position switching hands four times. The first one, Bhishma, was such a fierce warrior that he was impossible to defeat. However, on the tenth day of the battle, Shikhandi, described as transgender, stood in front guarding Arjuna. As war ethics demanded that women should not be attacked, Bhishma dithered, and Arjuna shot him down. Any warrior would have found his greatest honour in defeating Bhishma, whose prowess was equivalent to two Maharathis combined. It was not difficult for Shikhandi to make this his moment of glory, especially since he was at the forefront, while Arjuna hesitated to slay his grandfather. However, Shikhandi was glad to play second fiddle to Arjuna and let him be in the limelight.

This pattern of Panchala princes taking a back seat repeated itself when Karna, who took over as the Kuru Supreme Commander on the sixteenth day of the war, another acclaimed Maharathi, was killed by Arjuna. Shalya then took over on day eighteen, to be slain by Yudhishtira. All of this happened during the watch of Drishtadyumna, who commanded the combined Pandava and allied forces. It was all the Pandavas' glory and the Panchalas were willing to play a supporting role, though their kingdom contributed the maximum resources and took the highest risks.

Panchalas Unwilling to Compromise on Drona

But when it came to the second Supreme Commander, Drona, the teacher of both the Kauravas and the Pandavas, it was a different story altogether. After Bhishma fell, Drona took over the command on the eleventh day. He devised a successful strategy which managed to confine Arjuna to a remote part of the battlefield. But even when Arjuna, alongside the master-strategist Krishna, faltered, there was someone whose attention would not be diverted—Satyajit—a Panchala prince and younger brother of Draupadi. Satyajit stood firm and unruffled, and with great might continued to fight Drona on his own. He shot down Drona's charioteer first and then quickly went for his foe, piercing him with his arrows. Realising an unprecedented opportunity, one of his brothers arrived with reinforcements to back up Satyajit. But Drona, as the experienced warrior he was, made a comeback and finally managed to slaughter the Panchala prince.

Drona proved to be impossible to defeat, until the Pandavas played a psychological trick of lying to him that his son Ashwathama was slain. A heartbroken and purposeless Drona dropped his arms and alighted from his chariot. Just like the other Supreme Commanders—Bhishma, Karna or Shalya—Drona could then have been killed by any one of the Pandavas. It would have been easy for either Arjuna, Bhima or Yudhishtira, as they were the ones standing nearby and executing this plan. But in this case,

Dhrishtadyumna stood on his ground that only he would kill Drona. Under no circumstances would the Panchala prince let anyone else steal the opportunity to publicly behead Drona.

Draupadi and Dhrishtadyumna Groomed to Annihilate Drona

So, why would the Panchala princes allow the three other rival Supreme Commanders to be defeated by the Pandavas, but in the case of Drona they would insist on killing him themselves? In fact, it is said that during his early years, King Drupada desperately consulted several seers to bless him with a child powerful enough to kill Drona. As everyone failed, ultimately he approached two sages named Yaja and Upayaja. Though they initially refused, Drupada was so adamant in his resolve that he served them for a year until they relented. The fire sacrifice that followed resulted in the birth of his twins, Draupadi and Drishtadyumna. For the next several years, their father spent his time and resources to groom his children towards the single-minded mission of taking revenge against Drona. However, what enmity did the Panchala kingdom, the mightiest among the Indo-Gangetic plain Mahajanapadas, have against Drona, a poor Brahmin teacher?

Drona and Drupada: Childhood Friends

The story goes back a few years. Drupada was born the son of Prishata, the king of Panchala kingdom. As a child, he was sent to study at the hermitage of Bharadwaja, a revered Vedic Brahmin, and one of the authors of the Rig Veda. His son was Drona, and as children residing and learning together, they developed a great bond between each other. As the heir apparent of the Panchala kingdom, Drupada then promised his friend that he would always be there for him, come what may. Once he ascended the throne, his palace would be a home for Drona so that they could live together forever, assured Drupada. They parted ways after their education, and Drupada eventually took over the crown of his kingdom, the central power in the Indo-Gangetic basin at that point of time.

Drupada Forgot His Friendship and Publicly Insulted Drona

However, during the same time, Drona's life took a diametrically opposite turn. After the death of his father, he was impoverished and unable to feed his wife and child. Ridiculed and chided, he decided to take his childhood friend Drupada by his word. As Drona set out, walking for several miles to finally gain an audience with the king, he expected the same warmth from him that they had shared when they studied together at his father's hermitage. But upon the throne, Drupada was now a changed man. He had become acutely aware of the class differences between them, and haughtily refused to even recognize Drona. He publicly insulted him that there was no way a mighty king could ever be friends with a beggar like Drona. A deeply humiliated and wounded Drona walked out of Drupada's court, and bitterly swore to take revenge against his old friend.

Drona Cosied up to Rival Kuru Kingdom

On the west side of Panchala was the Kuru kingdom. Among all the various Mahajanapadas, these two were considered as the foremost—because they followed the ancient Vedic religion in its purest form. They were literally the guardians of the Vedic era. Hence, the other minor regions around them looked for their approval and yearned for an alliance with them. However, this also meant a constant rivalry between both these power centres. They were persistently at war with each other. When Drona visited Drupada, it was a period of Panchala supremacy. Hence as the Brahmin walked out as a much-humiliated man, it was obvious for him what his next step would be. He approached the rival Kuru court with a definite proposition, which in turn welcomed him with open arms. He was then entrusted the responsibility of training the young princes—the Pandavas and Kauravas. Under Drona all the princes excelled, but Arjuna emerged as the most accomplished and skilled archer.

Drona Repaid Drupada's Insult, Upsetting Regional Power Equation

Revenge is best served cold. Drona realized his moment had arrived when he was asked by the Kurus what fee he expected for his services to their kingdom. He went for the jugular and asked for the impossible—the arrest of Drupada. Though initially surprised at this strange request, Bhishma, the eldest of the Kuru kingdom, was only happy to oblige. He sensed an opportunity there, as the Kurus were now under the shadow of the mighty Panchala kingdom, their arch-rivals. Under the Kuru banner, a surprise attack by the young princes was meticulously strategized and put together by Bhishma and Drona. Surprise it was, because it led to the defeat of the Panchala king Drupada.

As Drupada was presented before Drona, it was time to return the favour. The mighty Panchala king was publicly insulted and his kingdom was split into two—the Southern Panchala continued under Drupada, while Northern Panchala adjoining the Kuru kingdom was now under the lordship of

Drona, a subordinate of the Kuru rulers. The centre of power in the Gangetic basin, held by the Panchala kingdom for generations together, now shifted to their fiercest adversary, the Kuru kingdom, that too in the most disgraceful manner.

A Glass of Milk Redefined a Nation

Drupada insulted Drona. Drona aligned with his arch-enemies and paid back in full measure, thereby upsetting the regional balance of power. However, what really triggered this geographical realignment might in reality would have been a tiny inconsequential incident. When Ashwathama, the son of Drona, was a young child, he longed to have a glass of milk. But Drona, a poor man, could not afford to keep a cow, and was heartbroken when he saw his child being humiliated by his friends with water mixed with flour. Unable to witness his child's plight, an impoverished Drona turned to his childhood friend Drupada for help. But once the king turned down Drona's request, a chain of events was set in motion. Much like a butterfly effect, a small incident such as a child crying for a glass of milk, eventually led to the destruction of mighty kingdoms and the reorganization of the entire history of a nation.

Drupada Co-opted Pandavas to Repay Kurus and Drona

As the Panchala chips were now down, Drupada carried the burden of revenge against Drona and the Kuru kingdom. His children were brought up as the breeding ground of this hatred. When Drupada saw a sliver of opportunity arise through the enmity between the Kauravas and Pandavas, he caught on to it. He focused on Arjuna, the young, valiant archer, whose prowess he had witnessed personally on the battlefield that had initially led

to his defeat. If he could win Arjuna over to his side, he stood
a great chance of tilting the scales of power yet again. As his
children grew up to be adults, Drupada realized that his time had
now arrived. Hence, a well-planned track and trace programme
was organized under the veil of choosing a groom for Draupadi.
However, there was still one more impediment. Since Arjuna
was only the third brother of the Pandavas, there was little chance
that Draupadi's children would inherit the Kuru kingdom unless
she was also wedded to the eldest Kuru prince Yudhishtira. But
if Draupadi was married to all the brothers, then not only did a
grandchild of Drupada have a shot at sitting on the Kuru throne,
they would also have a chance of putting up a united front.

Mahabharata Not a Kuru-Pandava War, Rather a Panchala-Kuru War

Hence, even if tens of thousands of lives needed to be sacrificed,
Draupadi would not hesitate to go to war. Drupada would
gladly take up all the risk—put all his sons and grandsons on
the battleground, committing all his military resources including
that of their vassal states. Panchala would then nominate
Drishtadyumna as the Supreme Commander of the combined
armies. All because in reality it was not a war between the
Pandavas and Kauravas, but between the great kingdoms of
Kurus and Panchala. All the other Mahajanapadas would join
the war as allies to either Kuru or Panchala, because this war
would redefine their existence in the Indo-Gangetic basin.

Panchala Won the War but Lost Their King

Unfortunately, the war resulted in a winner's curse. Though
the Panchalas and Pandavas eventually emerged victorious,

the losses they suffered were immense. Drupada's sons and grandsons were killed by the Kuru commanders Drona, Karna and Ashwathama. King Drupada himself was slain on the fifteenth day by Drona. To add to the woes of the kingdom of Panchala, on the last day of the war, Ashwathama attacked the Pandava camp at night and set it on fire. Those killed included Drishtadymna, Shikhandi and the children of Draupadi, all of who would have been in line to the throne and could have replaced Drupada. So, in effect, even after a much-yearned-for victory, the kingdom of Panchala was left without a rightful heir from their own bloodline.

Kurus Lost the War but Won Both the Kingdoms

The great war between the Panchala and the Kuru kingdoms changed the political landscape of the Indo-Gangetic basin. The Kurus, who had upset the regional status quo by taking over the Northern Panchala region, were now defeated. Panchala regained its former glory with its once-lost region annexed back. But the irony was that, as their king and two generations of his direct heirs were slain, there was no one from the Panchala kingdom who could take over the throne. Hence, now the region was consolidated under the banner of the Kuru kingdom of Hastinapura rather than the other way round, quite the contrary to what might have been the initial expectations of Drupada as they went into the war full force.

This single large kingdom of Panchala and Kuru passed over to the Pandavas under Yudhishtira, who incidentally belonged to the Kuru stock. So, the Panchalas won the war but lost their kingdom to their arch-rivals. However, the only saving grace for the victorious Panchalas would have been their princess Draupadi, who was now the queen of the joint kingdom of

Kuru-Panchala. In another twist of fate, after thirty-six years, the crown passed over to Parikshit, the son of Abhimanyu—the child of Arjuna from his wife other than Draupadi. The greater kingdom was now under the full lordship of the Kurus, with no trace of the Panchalas in sight.

The Kuru-Panchala Relationship

Just like the Kurus and the Pandavas were cousins engaged in a bitter feud, the Kuru and the Panchala dynasties also were closely related a few generations earlier. Both originated from the same lineage of Puru, who had inherited a kingdom in the Indo-Gangetic plain. He established his dynasty as Puruvamsha, which emerged as one of the most prominent during the Rigveda period. Puru's dynasty later split into many branches. Down the line, two of them—Panchala and Kuru—created their own separate kingdoms, though from the same bloodline.

Eventually, both of them emerged as the flagbearers of the Vedic religion in the geography, with a great reputation for religious wisdom and conservativism. So, naturally, there were continuous frictions and feuds, as these two closely related powerful dynasties next to each other competed for mind and territorial spaces. Through generations, their fortunes kept interchanging. Sometimes it was the Panchala kingdom that had the upper hand while during the other times, the Kurus took over. It was like displaying a typical case of narcissism of negligible differences—two closely related communities fighting each other to emphasize and reinforce their subtle differences which eventually culminated in a bloody war between two sets of cousins—one a closer relationship between the Kauravas and the Pandavas, and the other a distant one between the Panchalas and the Kurus.

Why Did Mahabharata Author Hide the Panchala Perspective?

The Mahabharata war in reality was fought between two mighty kingdoms of the region—Panchala and Kuru—who vied for geographical supremacy. However, in the epic Mahabharata, it was narrated as a bitter family feud between two sets of cousins. To uncover this mystery behind why it was narrated as the battle between Pandavas and Kauravas and not between Panchalas and Kurus, it might be helpful to know the author of this epic better.

This epic was composed by Krishna Dvaipayana, better known as Vyasa, meaning 'the compiler'. As a great, learned man, he not only wrote the Mahabharata, but is also credited with compiling the Veda into four separate books of Rig, Sama, Yajur and Atharva. He came from an illustrious family of Brahmin sages—his father Parasara was the author of the first Purana, the Vishnupurana, and his great grandfather, Vasishta, was counted amongst the most revered of the Vedic saints. However, this story of the Mahabharata had an intrinsic relationship with the author, making it rather a subjective one rather than an objective narration.

Vyasa's Connect to the Kuru Dynasty

The Kuru clan, a branch of the Puruvamsha, was established by King Kuru out of his capital at Hastinapura. One of his descendents was King Shantanu, who had a son named Bhishma, from his first marriage. Later, Shantanu met Satyavati, the daughter of a fisherman. But when Shantanu was enamoured by her beauty and wished to marry her, the shrewd fisherman put forward a condition that only Satyavati's children should be allowed to inherit the Kuru throne. This was a rather difficult proposition considering Bhishma was first in line. To resolve his father's predicament, Bhishma not only relinquished his right to the throne as the firstborn, but also vowed lifelong celibacy.

Shantanu then begot two sons—Chitrangada and Vichitravirya—from Satyavati. After his father's death, Chitrangada ascended the throne but was soon slain in a battle. Though Vichitravirya then took over the kingdom and married two princesses from another prominent kingdom, Kasi—he succumbed to excessive alcohol consumption. Unfortunately, both of Satyavati's children died young without leaving behind any heirs. Now, this posed a serious challenge as the throne was now vacant and Bhishma was tied by his vow. But Satyavati had a unique solution to this problem. Not known even to Shantanu, she had had an earlier relationship with a wise sage called Parasara before she met the king. From this she had a son, Vyasa, also called Krishna Dvaipayana. Vyasa was now on his own but nevertheless was willing to help his mother out of her dilemma.

Brahmins Claimed the Kshatriya Throne

To resolve the challenge of the vacant throne, Satyavati asked her first son Vyasa, a Brahmin, to be with the two widows of Vichitravirya so that the kingdom would have an heir. However, both the princesses, used to the luxury of a palace, were taken aback by the dark, unkempt look of Vyasa and reacted unpleasantly as he approached them. Each of them begot a son from Vyasa but unfortunately both the sons were born disabled—Dritharashtra was blind, while Pandu was pale and unhealthy.

Tracing back, though King Shantanu had three sons, Bhishma, Chitrangada and Vichitravirya, his two sons died young, and his eldest, Bhishma, could neither marry nor ascend the throne due to his vow. Hence, in reality, the Kuru bloodline ended with Bhishma and now, in a strange twist of fate, the kingdom had two claimants—Dhritarashtra and Pandu—from two different widows of Vichitravirya. But they were fathered by someone completely unrelated to the Kshatriya Kuru clan—Vyasa, a Brahmin sage.

Mahabharata Retold Vyasa's Own Family Tale

So, the Brahmin Vyasa was now grafted into the Kuru clan. And as Vyasa authored the Mahabharata, we need to remember that he was a grandfather to both the Pandavas and the Kauravas. Hence, he would have been subjectively involved in the battle, as it was his own family members who were fighting between each other. For him, it was not a battle between two Kshatriya clans—Kuru and Panchala—but rather a war between two prominent Brahmin clans—Pandava and Kaurava, who carried his bloodline. So, the author's intent might have been to retell a tale of his own family, where good triumphed over evil, rather than a story of two sets of Kshatriya kings going to war.

Vyasa's Favouritism Led to His Pandava Partisanship

Now, the next question is why Vyasa would be favourable towards the Pandavas and project them as good, and the Kauravas as evil, while in reality both were his grandchildren. To unravel this, we need to revisit the times when the widows of Vichitravirya gave birth to the sons of Vyasa. Seeing both the unhealthy babies—a blind Dhritarashtra and an unhealthy Pandu—their grandmother Satyavati was alarmed. Hence she wanted to give it another try. However, this time, the widows, who were already unhappy with the experience, replaced themselves with a handmaiden of theirs. Now, this maiden took to Vyasa happily, and they begot a healthy child named Vidura.

Though Vidura's social position might have been below his half-brothers, he might have been the favourite son of Vyasa. First, as his mother had been most respectful and pleasing to Vyasa, compared to the widow princesses, and second, Vidura grew up as a wise and knowledgeable young man, qualities that Vyasa would have appreciated as a Brahmin. Vidura, on his part, was favourable to the Pandavas probably because they were the underdogs, or possibly because being the prime minister in the Kaurava court, he was exposed to their arrogance on a continuous basis. Hence Vidura warned the Pandavas in advance about the devious Kaurava plot to burn them to death and the dangers of taking part in the game of dice. He even protested against the humiliation of Draupadi. At the onset of the war, Vidura took the risk of breaking away from the Kauravas, the rulers, putting his career at risk, and supporting the Pandavas, the challengers. Hence Vyasa, the author, would have merely reflected in his epic the perspective of his favourite child, thereby taking an approving view towards the Pandavas.

Figuring Out the Mahabharata War Period

Now, what could be the period when the great Mahabharata war occurred? There are several dates floating around. According to Romila Thapar, if we were to go by the date that the epic itself suggested, the war happened as the universe transitioned towards *kaliyuga*—hence around 3000 BCE. But if we were to trace the royal lineages, this would push the date to around 1200 BCE, while some archaeological evidence dates it to 800 BCE. But if we were to look carefully at further clues and references it could be at an even later date—around 350 BCE to 350 CE.

The Mahabharata, being an important epoch in the history of India, demands better thinking in order to gain clarity on these dates, which is now perched at a wide range between 3000 BCE to 300 CE.

Presence of Horses and Chariots in the War

The fortunes of the Mahabharata war revolved around horses and chariots. Krishna being the charioteer of Arjuna, Shikhandi standing guard for Arjuna to target Bhishma and Dhrishtadyumna beheading Drona as he alighted from his chariot are just a few of the incidents where horses are referred to. However, as we now know, horses were not indigenous to India but belonged to the Eurasian Steppes. Evidence suggests that the ancestors of the modern horses were domesticated between 3500 to 2200 BCE in the Steppes, after which they were used for food, transportation, agriculture and warfare. Chariots, meanwhile, were invented a few centuries later at around 2000 BCE, most probably in the Eurasian Steppes again, evidence of which is now unearthed from several of their burial sites. Horse-drawn chariots are believed to have reached South Asia around 1750 BCE. Hence, taking into consideration that horses and chariots prominently featured in the Mahabharata war, it could have happened only after 2000 BCE.

Absence of Horses in Indus Valley

The Indus Valley Civilization was at its height from 2600 to 1900 BCE. Though we now know a lot about the lives and times of this prominent world civilization, it makes no mention of horses, an animal of high religious, economic, social and political prominence during the Mahabharata period. At the same time, it was not that Indus Valley was a stranger to animals. Since their primary occupation was agriculture, oxen, cows and buffaloes were domesticated for ploughing of the soil and for transport. Cattle, along with sheep and goats, were also used for their milk and meat. We also have evidence of domesticated dogs, cats, fowl and pigs. Hence, it is reasonable to assume that horses and chariots arrived much later in India and not during the Indus Valley period. So, the war would have occurred in a period after 1900 BCE.

Lack of Urbanization after the Indus Valley

The Indus Valley Civilization covered large swathes of lands in the north-western part of South Asia. They built one of the world's first large-scale urban societies. The Indus Valley had sophisticated and technologically advanced urban culture with planned cities, homes, granaries, warehouses, public baths and urban sanitation systems. However, after the Indus Valley declined around 1600 BCE, until 600 BCE for a period spanning 1000 years, we see no evidence of any large-scale buildings or urban settlements. Around 600 BCE, the nomadic pastoral tribes of the late Vedic period started to settle themselves in communities centred around farming, triggered by the use of iron ploughshares ushered in by the Iron Age. Stable societies developed, and urban societies started to spring back again in the region, eventually organizing themselves into a political structure called Janas. Since urbanization of the region is an important evidence of the Mahabharata period, it could be reasonably assumed that the war occurred after 600 BCE.

A Phase of Consolidation in India

The emergence of the Iron Age resulted in two fundamental changes in the life of India as a region. First, farming gained popularity as productivity greatly increased with the use of ploughshares. It accelerated economic growth, trade and commerce, and ultimately tax collection. This enabled smaller tribal structures of Janas to organize themselves into sixty-nine small kingdoms known as Janapadas, a form of a republic state. Secondly, iron was used not only in agriculture but also in warfare, where superior weapons were developed. With the larger economic surplus derived from increased farming, some of these Janapadas were able to create bigger standing armies. Hence there was a constant power struggle between these kingdoms, resulting in smaller ones giving way to larger ones. Finally, sixteen of them emerged, known as the 'Mahajanapadas' around 550 BCE.

However, as armies improved and as territorial ambitions grew stronger, these Mahajanapadas continued warring with each other, out of which the biggest might have been the Mahabharata war. However, the Mahabharata was the beginning of this consolidation phase rather than the end. The Kuru-Panchala kingdom, a part of this unification process, was finally annexed by Magadha. Finally, four strong kingdoms emerged—Magadha, Kosala, Vatsa and Avanti. With this, the axis of power in India shifted to the east of the Ganges which was, until the Mahabharata war, centred on the Western and middle Ganges valleys.

Republics Gave Way to Universal Monarchies

Out of these four larger kingdoms, Magadha had several inherent advantages. First, under their command were several important trade routes, including the ones through the rivers of Ganges,

Gandak and Son, enabling them to generate a higher economic surplus compared to the others. Second, they controlled the iron ore deposits of south Bihar, helping them to develop better armouries and create a bigger army. Third, their capital of the time, Rajagriha, was strategically located, nestled between several hills and making external invasions difficult. Hence during the period between 500 to 350 BCE, Magadha conquered the rest and emerged as the first universal monarchy in ancient India.

Going by these clues we arrive at a shorter time range—after 550 BCE, coinciding with the development of Mahajanapadas, and 500 BCE, when Magadha started to consolidate its imperial dreams. Hence it might be reasonable to assume that the great Mahabharata war might have happened somewhere during the fifty-year span between 550 and 500 BCE.

Buddhism and Jainism Triggered Mahabharata Epic

This brings us to another reason why Vyasa would have authored the Mahabharata epic. Though the Kuru-Panchala kingdoms were exemplary Vedic societies, where Brahmins dominated the daily affairs of citizens through complex rituals and sacrifices, there was still a rising tide of resentment. Rituals like Rajasuya and Ashvamedha, and several others, demanded cattle sacrifice and donation of accumulated surplus. While these sacrifices underlined the monopoly and social domination of Brahmins, the other castes paid a price. For Kshatriyas, it meant forgoing the higher taxes; for Vysyas, lower trade prospects; and for Shudras, lower productivity. Hence, during the late sixth century BCE, around the same time that we are placing the Mahabharata war, there arose multiple new philosophies propagating vegetarianism and abhorring cattle sacrifice.

Among these, two religions gained the most popularity—Buddhism founded by Siddhartha Gautama and Jainism by Mahavira. They questioned the centralized authority of Brahmins, the rigid caste system and the traditions that they enforced on the layperson. Hence, through the epic of the Mahabharata, one of sage Vyasa's goals might have also been to underline the significance of these Brahminical rituals which were under threat. Several instances narrated in the Mahabharata point us towards this. Examples include Yudhishtira being asked to conduct the Rajasuya *yagna* after initially inheriting a portion of the Kuru kingdom, and once the war was won, Vyasa advising the newly crowned king to conduct an Ashvamedha ceremony, despite his plea that treasuries were empty. This overemphasis on such rituals can also be seen in the Ashvamedhika Parva, the fourteenth book of the Mahabharata, that describes the ceremonies in great length, spanning ninety-six chapters.

Through the Mahabharata, Brahminism Extended Support to a Universal Monarch

Many Mahajanapadas adopted a Vedic religious system where the king functioned under the guidance of an assembly of elders, mostly Brahmins. It had its own disadvantages, where the kingdoms remained unstable, small and constantly at war with each other. However, the mercantile class, which emerged on the back of increased agrarian outputs, demanded stability and preferred larger, powerful empires under a universal monarch. Buddhism, on its part, supported such a model, since a universal monarch would quell petty conflicts and establish peace and harmony, as against kingdoms under the older Vedic system. Through the Mahabharata, we can see that Vyasa extended support to the universal monarchy system, probably as a way to counter the Buddhist onslaught on Vedic dogmas. This might also be a reason why the epic talked at length about Rajasuya and Ashvamedha, sacrifices performed by ancient kings to be declared as the king of kings or as a universal monarch.

Mahabharata Period Similar to Chinese Warring States

Interestingly, India might not have operated in a vacuum even during ancient times. We see striking geopolitical similarities between India and its neighbouring regions during the Mahabharata age. From 770 to 476 BCE, its next-door neighbour China witnessed a period rife with battles, conflict and bloodshed. During this time several smaller kingdoms emerged, which kept battling each other for regional supremacy. Compared the to sixty-nine Janapadas in India, China had almost 100 autonomous states. This era eventually gave way to the Warring States Period in China, starting in 476 BCE, when these autonomous states were conquered and consolidated into seven major states—the Chu, Han, Qi, Qin, Wei, Yan and Zhao—similar to our sixteen Mahajanapadas, or like the four strong kingdoms of Magadha, Kosala, Vatsa and Avanti. Finally, in the case of India, while we see the kingdom of Magadha, one of the Mahajanapadas, emerging and consolidating India for the first time, in China, the Qin, one of the warring states, emerged and unified China.

Striking Similarities Between Confucius and Vyasa

In the period that led to the consolidation in India, changes were felt not just politically and geographically but also in the religious realm. There was widespread resentment towards the highly ritualistic Vedic religion and the social domination of the Brahmins. Hence several interpretations and philosophies sprung up, the major ones being the five heterodox schools of philosophy. As these changes swept over the land, Magadha broke away from the conservative clutches and embraced the new-age religions of Buddhism and Jainism. The dwindling lustre of Brahminism might have prompted Vyasa to compile the Vedas into four separate books. His objective of narrating the Mahabharata epic might have also been to make the principles and ceremonies narrated in these Vedas more palatable and appealing to the masses.

Coincidentally, neighbouring China went through a similar period of flux during the same era. Their ancient religious practices were challenged by new-age philosophies known as the Hundred Schools of Thought. Confucius, distressed with the social chaos, played a similar role as that of Vyasa. He read the classics, compiled them and adapted them into formats to encourage people to get back to their ancestral roots. He advocated the restoration of ritual institutions and the sanctity of Chinese orthodoxy. But immediately afterwards, the Qin dynasty that united China moved away from conformism and adopted principles from the newly founded Legalism for establishing a larger empire.

Ancient India and Ancient Rome Went through Similar Times

Ancient India's geopolitical similarities do not end with neighbouring China, but extend to a faraway Europe. The *jana* system adopted by many of the Janapadas and Mahajanapadas was, in reality, a form of republic. In this, an assembly of elders with full financial, administrative and judicial authority met regularly to discuss and decide on major state issues. The king coordinated his activities with this assembly to ensure that these decisions were percolated down to the administrative officers, who obeyed and executed orders. Mahajanapadas arose around 550 BCE. Coincidentally, just a few decades apart, in 509 BCE, ancient Rome came up with the concept of a state republic. Striking similarities apart, it is also reasonable to assume that the concept of a republic was prevalent in India much before Rome.

Mahabharata: A Part of the Global Climate Change Aftermath

Two immensely devastating climate changes preceded the Mahabharata war period. As elsewhere across the globe, these left a trail of transformations in the Indian subcontinent too. The Late Bronze Age Climate Change from 1900 to 1500 BCE catalysed the decline of the Indus Valley Civilization. The Iron Age Climate Change that followed closely after, unleashed its fury from 1200 BCE. These hostile weather conditions that lasted for a millennium triggered several waves of migration from the Eurasian Steppes towards north-west India. By 600 BCE, by the end of these climate changes, new urban settlements— Janas and then Mahajanapadas—started to take shape in the same geography where the infiltrations had taken place.

Meanwhile, as expected, these Steppe migrations were not limited to India but were also into other regions like the Near East, Europe and China, setting off similar changes. For example, in China, these nomads led to the fall of the Zhou dynasty in 771 BCE, which had until then provided stability in the region. Hence, we have to conclude that the period that led up to the Mahabharata age itself had similarities across the globe.

Mahabharata: An Integral Part of the Fountainhead Epoch

As the Mahabharata war brewed in the Indo-Gangetic basin, there were several other great geopolitical happenings across the world. These included Nebuchadnezzar conquering Jerusalem (597 BCE), the Achaemenid Empire being founded by Cyrus the Great (550 BCE), their conquest of Babylon (539 BCE) and the Spring and Autumn period and the Warring States Period in China. This was also a period of political innovations: democracy was established in Greece (508 BCE), the republic in Rome (509 BCE), the advanced administrative system called Satrapy came about in Persia and a meritocratic civil service system in China.

This era saw the rise of great philosophers and religious leaders across the world including Mahavira (599 BCE) Confucius (551 BCE) and Sun Tzu (544 BCE), the Buddha (528 BCE), Socrates (470 BCE) and Plato (428 BCE). During the same period, the foundations of the modern society were laid, with innovations like the establishment of a global trade network through the Persian Royal Road, the world's first postal and courier system in Persia, and a private banking system in Babylon. A template for human rights was established by Cyrus the Great with his cylinder, now considered as the first bill of human rights. Hence the Mahabharata war, a defining moment of India, occurred not in silos but during the Fountainhead epoch, an era when the whole world was getting reinvented through a period of churn.

6

The Fascinating Tale of How a Climate Change Altered Our Genetics of Women Empowerment

Keywords: *Climate Change, Pandemic, Steppe Migration, Genetics, Women's Rights, Women Empowerment, Sexism, Cradle of Civilizations, Global Collapse, Democracy, Republic, Colonialism*

Greece Built Europe's First Literate Civilization

The Bronze Age (3300–1200 BCE) was a period of inflection across the globe. Leveraging the new-found metal, several civilizations sprung up. They created new technologies, writing systems and urban settlements. Among them was the Minoan civilization, which thrived on a mountainous island called Crete in the Aegean Sea, now in Greece. The Minoans' primary occupation was agriculture: they grew wheat, barley and olives. The abundance of their produce opened up trade opportunities,

WOMEN'S OPPRESSION: A DATELINE

BEFORE ANCIENT CIVILIZATIONS AND EVENTS

- End of Glacial Age - 10,000 BCE
- Steppes's Human Settlements - 5000 BCE
- Old European Culture - 5000-3500 BCE
- Old Europe Climate Change - 4200-4000 BCE
- Early Bronze Age - 3300-2100 BCE
- Yamna Migration Climate Change - 3100-2800 BCE

ANCIENT CIVILIZATIONS AND EVENTS

- Minoan Civilization - 3500-1450 BCE
- Early Egypt, Old Kingdom And Middle Kingdom - 3150-1650 BCE
- Sumer Civilization - 3300-1900 BCE
- The Indus Valley Civilization - 3300-1600 BCE
- Middle And Late Bronze Age - 2100-1200 BCE

POST ANCIENT CIVILIZATIONS

- Mycenaean Civilization - 1750-1050 BCE
- Ancient Greek Civilization - 1200–323 BCE
- Egypt New Kingdom - 1550-1069 BCE
- Old Babylonian Empire - 1894-1595 BCE
- Indian Vedic Age - 1500-500 BCE

PRE-MODERN AGE CIVILIZATIONS

- Roman Kingdom and Republic - 753-27 BCE
- Hellenistic Greece - 323-146 BCE
- Achaemenid Empire - 550-330 BCE
- Hellenistic Ptolemaic Egypt - 332 to 30 BCE
- Hellenistic Seleucid Babylon - 312-141 BCE
- Magadha-Mauryan Empires - 500-185 BCE

MODERN EMPIRES AND EVENTS

- Roman Empire - 27 BCE-476 CE
- Christian Rome - 312-476 CE
- Byzantium - 330-1453 CE
- Middle/Dark Ages - 476–1453 CE
- Fall of Constantinople - 1453 CE
- Renaissance - 1453-1650 CE
- Age of Colonialism - 1488-1950 CE

complemented by the many natural harbours on their island. Leveraging these, they had commercial and cultural connections to other ancient civilizations like Egypt and Sumer. Their language, belonging to the Indo-European and Semitic families, used a script, now known as Linear A, which later evolved to Linear B, the predecessor of Greek. However, what is most remarkable about the Minoans was their ability to build complex urban landscapes starting from around 2000 BCE. According to Homer, the Greek poet, Crete had more than ninety cities connected by paved roads, water and sewage facilities, dotted with stone and mud wall buildings with flat, tiled roofs. The most interesting aspect of their cities were the magnificent palaces, which acted as economic and religious convergence points. The biggest of these was the one at Knossos. This great palace, built across three centuries starting from 1700 BCE, sprawled over 6 acres and rose to five stories, with almost 1300 interconnected rooms and hallways. Sir Arthur John Evans, the British archaeologist who unearthed this civilization, referred to the Minoans as 'Europe's first literate civilization' and 'Europe's first major experience with civilization'.

Minoans Provided an Ancient Feminist State Template

Minoans established a social structure closer to a matriarchy. Unlike many other societies, which viewed women as sexual objects, relegating their position to household chores, in the Minoan society, women had an important role to play, holding equal, if not higher, privileges compared to men and participating in all activities, even in administration. For example, both the wife and daughter of King Minos—the legendary ruler after whom the civilization is named—exerted considerable influence in their warfare, though the king was presumed to be the son of Zeus, the mightiest of all gods. In ancient Crete, there might not have been any limits to what women could be a part of. One of the frescoes found at their palatial palace in Knossos depicted two women holding back bulls alongside a man, which otherwise was thought of as a male-dominated sport. Minoan art represented women in the most beautiful and powerful ways. Typified images of domesticated, pregnant women and women taking care of children were completely absent. Rather, they were all about women in a milieu of social settings—on a throne, performing religious acts and even dancing away carelessly. While men were portrayed in their loincloths, women were presented in costumes like body-hugging blouses and skirts, bearing an astonishing resemblance to the modern times.

Minoans Emulated the Mighty Egyptian Civilization

Egypt, another ancient civilization, sprouted in the Nile Valley approximately at the same time—3150 BCE—as the Minoan civilization started to take roots in the island of Crete. However, compared to the Minoans, restricted to a few islands in the Mediterranean, Egypt was mightier and their impact larger. Their success came from their ability to tame the unpredictable waters of the Nile river for farming and producing surplus crops, which was then used to develop their society and culture. Though Minoans themselves made incredible progress, compared to the Egyptians, whose achievements included architecture and construction of formidable pyramids, temples and irrigation systems, they paled in comparison.

However, there is evidence that these two civilizations were not existing in silos, but rather had close links to each other. The first trading contacts between these two civilizations were made during the third millennium itself, now confirmed based on the hippopotamus ivory Egyptian scarabs unearthed from the Minoan burial tombs. There were also cultural exchanges, even marriage ties, resulting in several Egyptian customs and religious practices making their way to the Minoan civilization. Likewise, Minoan references could be found on many Egyptian frescoes, including on prominent tombs and temples. It is also speculated that Cretan hieroglyphs—the first-ever form of Greek writing system which predates even Linear A—could have been influenced by the Egyptian hieroglyphs. Now, the most important connection between these two civilizations is an yet to be proven theory that King Minos—the first king of Crete—might have been after all, King Menes, the first Pharaoh of ancient Egypt.

Ancient Egyptians also Empowered Their Women

The Minoan template of women empowerment was not really a unique one in the ancient world, as even ancient Egypt was also an epitome. Here, women were not subservient to men but rather held an equal footing, irrespective of their marital status. Women enjoyed the same legal and property rights as men. They were allowed to conduct all types of transactions, sign contracts, execute wills, be witness to documents and even adopt children in their own names. While economically backward women worked alongside their men in the fields or took up jobs as weavers, brewers, dancers or musicians, upper-class women even adorned the highest administrative and religious positions.

Women were also economically empowered; they were allowed to keep their wages, and run households and estates as they pleased. This gender equality percolated through families too: women could marry anyone or divorce whenever, with no fear of social backlash. They could enter into prenuptial agreements favouring them and divorcees were allowed to keep their children and were even eligible for an alimony. There were no taboos on premarital sex, birth control or abortion. Ancient Egypt would surprise even some of the modern societies with its feminist attitude.

Mycenaean Civilization Improvised on Its Minoan Predecessor

More than 250 years after the palace-centred civilization of the Minoans rose to its peak in the island of Crete, another advanced civilization—the Mycenaean—took roots in the Greek mainland in 1750 BCE. This new civilization was deeply influenced by its predecessors, partly due to its trading and cultural relations with people from Crete. However, in several aspects, the Mycenaeans were much more advanced compared to the Minoans. Since they came about during the final phase of the Bronze Age, they brought about several innovations in military and engineering, based on their improved knowledge and usage of this metal. They used purer clay and baked their wares in higher temperatures, enabling them to produce pottery of much higher durability. They also developed specialized skills in metalwork, far exceeding the Minoans. Their script, Linear B, was a more evolved form of Linear A, which was used by the Minoans.

Though the Mycenaeans borrowed certain aspects from their predecessors in their construction and architecture, they were better and different in some, for example, building heavily fortified citadels, a feature absent during the Minoan period. Their largest city, Mycenae, was built on a hill with an imposing entrance, with lion statues guarding it. Similarly, though there were similarities in burial practices between both the cultures, the Mycenaean tombs were much larger, elaborately decorated, subterranean with monumental doorways.

Like the Minoans, Mycenaeans Too Copied Egypt

During the rise of the Mycenaean civilization, ancient Egypt was at its pinnacle under its New Kingdom, also known as the Egyptian Empire. The most famous pharaohs of Egypt reigned during this time, including Hatshepsut, Amenhotep II, Akhenaten and Tutankhamun. At their greatest territorial extent, they expanded to the Levant and Nubia. Architectural marvels including Abu Simbel, Luxor Temple and the Valley of Kings were constructed during this period. Following their predecessors, the Minoans' footsteps, the Mycenaeans continued their ties with the mighty Egyptians. Of course, there were trade and cultural ties, where their artists travelled to Egypt and emulated the scale and expertise in art, sculpture and construction. However, their relationship was not limited, it expanded even to the military. Papyrus fragments depicted battle scenes of Egypt against their Libyan invaders, where Mycenaean soldiers adorning their typical boar tusk helmets, were represented fighting alongside Egyptians. Hence, it can very well be assumed that the relations between these two civilizations were not peripheral at all, but at a deeper level.

Though a Copy of Minoans and Egyptians, Mycenaeans Turned Out Sexist

Though the Mycenaeans copied and improved upon their predecessor, the Minoan civilization, in almost all aspects, and maintained deep ties with the mighty Egyptian civilization, in one area they regressed. While the Minoans were an idealistic matriarchal society and Egyptians empowered their women, Mycenaeans were extremely restrictive when it came to gender rights. In fact, this society took delight in the cruel oppression of women.

Professor Barbara A. Olsen, specializing in Greek archaeology and history, in her book *Women in Mycenaean Greece* examined the gender patterns in the Mycenaean civilization, and then commented that the inequalities were staggering, especially for the women labourers, who were considered amongst the lowest social classes. They were enslaved and subjected to the worst of working conditions. Many of them suffered from chronic ill health and had to survive on inadequate food supplies. They were devoid of all economic autonomy, denied all avenues of individualistic expression and contained in a highly restricted social role—household labour and rearing children. Even among the upper class, the role of women was limited, with no property rights. They were either completely controlled or owned by men, who incidentally had the freedom to engage in wide-ranging and socially prominent roles. Women were rarely represented in the artefacts, if at all; they were mostly passive spectators who had no access to exotic goods such as spices, ointments, ivory and gold, compared to men, who indulged in luxuries, hunting and games.

A Global Perspective to Understand the Reasons for Mycenaean Sexism

Now, we come to a critical question. Both the Minoan and the Mycenaean civilizations seem to be from the same stock— they were in the same Mediterranean geography, modelled after the most prominent civilization ever—Egypt. They were similar in their culture, art, architecture and even their outlook. They both emerged as the foundation stones for the later Greek civilization. However, while the Minoans happened to be the epitome of women empowerment, Mycenaean turned out to be just the opposite. How could this be so?

Now, to understand this phenomenon of differing perspectives of women empowerment, let us take a broader global perspective beyond Europe—represented by the Minoan and Mycenaean civilizations, and Africa—represented by the Egyptian Civilization. In order to complete this viewpoint we look at two more regions: Sumer from the Middle East and the Indus Valley from South Asia, both stalwart civilizations that existed in a similar time period as the other three.

Ancient Sumer Was an Embodiment of Women's Rights

Considering the time period that they existed in, though it could seem to be so, the Minoan and Egyptian civilizations were not outliers in terms of women empowerment. Sumer, which originated in a similar period, in 3300 BCE, is regarded among the cradles of civilization in the world. They flourished alongside the Euphrates and Tigris rivers, drained the marshes and perfected the art of agriculture. Just like their Egyptian and Minoan counterparts, they created an economic surplus out of their abundant grain produce, which they then used to develop urban settlements. In fact, it is thought that the Sumerians invented the concept of the city and developed the first-ever urban centre in the world, Uruk. Necessitated by their trade they developed the first writing system, initially as symbols on clay tablets.

Women in Sumer enjoyed similar amounts of freedom as their contemporaries. They were sexually liberated and were economically empowered, where they could own properties and businesses. Socially they enjoyed freedom—they could become priestesses, physicians, administrators and judges. Examples of their empowerment included Enheduanna and Ki-en-gir, both high priestesses and powerful people of their time. Enheduanna, incidentally, is also regarded as the first author and poet in the world; several Sumerian literature pieces identify her as their author.

Indus Valley Put Their Women on a Pedestal

The civilization in the Indus Valley also flourished at the same time as the Minoan, Egypt and Sumer—from 3300 BCE onwards and is considered alongside as one of the cradles of civilizations. Named after the river Indus, it thrived along the alluvial plains and its inhabitants were masters in agriculture. There is now evidence that they had at least two rounds of crops in a year: wheat and barley in the winter and rice and millet in summers. With the crop surplus they developed their trade systems, which spread out as far as Afghanistan, Persia and Mesopotamia. Like their counterparts elsewhere, the Indus Valley Civilization also is well known for its urban planning, baked brick houses, water supply systems and urban sanitation lines along with granaries, dockyards and warehouses. Meanwhile, the Indus script, found on their trading seals, pottery, jewellery and tools, is the earliest form of written script in the Indian subcontinent.

The women in the Indus Valley held positions of power and were influential. They enjoyed economic freedom, as the seals found at the excavation sites depicted women performing independent roles in agriculture, trade and commerce. Other women figures provided evidence of their social prominence and authority, including that of the high priestess.

Deepening Mystery Behind the Mycenaean Deviation

Four civilizations—Egypt, Sumer, the Indus Valley and the Minoan—chosen from Europe, Africa, the Middle East and

South Asia—practically laid the foundations of our world. All of them sprouted during the same time—end of the fourth millennium BCE. Three of them were river valley civilizations while the Minoan was an island-based coastal civilization. All of them initially started out as agrarian village communities, which allowed them to eventually take advantage of their advanced farming skills to create economic surpluses. Leveraging these abundant funds, they transformed themselves into complex urban societies. They invested in art, culture and architecture, and developed indigenous languages with unique written scripts to emerge as advanced civilizations. All of them truly empowered their women socially and economically.

However, the Mycenaean civilization, though it outwardly appeared similar to these older civilizations, differed in the fact that they were restrictive towards their women. Everything was the same, except their sexist attitude. What could have caused this?

As we investigate we find one significant difference— the time period. While Egypt, Sumer, the Indus Valley and the Minoan civilizations appeared around 3000 BCE, the Mycenaean civilization appeared almost towards the tail end of these four civilizations—in 1750 BCE. Is time, then, a factor for this sexist deviation?

Mycenaean Civilization Emerged During an Age of Global Collapse

By the time Mycenaean civilization emerged in 1750 BCE, three out of the four great civilizations were already past their prime. The Indus Valley Civilization had peaked around 2500 BCE when it supported a population of over 5 million. It started to decline by 1800 BCE, and by 1600 BCE, it was almost in an abandoned state. Coincidentally, the Sumerian Civilization rose and fell during almost the same period as the Indus Valley. It rose to its greatest height during 2600 BCE, when it had the largest city in the world, but collapsed by 1750 BCE. A few centuries down the lane, in 2000 BCE or so, the ancient Minoans reached their greatest splendour with the completion of their palaces. But by 1700 BCE, there were disturbances and the civilization was on its way down.

With its run across ages, Egypt seems to be an outlier, but during this period of boom and bust it went through a similar destiny. Under the Old Kingdom, Egypt was unified as a single state and witnessed remarkable growth, prosperity and geographical expansion. It reached its zenith around 2600 BCE under two rulers, King Sneferu and his son Khufu, who built great monuments including the Great Pyramid of Giza. But the region soon fell into a time of despair and the Old Kingdom collapsed by 2150 BCE. The Middle Kingdom succeeded to reunite the region and bring back a part of the glory in 2000 BCE, but it fell in 1700 BCE, exactly the same period when the other comparable civilizations were waning.

SIMULTANEOUS PEAK AND DECLINE OF ANCIENT CIVILIZATIONS

	PEAK PERIOD	DECLINE PERIOD
SUMER	2600 BCE	1750 BCE
EGYPT - OLD & MIDDLE KINGDOMS	2600 BCE	1700 BCE
INDUS VALLEY	2500 BCE	~1700 BCE
MINOAN	2000 BCE	1700 BCE

Sexism Increased across the World Following the Collapse

During the centuries around 1700 BCE, most of the stellar civilizations that had built our world until then collapsed or were in a state of decay. This was a phenomenon that spread across regions of the world: South Asia, the Middle East, Europe and Africa. The vacuum that arose due to this global fall would not be felt for long because upon the ancient rubble arose new cultures that replaced each one of them, like the Vedic civilization in South Asia or the Mycenaean civilization in Greece. Some of them would eventually reach greater heights than even their predecessors. However, in a rather curious case, except in the case of Egypt, which is anyway an outlier, in every other culture, women came to occupy a much inferior position than their forerunners. If this case was restricted to the Mycenaeans, this could be assumed as a deviation. But when we see this getting repeated across geographies and cultures, this should be nothing less than a pattern, rather than mere randomness. Why would this be so?

Ancient Civilizations Collapsed Owing to a Drastic Climate Change

For this, we need to answer one lingering question. What strange things happened during this period when the older civilizations collapsed and new ones arose? In the case of the Indus Valley, various theories suggest that changes in river patterns resulted in sporadic floods and droughts. Disruptions in the monsoons acted as a multiplier, finally turning the region uninhabitable. In Sumer, texts recovered from that period suggested movement in the Euphrates riverbed, as a consequence, the irrigation channels dried up and droughts ensued. Some reports proposed that these droughts could have persisted for two to three centuries. Fossil records indicated that the region came under extreme cold winters spells, eventually leading to a collapse. Egypt, meanwhile, struggled with its own challenges of harsh and unpredictable weather conditions, where a lower summer precipitation in the Ethiopian Highlands affected the headstream of the river Nile adversely, resulting in calamitously lower amounts of water discharges in the basin. The outcome was low floods and a catastrophic famine that lasted for centuries, causing the decline of their Old Kingdom.

While in the Mediterranean data analysis and simulations revealed that frequent, abnormally strong and longer-lasting El Niño events during the period led to drier conditions in the islands. Reported earthquakes and a catastrophic volcanic eruption in Thera, Santorini, in 1600 BCE, were death blows to the Minoan civilization. Hence we conclude that this period from 1900 to 1500 BCE was a period of great weather shift across the world, which we refer to as the Late Bronze Age Climate Change.

Climate Change Affected Ancient Agrarian Civilizations to the Core

These four ancient civilizations—Egyptian, Indus Valley, Sumer and Minoan—were distinctly agrarian and sedentary. The core reason for them sprouting and flourishing were their water sources—the Nile for Egypt, Indus for the Indus Valley, Euphrates-Tigris for Sumer and Aegean Sea for the Minoan. These sources enabled them to develop innovative farming and cattle-rearing techniques. Through centuries they perfected their craft, creating social stability and massive economic surpluses, which they then leveraged to create trade bases and sprawling urban landscapes. However, it also meant that their civilizations were built at the mercy of these water sources. Any changes in the stable weather conditions adversely affected and destabilized them. Exactly so, due to the Late Bronze Age Climate Change, as the river courses changed, in the cases of the Indus, the Nile and the Euphrates, and as tsunamis built in the Mediterranean, the situation quickly escalated and adversely affected the lives of the people on these valleys and coastal belts. And as these water bodies famished or raged, the people who relied on them for their sustenance either perished or fled.

A Perfect Storm Came Together to Destroy the Civilizations

Quite unfortunately, climate changes are not one-off incidents. They seem to follow a recurring pattern at almost regular intervals, the earliest of which had been recorded in 4200 BCE. Every time this wrath of the unfavourable climate was unleashed, it halted human progress and brought down civilizations. In his book *1177 B.C.: The Year Civilization Collapsed*, Eric H. Cline, historian and archaeologist, in reference to the Iron Age Climate Change, spoke about how complex these phenomena are, a perfect storm of sorts, a coming together of various disasters including droughts, famines, earthquakes, plagues, invasions and trade collapse, finally creating multiple interconnected failures. In the case of the Late Bronze Age Climate Change, we see the same pattern, the release of several disastrous events simultaneously. For example, droughts and famines in the Indus Valley, Egypt, Sumer and Minoan, earthquakes and volcanic eruptions in Crete and surrounding areas, and disruption of trade between the Minoans, Egyptians, Sumer and the Indus Valley.

A Plague at the Centre of the Perfect Storm

Every reported climate change has had an epidemic at the centre stage, acting as a devastation multiplier. The Late Bronze Age Climate Change would be no different. Excavations conducted in an ancient burial site, Hagios Charalambos in Crete, revealed genetic evidence of *Yersinia Pestis*, the bacterium responsible for bubonic plague, traced back to the Late Bronze Age Climate

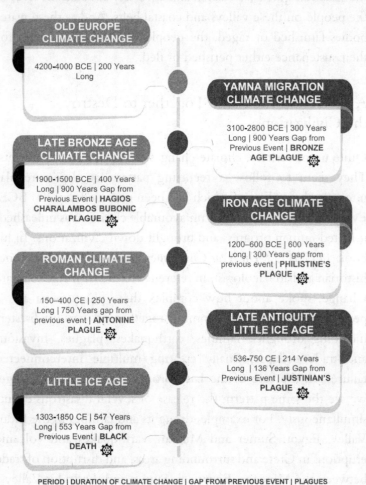

OLD EUROPE CLIMATE CHANGE

4200-4000 BCE | 200 Years Long

YAMNA MIGRATION CLIMATE CHANGE

3100-2800 BCE | 300 Years Long | 900 Years Gap from Previous Event | **BRONZE AGE PLAGUE**

LATE BRONZE AGE CLIMATE CHANGE

1900-1500 BCE | 400 Years Long | 900 Years Gap from Previous Event | **HAGIOS CHARALAMBOS BUBONIC PLAGUE**

IRON AGE CLIMATE CHANGE

1200–600 BCE | 600 Years Long | 300 Years gap from previous event | **PHILISTINE'S PLAGUE**

ROMAN CLIMATE CHANGE

150–400 CE | 250 Years Long | 750 Years gap from previous event | **ANTONINE PLAGUE**

LATE ANTIQUITY LITTLE ICE AGE

536-750 CE | 214 Years Long | 136 Years Gap from Previous Event | **JUSTINIAN'S PLAGUE**

LITTLE ICE AGE

1303-1850 CE | 547 Years Long | 553 Years Gap from Previous Event | **BLACK DEATH**

PERIOD | DURATION OF CLIMATE CHANGE | GAP FROM PREVIOUS EVENT | PLAGUES

Change period. Interestingly, it is proposed that the disease might have reached the eastern Mediterranean coast through the bacterium laden flea-infected rodents in the trade ships from Egypt. In Egypt, these rats were speculated to have arrived from the Indus Valley in South Asia or Sumer in Mesopotamia, inflecting the Nile rats. Papyrus manuscripts recovered from 1500 BCE, described symptoms such as black spots and swelling, pointing us to a bubonic outbreak. Meanwhile, in Sumer, transliterations of thousands of clay tablets have now given us an insight into the prevalence of an epidemic in the region at that time, whose symptoms were similar to that of bubonic plague. So, essentially, this plague circulated across multiple civilizations, especially the thickly populated ones, through generations in multiple waves.

Why Plagues Vanquished and Devastated Civilizations

The bubonic plague is mainly spread through parasitic infected fleas, residing in rodents. It typically enters human systems through flea bites, infecting the lymph nodes and causing them to swell, eventually leading to complications like muscle cramps, seizures, high fever and even death. Unfortunately, civilizations have been breeding grounds for the plague due to multiple reasons. Firstly, most of the ancient civilizations and in this particular case, all of them—Egypt, the Indus Valley, Sumer and the Minoan—have been agrarian. With their advanced farming skills and irrigation techniques, they created a farming surplus which was stored in granaries and large storage houses. These unfortunately were fertile breeding grounds for rats, who fed on the grains. As the agricultural surplus was traded for economic gains, these infected rats easily got transported to different corners of the world, typically to advanced civilizations that could afford to trade.

Secondly, these agrarian civilizations tended to be urban centres like Thebes or Memphis in Egypt, or Uruk in Sumer, with high population density, where often people lived alongside their cattle and sheep, providing an easy haven for pathogens to spread. A third factor was the low immunity of their populations, who were already reeling under famines and droughts. Hence, people who could have otherwise had a chance of survival, were now easily susceptible, increasing its virality and lethality. The epidemic could then sweep over, giving a devastating blow to these civilizations and leading to their eventual fall.

Going Back to the Steppes to Find Clues on Sexism

Though we figured out that the Late Bronze Age Climate Change and the Hagios Charalambos Bubonic Plague led to the fall of the ancient civilizations of Egypt, the Indus Valley, Sumer and the Minoan, we are yet to answer the core question: though not noticed in the earlier civilizations, why did sexism suddenly become prevalent in the newer ones? For this, we should figure out 'who' replaced the vacuum left by the collapse of the earlier civilizations. For clues, let us look at the previous waves of climate changes.

During 4200–4000 BCE, the harsh winters pushed a set of herders from the Eurasian Steppes to spread across the lower Danube valley, the centre of an early farming settlement called the Old European Culture, either causing or exploiting its collapse. During the Yamna Migration Climate Change Period, between 3100 and 2800 BCE, another set of pastoralists, along with their families and clans, migrated in search of better pastures. Their domesticated horses, superior weaponry and, most importantly, wheeled carts, enabled them to aggressively push forward and occupy new lands. Since we see the repeated pattern of Steppe migrations across climate changes, we ask ourselves the question whether this could have been a possibility during the Late Bronze Age Climate Change as well.

South Asian DNA Got 'Steppified' after the Climate Change

Multiple genetic studies have concluded that though there was no trace of Steppe ancestry present during the origins and heights of the Indus Valley Civilization, there was a large-scale injection of this parentage into the region during or after its decline phase. Several detailed research including 'The Formation of Human Populations in South and Central Asia' by Vageesh Narasimhan et al and 'An Ancient Harappan Genome Lacks Ancestry from Steppe Pastoralists or Iranian Farmers' by Vasant Shinde et al., have henceforth proposed that most South Asians of today carry an ancestry up to 30 per cent derived from Steppe pastoralists. Leading us to a conclusion that Steppe migration and mixing with the local population happened between 2000 and 1500 BCE, the same period as the Late Bronze Age Climate Change.

According to Roman Ghirshman, a French archaeologist renowned for his excavation in Iran and Afghanistan, at around 2000 BCE, different groups of herders, forced by the widespread aridization and water shortages in the Eurasian Steppes, started out on a migratory process. While some of them pressed on towards Mesopotamia, the other group passed the Karakum Desert in Central Asia and the Great Salt Desert in the middle of the Iranian plateau, crossed Afghanistan and the Hindu Kush mountains, eventually infiltrating into north-west India. This, of course, was not a single journey but across several successive waves involving numerous people, occupying different regions in their migratory path, including south-central Asia,

Afghanistan, Iran and finally India. As this coincided with the decline of the Indus Valley Civilization, again one part owing to the same climate change, this led to several deep-seated changes in the region, which also included a mixing of migrating people with the existing urban culture.

Steppe Genes Arrived in Sumer After the Climate Change

Decreased rainfall and enduring famines, induced by the Late Bronze Age Climate Change, left large parts of the ancient Mesopotamian settlements in the lurch. During this period, as one set of Steppe migrants entered the Indian subcontinent, the other reached northern Mesopotamia. Cuneiform sources indicate that during the Great Drought, which persisted for almost three centuries, several waves of predatory nomads penetrated in and plundered their capital city of Uruk. These migrations intensified after the death of Hammurabi, who ruled over the Old Babylonian Empire from 1792 to 1750 BCE.

Around the same period and region, we witnessed the rise of the Hurrian Empire of Mitanni. The Hurrians are now thought to have been carrying the Steppe-related ancestry, who later migrated to occupy the upper valleys of the Euphrates and Tigris. They claimed aristocratic origins, and with the collapse of the older empires established their own independent state. The Mitannis then introduced cultures typical to the Steppe region including their gods and linguistic terms of Indo-Aryan origin, sprinkled with their equestrian terminology. A study on the genomic history of the Middle East found that the present-day population derived its ancestry from four ancient populations: the Levant, Neolithic Iranians, Eastern Hunter-Gatherers and East Africa. While the rest of the Arabian population had an excess of

African ancestry, in the Levant and Mesopotamian regions, they carried a higher Steppe-related lineage that arrived during the late Bronze Age, around the same time as the climate change.

Compared to Native Minoan, the Mycenaean Carried a Steppe Ancestry

According to genetic studies conducted in Crete, it had no traces of any Steppe ancestry during the Middle and Late Bronze Ages. A specific study that spoke about all published individuals from the Minoan culture dating 2400–1700 BCE reiterated this finding—that Minoans had no linkages to Steppe ancestry. Now the Mycenaeans, the civilization that succeeded and resembled the Minoans but deviated from them in women empowerment, were found to be genetically similar to their predecessors in three quarters of their ancestry. Both of them derived their related genes from the Neolithic farmers of western Anatolia and Aegean.

However, the Mycenaeans had one difference from the Minoans: they traced their remaining lineage back to the pastoralists of Eurasian Steppe. In a landmark study 'Genetic Origins of the Minoans and Mycenaeans' published in the journal *Nature*, Losif Lazaridis, an evolutionary biologist, noted that 'the Mycenaean gene pool was not monolithic' as it carried traces of Steppe ancestry across individuals of all social classes. Now the interesting part is that, according to DNA evidence, the modern Greeks are descendants of the Mycenaeans and hence continue to carry more or less the same genetic structure that included the Steppe ancestry.

Egypt Was an Outlier Among All Ancient Civilizations

A genome sequencing of several individuals from the Near East to study their genetic history in the past 4000 years found

Steppe-like ancestry appearing during the late Bronze Age period. However, in the case of Egypt, strangely it was found to be significantly negative, suggesting that ancient Egyptian civilization did not receive this inflow of Eurasian genes that others in the region were a part of. However, Egypt might not have been completely insulated as well. Another DNA study published in 2020 analysed Egyptian human mummies, especially belonging to the royal families. They found Steppe-related ancestry associated with Amenhotep III, also known as Amenhotep the Great, who ruled from 1391 to 1353 BCE. It is now speculated that the pharaoh might have received this lineage from his mother, thought to have been the daughter of the king of the Mitanni Empire. The Hurrians, who built the Mitanni Empire, incidentally, carried Steppe genetics.

However, these interactions might have been limited and strategic rather than a widespread phenomenon, as both the Egyptian and the Mitanni empires were protecting their own interests from a mutual enemy, the Hittites. Despite being part

STEPPE ANCENSTRY IN ANCIENT CIVILIZATIONS

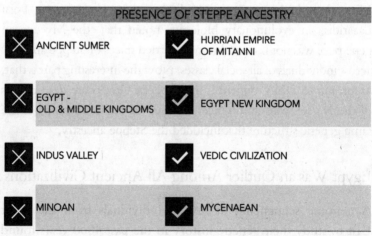

PRESENCE OF STEPPE ANCESTRY	
✕ ANCIENT SUMER	✓ HURRIAN EMPIRE OF MITANNI
✕ EGYPT - OLD & MIDDLE KINGDOMS	✓ EGYPT NEW KINGDOM
✕ INDUS VALLEY	✓ VEDIC CIVILIZATION
✕ MINOAN	✓ MYCENAEAN

of several historical population movements, the people of the Near East, including the Egyptians, retained 90 per cent of their Bronze Age ancestry. Hence compared to the other regions of South Asia, Mesopotamia and Greece, which underwent a change in its genetic make-up owing to the Steppe migrations during the Late Bronze Age Climate Change, Egypt remained an outlier.

Surprisingly, the Steppe Ancestry Replaced Only Males, Not Females

Before the advent of the Late Bronze Age Climate Change, Steppe ancestry was not noticed in the ancient civilizations of the Indus Valley, Sumer, Minoan as well as Egypt. However, after this catastrophe, except in the case of Egypt, there was a substantial infiltration of Steppe genetics into these regions. Though this was a noticeable change, how do we conclude with certainty that this Steppe migration had anything to do with the sexism that the world acquired after the climate change? To find a conclusive answer, let us look outside these four civilizations to other locations which have again been affected by these large-scale migrations. In the case of the British Isles, though the incoming populations during the Late Bronze Age period replaced the native people, strangely, it was the male lineages that were almost completely replaced rather than the females.

Meanwhile, the Iberian Peninsula, consisting of Spain and Portugal, witnessed 40 per cent of its inhabitants getting replaced by the immigrants by the second millennium BCE. Coincidentally, here again, the Y chromosome, corresponding to males, underwent replacement. Meanwhile, another study published in the journal *Annals of Human Biology* quantified male and female genetic contribution into European Bronze

Age populations from the Steppe-related ancestry. It concluded that not only this migration from the Steppe region had a considerable impact on the European population, but also predominantly replaced its male population compared to females.

Steppe Undertook Male-dominated Migration

Considering both genders are evenly distributed in any population, why would the Steppe migrants across the world overridingly replace the males and not females? A landmark paper, 'Familial Migration of the Neolithic Contrasts Massive Male Migration during Bronze Age in Europe Inferred from Ancient X Chromosomes', written by Amy Goldberg and team, studied population dynamics and evolution, and then came to the conclusion that the previous Yamna Migration Climate Change that took place between 3100 and 2800 BCE had not produced this strange phenomenon of higher male replacement. According to this paper, the Europeans who existed during this period inherited equal amounts of DNA from the males and females. This enables us to conclude that similar proportions of men and women, or even entire families, might have been part of this previous migratory process.

However, during the Late Bronze Age Climate Change migration, there was an extreme skew towards male among the migrant members. Goldberg and team, after extrapolating the data, proposed that there were approximately fourteen male migrants for every female migrant—a staggering and lopsided gender aberration. Hence, quite contrary to the earlier instance, during the Late Bronze Age Climate Change, women were left behind, and predominantly men migrated from the Steppes.

Solving the Mystery of Women Being Left Behind in Steppes

While the Steppe migration during 3000 BCE was undertaken alongside entire clans and families, during the Late Bronze Age, in contrast, it was male dominated. One explanation is that, since a warrior culture prevailed in the Steppes rather than a passive migration, this round might have been driven by a thirst for conquest and aggressive acquisition of new territories. If that was the intent, then it made sense that only men start out on it, well-equipped on their horses and wagons, leaving their women behind. Another hypothesis is of a population explosion in the Steppes, where there might have been an intense resource scarcity or even a competition for females, as theirs was male-kinship oriented, the strongest-take-it-all society. Such a scenario could have prompted several groups of side-lined men to start out on missions to take over new lands and procure new mates. This theory of overpopulation is a highly possible one as the gap between the last migration and the Late Bronze Age one was almost 1000 years, where the Steppe herders enjoyed stable weather conditions for almost a millennium. A third hypothesis could be that the Steppe herders deliberately left their women behind to tend to their children, herds and wealth but then refused to turn back around, as they wandered too far away into other civilizations. This theory is equally as plausible as the others because in many Steppe cultures, women are put in charge to guard the existing territories and wealth, as their men venture out for longer periods of time.

Steppe Males Won Over the Native Women

Though the Steppe migrants might have been more male-dominated, they still needed to become a part of the native population for their genetics to turn up in the future studies. There are two ways in which this would be possible: firstly, is by coercion, which might not have been hugely difficult since the native population of each of these civilizations were already weak due to the ongoing famines, droughts and plagues. In fact, researchers suggest that the natives could have contracted the epidemic from the pastoralists themselves. Genetic studies have now identified the presence of *Yersinia pestis*, a bacterium responsible for bubonic plague, in the Steppe tombs. As the herders lived alongside animals, it was easier for them to develop a tolerance, but as they continued to carry these microbes, they infected the outsiders they came in contact with. These conditions could have helped the migrants overpower the native men in order to take over their women and wealth.

A population geneticist, Mattias Jakobsson, says that their infiltration process itself might have been warlike rather than a peaceful process. Ann Gibbons quoted him in her article 'Thousands of Horsemen May Have Swept into Bronze Age Europe, Transforming the Local Population' published in *Science* that: 'It can be called an ancient thousand-man march. It would have looked like males migrating in war, leaving their women behind, sweeping into new lands, on horses, and in horse driven wagons, swirling their weapons.' A second possibility, according to Goldberg is that these swashbuckling, horse-riding Steppe men, better built compared to the sedentary native farmers, could have been more attractive as mates and hence had an advantage with the native women. Whether it is one of these or a combination of both, more and more native males, through multiple generations and waves, were replaced with the migrants, whose genetics then became an integral and dominant part of that land's future. The world after the Late Bronze Age Climate Change, in a way, became Steppe male-oriented.

Unravelling the Mystery Behind Global Sexism

It was not only the existing genetics of these ancient civilizations that were pushed aside by the migrants but also their deeply entrenched, centuries-old culture. Egypt, Sumer, the Indus Valley and the Minoan, all were agrarian in nature and relied on the fertility of their lands for their wealth and well-being. Here, women were socially and politically important, considering their contribution in food production, an aspect central to the economy, family and society. Compared to men, women put in equal, if not more effort, in planting, harvesting and processing crops as well as caring for their livestock, which eventually formed the backbone of the economy, producing surplus and improving trade prospects. Hence, it was only natural that they enjoyed economic freedom, property rights and equality before the law.

Steppe men came from the opposite end of the spectrum. In order to survive the hostility of the Steppe terrain, their communities valued a warrior culture, emphasized martial skills, horsemanship and physical strength. Though these aggressive values helped them immensely in their conquests and acquisitions, they tended to be physically demanding, unfortunately, making these societies highly male dominated. In their patriarchal societies, lineage, wealth and power were strictly passed from fathers to their sons. Women often had no political or economic rights and were merely responsible for domestic duties. Glimpses of these can be seen in the Steppe male-centric pantheon and the disproportionate number of male burial mounds. Hence, as the Steppe men cohabited with the native women, they applied the same social template that they had grown up with and were used to, which viewed women in a subservient role.

Sexism: An Unintended Global Consequence from the Steppes

However, using a broad brush to brand the entire Steppe culture of the time as sexist might not be correct because their women had their own sets of responsibilities and social roles. They took charge of guarding flocks and families as their men stepped out for adventures and conquests. And as they moved between pastures and camping grounds to save themselves from the harsh winters, these women managed the meticulous movement of men and materials.

Then why would the Steppe men not consider the native women worthy? One hypothesis could be that since the native women did not belong to their own communities and clans, they did not adhere to the same perceptions of beauty that the Steppe men were used to back home. This could have adversely affected their interactions with them. Another theory is that, in many cases, these men could have forced the natives to have sexual relations with them without any intent of any permanent marriage of sorts. This could have again resulted in a deterioration of women's rights. As the Steppe men were stronger and combative, it was easier for them to impose their viewpoints on the rest of the society, ultimately leading to the institutionalization of these practices. Among them, unfortunately, sexism became the one that would most critically affect the future generations.

Mycenaean Civilization Inspired the Greeks

The Mycenaean civilization collapsed around 1050 BCE, probably due to internal strife, political instability or overpopulation. Less than three centuries later, on its foundation, the Greek civilization started to take form. The Greeks shared not only the same genetic lineage from ancient Mycenaean but also their culture and practices. They were so inspired by the Mycenaeans, that they considered it as the Golden Age. Several elements of the Greek civilization could be traced back to Mycenaean, including their language, religion, art and architecture. While Mycenaean Linear B script was the predecessor for the Greek written text, their palace culture served as a model for the later Greek city-states and influenced the development of the classical temples and monumental architecture of the Greek world. Homer, one of the most influential authors in history, whose epics sparked the Greek resurgence, idealized the Mycenaean forefathers. He glorified the life and times of the Mycenaeans. In the *Iliad*, he narrated the Trojan war and the quarrel between King Agamemnon and the invincible warrior, Achilles, based on the Mycenaeans conflict with their arch enemies, the Hittites. In his other epic, the *Odyssey*, he glorified the adventures of Odysseus and his adventurous journey back home after the Trojan war.

Greek Democracy Ushered in a Political Revolution

Due to its peculiar geography, Greece was divided into many city-states and self-governing communities. Trade and commerce contributed to the overall prosperity, and by the sixth and seventh centuries, there was the rise of a new aristocratic class that wielded economic and political power. To claim legitimacy as rulers, many of them traced back their lineage to the legendary Mycenaean heroes Herakles, Neleus or Nestor. However, soon, Athens, one of the city-states, fell under the tyranny of one such noble family, the Peisistratids. When another city-state, Sparta, got involved and took advantage of the situation, Cleisthenes, an aristocratic Athenian, proposed the radical idea of democracy, which promised equality and participation of citizens directly in the political process. With time, the Athenian democracy evolved, through a series of reforms, including the creation of an assembly called Ecclesia, for citizens to vote on legislation, and a council of citizens called Boule, which prepared the agenda for the assembly and kept a check on the power of individual politicians.

Now, the concept of democracy that the Greeks invented, has had a profound and lasting influence on the world in several ways. It introduced the idea of popular sovereignty, where power is held by the people and not by a monarch or oligarchy. This idea laid the foundation for modern democratic systems and inspired later political philosophers such as John Locke and Jean-Jacques Rousseau. In fact, it so deeply influenced the founding fathers of the United States that they sought to establish a democratic system based on Athenian principles.

With Democracy, Sexism Got Its Arms and Legs

Democracy is often referred to as the elixir of life, a magical cure for many of the communal ills, as it provided a voice for the citizens, promoting fairness, equality and freedom, and laying the foundations of a just society. Ideally it should have sounded a death knell for sexism, which is against everything that democracy stands for, but unfortunately, it proved to be just the opposite. The Greeks built their cultural bedrock on the Mycenaean civilization, including their sexual oppression. Sexism, which was until then just a social undercurrent—with unwritten cultural rules and regulations—suddenly became institutionalized with the establishment of democracy. Now legally, women were excluded. Women were not allowed to speak in public and were discouraged from expressing political opinions. They were not allowed to participate in assembly or vote on political matters. They were not eligible to hold political office or serve elected officials. They were often excluded from formal education—a necessity for political participation. They had limited property rights and were often unable to own or inherit property. Women were already relegated to an inferior position after the Late Bronze Age Climate Change but with the advent of democracy, they found themselves in an even more precarious state.

Alexander the Great Placed Greece at the Centre of the Global Stage

As a tiny piece of land, alongside numerous islands, located at the southern end of the Balkan Peninsula, with the Aegean and Ionian Seas surrounding it, Greece and its culture might have gone unnoticed in history. Unless for one man—Alexander the Great—who started on his conquests with probably the world's first cerebral army, represented by a disproportionate number of intellectuals including historians, philosophers, cartographers, poets and authors. Enabled by the multiplier effect of these thinkers and philosophers, he spread Hellenistic values through the world by establishing a large empire that covered much of the Mediterranean region, Southwest Asia and Egypt. He commissioned Greek-style cities across the world, many of which became centres of Hellenistic culture and beliefs.

After Alexander's untimely death, his empire split into several Hellenistic empires including the Seleucid Empire, which controlled much of the Near East and parts of Central Asia, the Ptolemaic Empire with Egypt and parts of the eastern Mediterranean, the Antigonid Kingdom of Greece, Macedonia, and parts of the Balkans and the Attalid kingdom of parts of Asia Minor. These kingdoms continued the Hellenistic cultural diffusion throughout the world, influencing art, science, philosophy and religions of the world for centuries to come. It was an age that saw the meteoric rise of a global Greece. But unfortunately, it also meant a rapid proliferation of this value that kept women suppressed and oppressed—from Greece to wherever the Greeks went.

Rome Rose Up as the New Greece

As Alexander the Great conquered the entire known world and spread Hellenistic ideas on the other side of the Mediterranean Sea, the Romans were their biggest admirers. They were already in contact with each other from the ancient times, especially after the Greeks had settled in Sicily since the eighth century BCE. But as the Romans rose in their influence across the globe, they built themselves on the Greek ideas, whom they considered their predecessors. For example, Roman literature was heavily influenced by Hellenistic ideas. Virgil, among Rome's greatest poets, was inspired by Homer, whom he modelled himself after. Cicero, the Roman statesman and orator, acknowledged how Greek ideas inspired the development of the Roman civilization. When it came to art and design, the Romans emulated the Greek form and even decorated their own buildings with Hellenistic statues. In architecture, the Romans followed the Greek concepts of colonnades and rectangular shapes. In religion, Romans followed a polytheistic system of worship, where many of their myths were similar in narratives, and their gods, similar in characteristics to the Hellenistic ones. In more ways than one, Rome was the new Greece.

Rome Umbilically Connected to Greece

Interestingly, Rome might not have been just connected to Greece culturally, but genetically too. A study titled 'Ancient Genomes Reveal Structural Shifts after the Arrival of Steppe-Related Ancestry in the Italian Peninsula', conducted by Tina Saupe and her team published in the journal *Current Biology*, revealed that the Italian Peninsula was shaped—as with many other regions elsewhere in the world—by continuous events of migrations. This paper specifically delved into a period around 1600 BCE, during the Late Bronze Age, when large-scale migrations occurred towards Central Italy from the Steppe herders, the result of which changed the DNA structure of the existing population in the region, which was until then composed predominantly from the Early Neolithic Farmers in Eastern Europe. The study also suggested that this occupation from the Steppes drove social structural changes, reflected through changes in burial practices and patrilineal kinship structures, indicating that the populations shared not only genes but also their culture. Hence, when the Romans emulated the Greeks, in a way, they were merely mirroring the behaviour of their same stock—the Steppe ancestry—which the Greeks inherited from Mycenae but which the Romans inherited directly.

Rome Provided More Credibility to Sexism

Ancient Rome had its beginnings in the eighth century BCE as a settlement beside the river Tiber. As it grew to a kingdom, a series of kings took over its rule. However, the seventh one—Tarquinius Superbus—proved unpopular, and hence was deposed in an uprising. Henceforth, his nephew Lucius Junius

Brutus brought the people of Rome together in order to never allow any man to take over as the King of Rome again. He then established a system called the Republic, where elected representatives would be a part of the assemblies. The system ensured that all the people holding positions were kept under check by a separation of powers. The concept of the Republic set a precedent for representative government. It gave the world the concept of citizenship and the rule of law—how the law applied equally to all the citizens—thereby contributing to the development of the modern legal system.

Ironically, beyond all this high-level idealistic talk, women faced further exclusions. In the Roman Republic, women were not allowed to participate in political life or hold public office. They were considered the property of the male members and shut out from all citizenship rights, including the right to vote, speak in public or to be represented in courts of law. If women were denied all the rights in the Greek democracy, their successor, the Roman Republic, would ensure that they were handed out no greater privileges.

With Pax Romana, a Global Rome Rose at the Global Stage

Though it started out as a small city-state in central Italy, by 27 BCE the Roman Empire had expanded to include most of Italy, parts of Spain, France, Greece and North Africa. Under Augustus Caesar, it added regions across Europe, including France, and the eastern Mediterranean. In the following two centuries, known as the Pax Romana period, an age of unprecedented peace and prosperity, the Roman Empire stretched from Western Europe to the Near East and North Africa, becoming one of the largest and most powerful empires in world history. Alongside the expansion of its borders through conquests and diplomacy, the Roman culture, language, law and religion spread, influencing the future of the world in an unprecedented manner. As Rome was culturally connected to the Greeks, with this rise, the world now came to be built on a twin foundational structure—Greek and Roman values.

Christianity Took Over the World from Rome

Christianity, which initially started out as a small Jewish sect, took root in the eastern provinces of Rome and adapted the Greco-Roman culture, including many of the popular philosophies of the time. However, their decisive moment arrived, as Constantine conquered his rival in the Battle of the Milvian Bridge to take over the throne of the Roman Empire. As he believed a miracle from Jesus Christ turned around this impossible battle for him, he accorded an official status to the religion, and extended to Christianity several imperial favours including tax exemptions and access to the treasury funds. Through the First Council of Nicaea, he tried to bring in the much-required unity among the divided Christian factions. Constantine's reign catapulted Christianity to a position of power. Christians filled the social and political seats of authority across the empire. The voice of the clergy reigned supreme in matters of statecraft and diplomacy.

Meanwhile, Constantine reorganized his empire into eastern and western parts. He moved the power centre to Constantinople, a strategically located region at the intersection of the European and Asian trade routes. Later known as the Byzantine Empire, officially a Christian State, it accelerated the spread of Christianity even further, especially to the eastern parts of the empire. Though the Western Roman Empire fell in 476

CE, Christianity continued to rise even higher. The bishop of Rome, the Pope, was at the helm now, and the religion spread its wings across Europe, Africa and Asia. After Greece and Rome, the next centuries belonged to Christianity.

Christianity Inherited Sexism from Rome and Greece

Oppression of women in the civilizations after the Late Bronze Age thrived on the basis of the cultural nuances of the Steppe ancestry. However, with Christianity, another leg was added to this: a divine-centric, religious one. The philosophical underpinning on which Christianity was built itself was anti-feminist. According to the idea of original sin, it was the act of Eve succumbing to the temptation from the serpent in the Garden of Eden that was responsible for the fall of humanity. Hence women came to be perceived as inherently sinful and inferior. Further philosophies were then built on this to justify the exclusion of women from the positions of authority and leadership. The New Testament contained passages that were interpreted to support male authority over women, and this interpretation was reinforced by early Christian leaders such as Paul and Tertullian. Their teachings that celibacy was superior to marriage and that women who chose to remain single and devoted to God were especially holy, reinforced the idea that women's place in the society was restricted, and not in the public sphere. Some Christian teachings placed a heavy emphasis on modesty and sexual purity for women, often excluding men from all these strict regulations. This was then used to justify restrictions on women's dress, mobility and participation in public life, and has then reinforced the idea that women's bodies and sexuality are a source of shame and danger. Overall, Christianity not just inherited the Greco-

Roman values, but also reinforced them. With God on their side, now these values could be institutionalized across the world, in every society and community and family that adopted Christianity.

Western Civilization Built Itself on Rome, Greece and Christianity

Together, these three—the Greek and Roman civilizations and Christianity—have had a disproportionate influence on the world that we live in. It does not matter whether you are a Christian or not, and whether you are thousands of miles away from Europe, in more ways than one, our daily lives are affected by these three forces. For example, if you live in a democratic country, you enjoy the freedom and accountability prescribed by ancient Greece. Individualism and the pursuit of excellence, which many of us take for granted, draw inspiration from this eastern Mediterranean civilization, which believed that each person had the potential to achieve greatness. Modern philosophy, biology, medicine and physics draw upon the foundations laid down by Socrates, Plato, Aristotle and Hippocrates.

The Romans, on their part, have left us the legacy of law and justice. Their comprehensive legal system known as the Corpus Juris Civilis served as a model for modern legal systems. Their engineering and architectural feats including roads, aqueducts, public baths and monumental arches continue to inspire countless imitations and adaptations over the centuries.

Christianity, meanwhile, has played a key role in the development of modern education and research. The many universities established by the church enabled the scientific revolution. It has also been a driving force behind many social justice movements throughout history, from the anti-slavery to the civil rights movement. Together, Greece, Rome and Christianity formed the three pillars upon which our modern world is founded. They gave us all the values that we continue practising—democracy, individualism, justice, philosophy, scientific temperament, and incidentally, sexism.

Easy for all Nations to Adopt, As All Belonged to the Same Stock

The biggest baggage these civilizations left us with, which continue to haunt us, is sexism. It is rather strange how countries and nations that are far away from each other, in time and space, still fell for this. It is even stranger that these regressive ideas persist after these cultures are long gone. How could a set of people take to it if they did not inherently believe in it? Quite the contrary, they are indeed genetically a part of the same culture, the same Steppe stock, and hence adoption and practice might have been easier.

In Finland, Norway, Iceland, Russia, Lithuania and Estonia, a majority of the population carries the Steppe ancestry, while in the Czech Republic, England, France, Poland, Hungary, Bulgaria, Spain and Portugal, it is at least half or less, and in South Asia, it is up to 30 per cent of the population who carry these genetics. In the US, as the largest population groups in most states trace their ancestral roots back to European countries like Germany, England, France, Italy or Ireland, they link again back to the Steppes. Hence, the larger conclusion is that similar ancestry meant similar cultural memories for populations, enabling all of them to collectively relate to and then follow through a repressive policy towards women for several centuries.

EUROPEAN STEPPE STOCK

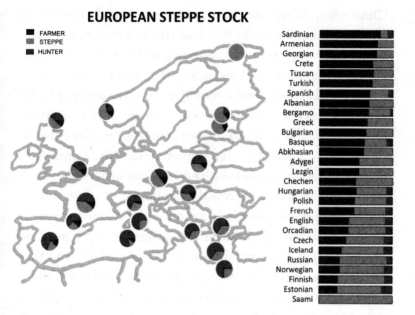

■ FARMER
■ STEPPE
■ HUNTER

Sardinian
Armenian
Georgian
Crete
Tuscan
Turkish
Spanish
Albanian
Bergamo
Greek
Bulgarian
Basque
Abkhasian
Adygei
Lezgin
Chechen
Hungarian
Polish
French
English
Orcadian
Czech
Iceland
Russian
Norwegian
Finnish
Estonian
Saami

Western Colonialism Enabled Sexism to Spread to the Non-Steppe Geographies

Though the majority of the European world shared the Steppe ancestry, there was still a wider world out there, which was still not part of its culture. This defining moment came in 1453 CE, as Constantinople fell to the Ottomans. The resulting blockade of the European trade routes to Asia pushed the western powers to explore alternative trade routes. Thus started the age of colonialism—initially led by the Portuguese and the Spanish Empires—but quickly followed by the other European powers like the Netherlands, England, France and Belgium.

Alongside their desire to expand to new territories, markets, resources and trade centres, another major factor that drove them was their intense desire to see the world converted to

Christianity. While the Portuguese and Spanish focused on spreading Catholicism, the Dutch and the British were motivated by an opposing faction of Christianity, Protestantism. They not only used their religious missions to exert control over the native populations and institutions, but also used philosophies to justify this coercion. Unfortunately, many of these conversions used violence and intimidation during the process. For example, the Spanish conquest of the Americas was characterized by military campaigns against the natives. Many indigenous people were often subjected to brutal punishments, such as torture and execution. In some cases, colonial powers used slavery as a means of spreading Christianity. For example, the Portuguese empire forcibly enslaved large numbers of Africans and then used their enslavement as an opportunity to convert them. Colonial nations also often attempted to stamp out indigenous cultural practices and beliefs, and destroyed their religious sites and cultural artefacts. They often used these in conjunction with other methods, such as missionary work and education.

In a span of about four centuries, many of the regions and populations, otherwise outside the gambit of the Steppe migrations, including Latin America, Africa, Southeast Asia and the Pacific Islands, were now at least symbolically part of the same culture.

Centuries After, Women Continue to Struggle

In one fell swoop, a set of aggressive male herders who migrated from the Steppe regions to escape the harshness of the Late Bronze Age Climate Change altered the global perceptions about women. As they travelled, leaving their women behind, they explored new regions, occupied newer lands and probably not deliberately but eventually created a lopsided masculine genetic ancestry and culture. From then on, the world moved ahead at a breakneck speed; tremendous progress was made in all the spheres but unfortunately the culture of sexism lingered on.

Though Hatshepsut, a woman, could ascend the throne of Egypt in 1478 BCE, it took another 3500-odd years for Sirimavo Bandaranaike to take over as the first elected head of a nation; though Aglaonice gained fame as an astronomer in 1700 BCE, it took us another three-and-a-half millenniums to get a modern lady on the same task; though Tapputi-Belatekallim was the first chemist in history from Mesopotamia, it took us several centuries before Marie Curie won the Nobel Prize. And though Enheduanna was the head priestess in the city of Uruk in 2285 BCE, a female Pope, or a female bishop in the Catholic church, still continues to be a faraway dream.

Hidden Randomness: Our Bridge from the Past to the Present

As human beings, we pride ourselves as the most successful species to have ever existed on our planet. Though we might not have had the longest run compared to the rest, these few thousands of years we have been flourishing, we have created a considerable impact. However, our influence might just be a bit overrated. Many things that have a disproportional influence on our daily lives could be the result of some blind, random events than anything which we have created with a specific purpose or intent. We are so infallible that these random events affect our lives in more ways than one—while some of them help us continue our progress, some others keep us subjugated or divided. Having examined a few such random events from history having a great influence on our lives, these are a few key insights we have gained.

Persistence of the Past

Most of us think of history in events. However, these events do not exist in silos but rather are a result of many other related and unrelated episodes in time. Our inability to connect past incidents to those occurring here and now is partly due to the gradual nature of time itself. These events happen so slowly that they are not apparent to either human memory or archaeological records, making it difficult for us to trace back their growth path. Hence, in order to understand the causes of events—like philosophies, religious ideas and social structures—we should look at them further back, their changing relationships with time and how they all fit together in the big picture. Once we unravel these, we start noticing a lingering persistence of our past on our present lives—for example, the long shadow cast on us by the Fountainhead epoch or the widespread prevalence of the nomadic Xiongnu stock—across geographies, across populations, across time periods.

The Curse of the Black Swan

Black Swans, according to the proponent of the term, Nassim Nicholas Taleb, are 'unexpected events, particularly negative ones, having disproportionate impact on individuals and societies on the longer term'. According to Taleb, the Curse of the Black Swan 'arises because people tend to underestimate the probability of these rare, unpredictable events, and as a result, fail to prepare adequately for them'. Hence, when such events do occur, they cause significant damage and disrupt entire systems. Climate change is one such, but interestingly, as we look deeper, there are distinguishable recurring patterns that can enable us to be ready for the unexpected. For example, in this book, we have recorded seven periods of climate history starting from 4200 BCE until 1850 CE. These changes seem to occur at an average gap of around 550 years from each other (though with a caveat that some of them were as close as a century, while some others as far as a millennium). There are even more interesting patterns—on an average, each of them lasted for 350 years and was accompanied by pandemic infection, resulting in mass migrations and wars, and eventually leading up to the collapse of existing orders and hegemons. In fact, if you make the mistake of reading a bit too much into the data, then extraordinary civilizations, formidable empires and great nations—all of which have been obvious evidences of human triumphs, look nothing more than mere fillers between climate change events.

Domino Chain Reactions

The domino effect is a phenomenon where a small action or event can trigger a sequence of related events, causing a much larger and often unforeseen outcome. This concept is named after the game of dominoes, where knocking over one piece can cause a chain reaction resulting in the toppling of all the pieces. In real-life scenarios, the domino effect can manifest in various ways. For example, a small error or oversight in a complex system can trigger a chain of events, leading to a catastrophic failure. Similarly, a small economic disruption in one region can cause a ripple effect across the global market, affecting businesses and individuals worldwide. We see such a typical case unravelling as a small revolt in the minor Judean territory of the Roman Empire disrupted its normal systems, which then led an emperor—regarded as one of the greatest Stoic philosophers— into taking two decisions, thereby accidentally overturning the future of our world for ever. Another such incident we can see in ancient India: an unsuspecting child was bullied by his friends over a glass of milk, eventually upsetting the territorial balance of power, leading to one of the greatest wars during that period and then to the unification of India. For us authors, the most surprising case of such a chain reaction was an ancient male dominated migration from the Eurasian Steppes—finally leaving humanity with a heavy baggage of sexism—that many cultures are still struggling with.

Chaotic Interconnectedness

Chaos theory suggests that seemingly unrelated events, though they appear to be unexpected and unpredictable, connect back in surprising ways. Random events, though they appear to be disconnected at first glance, are often characterized by feedback loops and non-linear dynamics, where patterns and structures emerge from the interactions between individual agents within the system. In this book, we have observed unbelievable cases of such interconnectedness, examples being the sixteen warring Mahajanapadas and the consolidation of India happening in a similar era as the Seven Warring States and unification of China, and three religions from different spaces and times, looking alike, as if they shared an umbilical cord.

Our world is more random and mysterious than we think. It hides infinitely more than what it reveals.

Acknowledgements

This book came out differently than what we initially imagined it to be. We would like to thank each other for professionalism and commitment throughout this project.

V.R. Ferose, Sridhar Sundaram, Vidyadhar Prabhudesai, Jagan Girisaballa and Saurabh Nanda, for being excellent bouncing boards.

Dr D. Sambandhan for his unwavering support and infectious passion.

Vadlapudi Srinivas Praveen Kumar and Sumit Kumar Bhoi, for conceptualizing and turning around the infographics.

Milee Ashwarya and Manish Kumar, for believing in the potential of this book, though it was quite unconventional to start with.

Manali Das and Yash Daiv for their careful edits and wonderful guidance.

Zac would like to thank his grandparents, uncles, aunts, cousins, teachers, and friends, especially Shiva, Sammy and Aditya.

Bibliography

Acta Theologica Supplementum 7. 'Causes of Death Among the Caesars (27 BC–AD 476).' 2005. https://www.ajol.info/index.php/actat/article/view/52565# (accessed March 9, 2023).

Almarri, Mohamed A., et al., 'The Genomic History of the Middle East. The Genomic History of the Middle East'. *Science Direct*, August 4, 2021. https://doi.org/10.1016/j.cell.2021.07.013 (accessed March 9, 2023).

Ambedkar, B.R., *The Untouchables: Who Were They and Why They Became Untouchables*. New Delhi: Gyan Books, 2017.

Andrade, Tonio. *The Gunpowder Age: China, Military Innovation, and the Rise of the West in World History*. Princeton: Princeton University Press, 2017.

Ansede, Manuel. 'The Invasion That Wiped out Every Man from Spain 4,500 Years Ago'. *El Pais*, English Edition, October 4 2018, https://english.elpais.com/elpais/2018/10/03/inenglish/1538568010_930565.html (accessed March 9, 2023).

Answering-Islam.Org. 'The Nature of Muhammad's Prophetic Experience', https://answering-islam.org/Gilchrist/Vol1/3b.html (accessed March 9, 2023).

Avichai Katz Sinvany, Benjamin. 'Notes on the Invention of the First Gun: Conflict and Innovation in the Song Warring States Period (960–1279)'. *Journal of Chinese Military History*, May 17, 2019. https://brill.com/view/journals/jcmh/8/1/article-p1_1.xml (accessed March 9, 2023).

Barber, Elizabeth J.W. 'Half-Clad Minoan Women, Revisited'. *Kadmos* 44, no. 1–2 (January 1, 2005): 40–42, https://doi.org/10.1515/kadm.2005.007 (accessed March 9, 2023).

Barua, Kazal. 'Tracing the Socio-Economic Roots of the Buddhist Concept of Universal Monarch (Cakkavatti)'. *South Asia Culture, History & Heritage*, 2015, http://repository.kln.ac.lk/bitstream/handle/123456789/11473/4-12.pdf?sequence=1&isAllowed=y (accessed March 9, 2023).

Beaujard, Philippe. 'The Worlds of the Indian Ocean: A Global History'. Cambridge University Press, 2019.

Betancourt, Philip P., Heidi M.C. Dierckx, Susan C. Ferrence, Panagiotis Karkanas, Louise C. Langford-Verstegen, Tanya J. McCullough, James D. Muhly et al. *Hagios Charalambos: A Minoan Burial Cave in Crete: I. Excavation and Portable Objects.* Edited by Philip P. Betancourt, Costis Davaras and Eleni Stravopodi. INSTAP Academic Press, 2014.

Berzin, Alexander. 'Indian Society and Thought at the Time of Buddha'. Study Buddhism, https://studybuddhism.com/en/advanced-studies/history-culture/buddhism-in-india/indian-society-and-thought-at-the-time-of-buddha (accessed March 9, 2023).

Blakemore, Erin. 'Surprising DNA Found in Ancient People from Southern Europe'. *National Geographic*, March 14, 2019, https://www.nationalgeographic.com/science/article/ancient-iberians-dna-from-steppe-men-spain (accessed March 9, 2023).

Biello, David. 'Rise and Fall of Chinese Dynasties Tied to Changes in Rainfall'. *Scientific American*, November 7, 2008, https://www.scientificamerican.com/article/monsoon-climate-change-chinese/ (accessed March 9, 2023).

Boardman, John. '1177 B.C.: The Year Civilization Collapsed'. Common Knowledge 23, no. 2 (April 1, 2017): 346–47. https://doi.org/10.1215/0961754x-3815882 (accessed March 9, 2023).

Borghini, Andrea. 'The 5 Great Schools of Ancient Greek Philosophy'. ThoughtCo, August 27, 2020, thoughtco.com/five-great-schools-ancient-greek-philosophy-2670495 (accessed March 9, 2023).

Callaway, E. 'Bronze Age Skeletons Were Earliest Plague Victims'. *Nature* (October 22, 2015). https://www.nature.com/articles/nature.2015.18633 (accessed March 9, 2023).

Cascio, Elio Lo. 'The New State of Diocletian and Constantine: From the Tetrarchy to the Reunification of the Empire'. In *The Cambridge Ancient History*, edited by Alan Bowman, Averil Cameron and Peter Garnsey, Second ed., pp. 170–83. Cambridge: Cambridge University Press, 2005.

Christ, Karl. 'The Minoan Civilization of Ancient Crete'. *Philosophy and History* 2, no. 2 (1969), https://doi.org/10.5840/philhist196922112 (accessed March 9, 2023).

Christian, David. 'Silk Roads or Steppe Roads? The Silk Roads in World History'. *Journal of World History* 11, no. 1 (Spring, 2000): 1–26.

Chyla, J. '1739 BC – Year when the Sumerian Civilization Collapsed'. Archeowieści.Pl - Information from the World of Archeology, October 25, 2021, https://archeowiesci.pl/en/1739-bc-year-when-the-sumerian-civilization-collapsed/ (accessed March 9, 2023).

Cline, Eric. *1177 B.C.: The Year Civilization Collapsed: Turning Points in Ancient History*. Princeton University Press, 2021.

Conliffe, Ciaran. 'The Turkic Khaganate'. Daily Scribbling, https://dailyscribbling.com/forgotten-empires/the-turkic-khaganate/ (accessed March 9, 2023).

Craig, Erin. 'Why Genghis Khan's Tomb Can't be Found', BBC.com, July 19, 2017. https://www.bbc.com/travel/article/20170717-why-genghis-khans-tomb-cant-be-found (accessed May 9, 2023).

Dandekar, R.N. *The Mahabharata Revisited*. Sahitya Akademi, 2011.

Darian, Jean C. 'Social and Economic Factors in the Rise of Buddhism'. *Sociological Analysis* 38, no. 3 (1977): 226–38.

Dean, Riaz. 'We Know Very Little of the Kushans: Middlemen of Silk Road & Empire that Gave India Kanishka'. *Print*, March 6, 2022, https://theprint.in/pageturner/excerpt/we-know-very-little-of-the-kushans-middlemen-of-silk-road-empire-that-gave-india-kanishka/858784/ (accessed March 9, 2023).

Dikov, Ivan. '6th Century Justinian Plague May Have Originated with Hun Migrations in Asia'. Brewminate, November 15, 2018, https://brewminate.com/6th-century-justinian-plague-may-have-originated-with-hun-migrations-in-asia/ (accessed March 9, 2023).

Dobroruka, Vicente. 'Theriac and Tao: More Aspects on Byzantine Diplomatic Gifts to Tang China'. *Journal of Literature and Art Studies* 6, no. 2 (February 2016): 170–77, http://www.davidpublisher.com/Public/uploads/Contribute/568e0c167171f.pdf (accessed March 9, 2023).

Dong, Guanghui, Leibin Wang, David Dian Zhang and Fengwen Liu. 'Climate-Driven Desertification and Its Implications for the Ancient Silk Road Trade'. Climate of the Past, June 2021, https://cp.copernicus.org/preprints/cp-2020-102/

cp-2020-102-manuscript-version5.pdf (accessed March 9, 2023).

Doyle, Alister. 'Roman, Han Dynasty Kick Started Climate Change'. *ABC Science*, October 4, 2012.

Drake, H.A. 'Lambs into Lions: Explaining Early Christian Intolerance'. *Past & Present*, no. 153 (1996): 3–36. http://www.jstor.org/stable/651134 (accessed March 9, 2023).

Economic Times, 'Steppe Migration to India Was between 3500–4000 Years Ago: David Reich'. October 12, 2019, https://economictimes.indiatimes.com/news/science/steppe-migration-to-india-was-between-3500-4000-years-ago-david-reich/articleshow/71556277.cms (accessed March 9, 2023).

Encyclopedia Britannica. 'Moses: Years and Deeds', https://www.britannica.com/biography/Moses-Hebrew-prophet (accessed March 9, 2023).

Erdem, Cagri. 'Pax Sinica along the Silk Road: Avant-Garde Perspectives on Eurasian Geopolitics'. *Acta Via Serica*, December 2018, https://doi.org/10.22679/avs.2018.3.2.009 (accessed March 9, 2023).

Facts and Details. 'After the Gupta Empire: Hunas (Huns) and Pratiharas.' September 2020. https://factsanddetails.com/india/History/sub7_1b/entry-4108.html (accessed March 9, 2023).

Fernandes, D.M. et al., 'The Spread of Steppe and Iranian-Related Ancestry in the Islands of the Western Mediterranean'. *Nature Ecology & Evolution* 4, no. 3 (March 2020): 334–45.

Freemon, F.R. 'Bubonic Plague in the Book of Samuel'. *Journal of the Royal Society Medicine* 98, no. 9 (September 2005): 436.

Freewalt, Jason. 'Justinian and China: Connections between the Byzantine Empire and China during the Reign of Justinian I'. Academia.edu.

Garnsey, Peter, Richard Saller, Jaś Elsner, Martin Goodman, Richard Gordon, Greg Woolf and Marguerite Hirt. *The Roman Empire: Economy, Society and Culture*. Second ed. University of California Press, 2015.

Geggel, Laura. 'The Weird Reason Roman Emperors Were Assassinated'. livescience.com, December 4, 2021.

GenomeWeb. 'Ancient DNA Points to Plague, Typhoid Pathogens on Greek Island during Bronze Age Transition Period'. 2022, https://www.genomeweb.com/sequencing/ancient-dna-points-plague-typhoid-pathogens-greek-island-during-bronze-age-transition (accessed March 9, 2023).

Ghose, Tia. '200-Year-Long Drought May Have Killed Sumerian Language'. NBC News, December 4, 2012, https://www.nbcnews.com/id/wbna50073177 (accessed March 9, 2023).

Gibbons, Ann. 'The Greeks Really Do Have Near-Mythical Origins, Ancient DNA Reveals'. *Science*, August 2, 2017.

Gibbons, Ann. 'Thousands of Horsemen May Have Swept into Bronze Age Europe, Transforming the Local Population'. *Science*, February 21, 2017, https://www.science.org/content/article/thousands-horsemen-may-have-swept-bronze-age-europe-transforming-local-population (accessed March 9, 2023).

Global Security.org. 'Hurrian - 2400 BC - 1200 BC. Hurrian - 2400 BC - 1200 BC', https://www.globalsecurity.org/military/world/europe/tu-history-hurria.htm (accessed March 9, 2023).

Goldberg, Amy, Torsten Günther, Noah A. Rosenberg and Mattias Jakobsson, 'Familial Migration of the Neolithic Contrasts Massive Male Migration During Bronze Age in Europe Inferred from Ancient X Chromosomes'. bioRxiv,

September 30, 2016, doi: http://dx.doi.org/10.1101/078360 (accessed March 9, 2023).

Grammatikakis, I.E. 'The Woman in Minoic Crete'. *Journal of Maternal-Fetal and Neonatal Medicine* 24, no. 7 (July 2011): 968–72.

Haak, W., Lazaridis, I., Patterson, N. et al. 'Massive Migration from the Steppe Was a Source for Indo-European languages in Europe'. *Nature* 522, 207–211 (2015). https://doi.org/10.1038/nature14317

HAAW Workplace. 'Gunpowder: Origins in the East'. https://www.brown.edu/Departments/Joukowsky_Institute/courses/13things/7687.html (accessed March 9, 2023).

Haber, Marc et al., 'A Genetic History of the Near East from an aDNA Time Course Sampling Eight Points in the Past 4,000 Years'. *American Journal of Human Genetics* 107, no.1 (2020): 149–57.

Hakenbeck, Susanne E., and Ulf Büntgen. 'The Role of Drought during the Hunnic Incursions into Central-East Europe in the 4th and 5th c. CE'. *Journal of Roman Archaeology* 35, no. 2 (2022): 1–21.

Handwerk, Brian. 'Rare Ancient DNA Provides Window into a 5,000-Year-Old South Asian Civilization'. *Smithsonian Magazine*, September 5, 2019. https://www.smithsonianmag.com/science-nature/rare-ancient-dna-south-asia-reveals-complexities-little-known-civilization-180973053/ (accessed March 9, 2023).

Hassan, Fekri. 'Climate Change and Our Common Future: A Historical Perspective'. UN Chronicle. Accessed December 21, 2022. https://www.un.org/en/chronicle/article/climate-change-and-our-common-future-historical-perspective (accessed March 9, 2023).

Haw, Stephen. 'The Mongol Empire: The First "Gunpowder Empire"?' *Journal of the Royal Asiatic Society*, 23, no. 3 (August 2013): 441–69, https://doi.org/10.1017/S1356186313000369 (accessed March 9, 2023).

Hill, Bryan, 'The Rise and Fall of Sumer and Akkad. Ancient Origins Reconstructing the Story of Humanity's Past'. 2020. https://www.ancient-origins.net/ancient-places-asia/rise-and-fall-sumer-and-akkad-003192 (accessed March 9, 2023).

Hindustan Times. 'Who Are the Gujjars?' June 3, 2007.

Huzaifa, Abu. 'Monastery of Bahira the Monk'. Islamic Landmarks.com, https://www.islamiclandmarks.com/monastery-of-bahira-the-monk/ (accessed March 9, 2023).

Indian Saga Info. 'Huns and Other Tribes'. http://indiansaga.com/history/post_gupta.html (accessed March 9, 2023).

Ismaili.Net. 'Pre-Islamic Conditions'. https://www.ismaili.net/histoire/history03/history304.html (accessed March 9, 2023).

Ivy Panda. 'Effect of Gunpowder on the Mongolian Invasion of the Europe before 1850 Term Paper'. https://ivypanda.com/essays/effect-of-gunpowder-on-the-mongolian-invasion-of-the-europe-before-1850/ (accessed March 9, 2023).

Jackson, Eleanor. 'Ancient Greek and Egyptian Interactions'. OUPblog, 2016, https://blog.oup.com/2016/04/greek-egyptian-interactions-literature/ (accessed March 9, 2023).

Jones, Evan Jeffery. 'Long Distance Trade and the Parthian Empire: Reclaiming Parthian Agency from an Orientalist Historiography'. *WWU Graduate School Collection*, 2018.

Khalil, R., A.A. Moustafa, M.Z. Moftah and A.A. Karim. 'How Knowledge of Ancient Egyptian Women Can Influence

Today's Gender Role: Does History Matter in Gender Psychology?' *Frontiers in Psychology* 7 (2017).

King, Anthony, 'How Did the Plague Reshape Bronze Age Europe?' *Horizon: The EU Research & Innovation Magazine*, December 3, 2019, https://ec.europa.eu/research-and-innovation/en/horizon-magazine/how-did-plague-reshape-bronze-age-europe (accessed March 9, 2023).

Koy, Michael. 'Egyptian Influence on Ancient Greece'. Medium, 2021, https://medium.com/the-history-inquiry/egyptian-influence-on-ancient-greece-289bf985d3c (accessed March 9, 2023).

Lazaridis, I. et al., 'Genetic Origins of the Minoans and Mycenaeans'. *Nature* 548, no. 7666 (August 10, 2017): 214–18.

Li, Tianze. 'Sasanian's Role in the Trading Network of the Silk Roads: An Insight into the Coins Found along the Silk Roads'. *Frontiers of Society, Science and Technology* 3, no. 2 (n.d.), https://francis-press.com/uploads/papers/IR4ZBfsLvCOQcjvaIFalqRrBK6kbBCNCwLeNyzf8.pdf (accessed March 9, 2023).

Liritzis, Loannis. 'The Ancient DNA of the N.E. Mediterranean/Euro-Asian Cultures and the Position of the Mycenaean Greeks among the First Cultures'. PEASA, August 29, 2022. https://www.peasa.eu/ancient-dna-of-the-mediterranean-euro-asian-cultures/ (accessed March 9, 2023).

LiveScience. 'The Worst Epidemics and Pandemics in History'. 2022, https://www.livescience.com/worst-epidemics-and-pandemics-in-history.html (accessed March 9, 2023).

London Buddhist Vihara. 'Pre Buddhist Indian Society'. https://www.londonbuddhistvihara.org/teachings/pre-buddhist-indian-history/.

Lynch, Joseph H. *The Greek and Roman Context of Early Christianity*. *Early Christianity: A Brief History*. New York: Oxford University Press, 2010.

M, Monalisa. 'Rise of Christianity with Fall of Roman Empire'. Political Science, https://www.politicalsciencenotes.com/medieval-political-thought/rise-of-christianity-with-fall-of-roman-empire/1049 (accessed March 9, 2023).

Mark, Joshua J. 'Aristotle'. World History, May 22, 2019, https://www.worldhistory.org/aristotle/ (accessed March 9, 2023).

Mark, Joshua J. 'The Crisis of the Third Century'. World History, November 9, 2017, https://www.worldhistory.org/Crisis_of_the_Third_Century/ (accessed March 9, 2023).

Maróti, Zoltán, et al., 'The Genetic Origin of Huns, Avars, and Conquering Hungarians'. *Current Biology* 32, no. 13 (July 11, 2022), https://www.sciencedirect.com/science/article/pii/S0960982222007321 (accessed March 9, 2023).

McBride, Richard D. 'Making and Remaking Silla Origins'. *Journal of the American Oriental Society* 140 (2021): 531–48. https://doi.org/10.7817/jameroriesoci.140.3.0531.

McCormick, Michael. 'Climate Change during and after the Roman Empire: Reconstructing the Past from Scientific and Historical Evidence'. *Journal of Interdisciplinary History*, Autumn (2012): 169–220.

McGiffert, Arthur Cushman. 'The Influence of Christianity upon the Roman Empire'. *Harvard Theological Review* 2, no. 1 (1909): 28–49, http://www.jstor.org/stable/1507353 (accessed March 9, 2023).

Medievalists.net. "Genghis Khan Died of the Plague, Researchers Suggest." Accessed December 21, 2022. https://www.

medievalists.net/2021/12/genghis-khan-died-plague/ (accessed March 9, 2023).

Mishra, Ravi K. 'The 'Silk Road: Historical Perspectives and Modern Constructions'. *Indian Historical Review* 47, no. 1 (June 26, 2020), https://journals.sagepub.com/doi/full/10.1177/0376983620922431 (accessed March 9, 2023).

Modi, Jivanji Jamshedji. *The Early History of the Huns and Their Inroads in India and Persia.* Times Press, 2014.

Mortlock, Stephen. 'The Ten Plagues of Egypt'. *BioMedical Scientist*, 2019. https://thebiomedicalscientist.net/science/ten-plagues-egypt (accessed March 9, 2023).

N.S., Gill. 'Parthians and the Silk Trade'. ThoughtCo. January 4, 2020, https://www.thoughtco.com/parthians-intermediaries-china-rome-silk-trade-117682 (accessed March 9, 2023).

Nagle, John, and Mary-Alice C. Clancy. *Conclusion: The Narcissism of Minor Differences? Shared Society or Benign Apartheid?* First edition, Palgrave Macmillan London, 2010.

New Zealand Foreign Affairs and Trade, 'The Importance of the Suez Canal to Global Trade'. April 18, 2021, https://www.mfat.govt.nz/en/trade/mfat-market-reports/market-reports-africa/the-importance-of-the-suez-canal-to-global-trade-18-april-2021/ (accessed March 9, 2023).

Niazi, Amjad Daoud. 'Plague Epidemic in Sumerian Empire, Mesopotamia'. *The Iraqi Post Graduate Medical Journal* 31, no. 3, https://www.iasj.net/iasj/download/8a1dcc441979a3f0 (accessed March 9, 2023).

Norrie, Philip. 'How Disease Affected the End of the Bronze Age'. PubMed Central, 2016. https://doi.org/10.1007/978-3-319-28937-3_5 (accessed March 9, 2023).

Olsen, Barbara A. 'Women, Children and the Family in the Late Aegean Bronze Age: Differences in Minoan and

Mycenaean Constructions of Gender'. *World Archaeology* 29, no. 3 (1998): 380–92. http://www.jstor.org/stable/125037 (accessed March 9, 2023).

Olsen, Barbara. *Women in Mycenaean Greece*. First edition. Taylor and Francis, 2014. https://www.perlego.com/book/1664422/women-in-mycenaean-greece-the-linear-b-tablets-from-pylos-and-knossos-pdf. (accessed March 9, 2023).

Orton, Kyle. 'How Many Christians Were There in the Roman Empire?' Kyle Orton's Blog, June 11, 2021. https://kyleorton.co.uk/2021/06/11/how-many-christians-were-there-in-the-roman-empire/ (accessed March 9, 2023).

Pfeiffer, Stephan. 'Egypt and Greece Before Alexander'. *UCLA Encyclopedia of Egyptology* 1, no. 1 (2013), https://escholarship.org/uc/item/833528zm (accessed March 9, 2023).

Phys.Org. 'Drought Encouraged Attila's Huns to Attack the Roman Empire, Tree Rings Suggest'. December 15, 2022, https://phys.org/news/2022-12-drought-attila-huns-roman-empire.html (accessed March 9, 2023).

Qing, Yan, Zhongshi Zhang, Huijun Wang and Dabang Jiang. 'Simulated Warm Periods of Climate over China during the Last Two Millennia: The Sui-Tang Warm Period versus the Song-Yuan Warm Period'. *AGU*, February 19, 2015. https://agupubs.onlinelibrary.wiley.com/doi/full/10.1002/2014JD022941 (accessed March 9, 2023).

Quran Reading. 'Some Major Events from the Prophet's (PBUH) Life (After Revelation)'. 2022. http://www.quranreading.com/blog/some-major-events-from-the-prophets-pbuh-life-after-revelation/ (accessed March 9, 2023).

Razwy, Sayyid Ali Asghar. 'Arabia before Islam'. Al-Islam.org, https://www.al-islam.org/restatement-history-islam-and-muslims-sayyid-ali-asghar-razwy/arabia-islam (accessed March 9, 2023).

Retief, F.P., and L. Cilliers. 'Causes of Death among the Caesars (27 BC–AD 476)'. *Acta Theologica* 26, no. 2 (2006): Supplementum 7.

Rezakhani, Khodadad. 'The Land of Iran and Early Civilisations'. Iranologie, https://iranologie.com/the-history-page/the-land-of-iran-and-early-civilisations (accessed March 9, 2023).

Rincon, Paul, 'Hun Migrations "Linked to Deadly Justinian Plague"'. BBC News, May 10, 2018, https://www.bbc.com/news/science-environment-44046031 (accessed March 9, 2023).

Rodrigues, Tensing Carlos. 'The Mesopotamian Connection'. figshare, July 21, 2019. doi:10.6084/m9.figshare.8970314.v2 (accessed March 9, 2023).

Savelyev, Alexander, and Choongwon Jeong. 'Early Nomads of the Eastern Steppe and Their Tentative Connections in the West'. *Evolutionary Human Sciences* 2 (2020), e20. doi:10.1017/ehs.2020.18 (accessed March 9, 2023).

Saltré, Frédérik and Corey J.A. Bradshaw. 'Climate Explained: What Was the Medieval Warm Period?' The Conversation, April 20, 2021, https://theconversation.com/climate-explained-what-was-the-medieval-warm-period-155294 (accessed March 9, 2023).

Sandoiu, Ana, 'Bubonic Plague 1,000 Years Older than Previously Thought'. Medical News Today, June 11, 2018, https://www.medicalnewstoday.com/articles/322102 (accessed March 9, 2023).

Saupe, Tina. 'Ancient Genomes Reveal Structural Shifts after the Arrival of Steppe-Related Ancestry in the Italian Peninsula'. *Current Biology* 31, no. 12 (June 21, 2021): P2576–2591. E12, https://doi.org/10.1016/j.cub.2021.04.022 (accessed March 9, 2023).

Schmidt, Ryan. 'Unravelling the Population History of the Xiongnu to Explain Molecular and Archaeological Models of Prehistoric Mongolia'. Montana, US: University of Montana, 2012.

Science News Explores, 'The Earliest Evidence of Plague', 2015. https://www.snexplores.org/article/earliest-evidence-plague (accessed March 9, 2023).

Scorrano, G., et al., 'The Genetic and Cultural Impact of the Steppe Migration into Europe'. *Annals of Human Biology* 48, no.3 (May 2021 May): 223–33.

Self Study History. 'The Factors That Played an Important Role In the Process of Urbanization After the Late Vedic Period'. February 2, 2021.

Semple, Ellen Churchill. 'The Ancient Piedmont Route of Northern Mesopotamia'. *Geographical Review* 8, no. 3 (1919): 153–79. https://doi.org/10.2307/207405 (accessed March 9, 2023).

Singh Bal, Hartosh. 'After the Harappans, Large Influx Brought Steppe DNA into South Asia: Geneticist Vagheesh Narasimhan'. *Caravan*, November 22, 2019. https://caravanmagazine. in/science/after-harappans-influx-steppe-dna-south-asia-vagheesh-narasimhan (accessed March 9, 2023).

Singley, Richard Lawson. 'The Origins of Greece: Minoan, Mycenaean and Egyptian Influence'. *Medium*, 2020. https://medium.com/swlh/the-origins-of-greece-minoan-mycenaean-and-egyptian-influence-5b256e5baf50 (accessed March 9, 2023).

Slawson, Larry. 'Greek Influence on the Roman Empire'. Owlcation, January 2, 2023, https://owlcation.com/humanities/Greek-Influence-on-Rome (accessed March 9, 2023).

Smith, Kiona N. '4,000-Year-Old Genomes Point to Origins of Bubonic Plague'. *Ars Technica*, 2018, https://arstechnica.com/science/2018/06/4000-year-old-genomes-point-to-origins-of-bubonic-plague/ (accessed March 9, 2023).

Sommer, Bec. 'An Analysis of Minoan and Mycenaean Gender Representations'. Academia, April 12, 2018, https://www.academia.edu/37191961/An_Analysis_of_Minoan_and_Mycenaean_Gender_Representations (accessed March 9, 2023).

South China Morning Post. 'Climate Link to Fall of Tang Dynasty Questioned', November 30, 2007, https://www.scmp.com/article/617611/climate-link-fall-tang-dynasty-questioned (accessed March 9, 2023).

Shinder, Vasat, et al. 'An Ancient Harappan Genome Lacks Ancestry from Steppe Pastoralists or Iranian Farmers. An Ancient Harappan Genome Lacks Ancestry from Steppe Pastoralists or Iranian Farmers'. *ScienceDirect* 179, no. 3 (October 17, 2019): P729–735.E10, https://doi.org/10.1016/j.cell.2019.08.048 (accessed March 9, 2023).

Spyrou, Maria A. et al. 'Analysis of 3800-Year-Old *Yersinia Pestis* Genomes Suggests Bronze Age Origin for Bubonic Plague'. *Nature Communications* 9, no. 1 (2018).

Stark, Rodney. *The Rise of Christianity: How the Obscure, Marginal Jesus Movement Became the Dominant Religious Force in the Western World in a Few Centuries.* Harper San Francisco, 1997.

Starr, Michelle. 'Extinct Pathogens Ushered the Fall of Ancient Civilizations, Scientists Say'. *ScienceAlert*, August 6, 2022.

https://www.sciencealert.com/thousands-of-years-ago-plague-may-have-helped-the-decline-of-an-ancient-civilization (accessed March 9, 2023).

Su, Y., L. Liu, X.Q. Fang and Y.N. Ma. *The Relationship between Climate Change and Wars Waged between Nomadic and Farming Groups from the Western Han Dynasty to the Tang Dynasty Period*. Copernicus Publications, January 29, 2016.

The Archaeologist, 'Mycenaean Warriors in the Egyptian Army of 18th Dynasty?' July 8, 2022. https://www.thearchaeologist. org/blog/x4z1qi7hp27q8mjvo74cbzz9uc8irm (accessed March 9, 2023).

Thakur, Pallavi. 'Status of Women in Ancient Egypt and Vedic India: Dependent or Independent of Gender Norms'. *Palarch's Journal of Archaeology of Egypt/Egyptology* 18, no. 7, 3535–44.

Thapar, Romila. 'The Epic of the Bharatas'. India-seminar.com, https://www.india-seminar.com/2010/608/608_romila_ thapar.htm (accessed March 9, 2023).

Thapar, Romila. 'War in the 'Mahabharata'. *PMLA* 124, no. 5 (2009): 1830–33, http://www.jstor.org/stable/25614409 (accessed March 9, 2023).

Thea, Baldrick, 'Could Akhenaten's Monotheism Have Been Due to the Plague in Egypt?' The Collector, March 8, 2022, https://www.thecollector.com/akhenaten-monotheism-plague-egypt/ (accessed March 9, 2023).

The Palace Museum. 'Across the Silk Road: Gupta Sculptures and Their Chinese Counterparts during 400-700 CE'. September 28, 2016. https://en.dpm.org.cn/exhibitions/ current/2016-03-28/2404.html (accessed March 9, 2023).

Tsonis, A.A., K.L. Swanson, G. Sugihara and P.A. Tsonis. 'Climate Change and the Demise of Minoan Civilization',

Climate of the Past 6, no. 4 (2010): 525–30, https://doi. org/10.5194/cp-6-525-2010 (accessed March 9, 2023).

UW Departments. 'The Ming Dynasty'. https://depts. washington.edu/silkroad/exhibit/ming/essay.html (accessed March 9, 2023).

UShistory.Org. 'Women of Ancient Egypt', https://www. ushistory.org/civ/3f.asp (accessed March 9, 2023).

Vishnoi, Anubhuti. 'Indus Valley Civilisation Is Largest Source of Ancestry for South Asians: David Reich'. *Economic Times*, n.d. https://economictimes.indiatimes.com/news/politics-and-nation/indus-valley-civilisation-is-largest-source-of-ancestry-for-south-asians/articleshow/71042072.cms (accessed March 9, 2023).

Vymazalová, Hava and Miroslav Bárta (eds). 'Beetles and the Decline of the Old Kingdom: Climate Change in Ancient Egypt'. In *Chronology and Archaeology in Ancient Egypt (The Third Millennium B.C.)*, pp. 214–22. Prague: Czech Institute of Egyptology, Faculty of Arts, Charles University, 2008.

Watts, Edward. 'What Rome Learned from the Deadly Antonine Plague of 165 A.D'. *Smithsonian Magazine*, April 28, 2020, https://www.smithsonianmag.com/history/what-rome-learned-deadly-antonine-plague-165-d-180974758/ (accessed March 9, 2023).

Waxman, Olivia B. 'Did the 10 Plagues of Egypt Really Happen? Here Are 3 Theories'. *Time Magazine*, April 13, 2022, https://time.com/5561441/passover-10-plagues-real-history/ (accessed March 9, 2023).

Welc, Fabian, and Marks, Leszek. 'Climate Change at the End of the Old Kingdom in Egypt around 4200 BP: New Geoarcheological Evidence'. *Quaternary International* 324 (2014): 124–33. 10.1016/j.quaint.2013.07.035 (accessed March 9, 2023).

Whitfield, John, 'Did Plague Start Between the Pyramids?' Science, February 13, 2004, https://www.science.org/content/article/did-plague-start-between-pyramids (accessed March 9, 2023).

Williams IV, Dan. 'Christianity in The Roman Empire'. October 2020, https://www.researchgate.net/publication/344728292_Christianity_In_The_Roman_Empire (accessed March 9, 2023).

Wilson, Paul. *The Kushans and the Emergence of the Early Silk Roads*. Australia: University of Sydney, Faculty of Arts and Social Sciences, 2020.

Witty Chimp. 'From Janas to Mahajanapadas: Questions and Answers'. September 2020, https://www.wittychimp.com/from-janas-to-mahajanapadas-questions-answers-2/ (accessed March 9, 2023).

Wolfgang, Haak, et al., 'Massive Migration from the Steppe Was a Source for Indo-European Languages in Europe'. *Nature* 522, no. 7555 (June 11, 2015): 207–11.

Xumeng, Sun. *Identifying the Huns and the Xiongnu (or Not): Multi-Faceted Implications and Difficulties*. PRISM: University of Calgary's Digital Repository, September 14, 2020.

Yirka, Bob. 'Genetic Analysis of Neolithic People from Mesopotamia Shows Blend of Demographics'. Phys.Org, https://phys.org/news/2022-11-genetic-analysis-neolithic-people-mesopotamia.html (accessed March 9, 2023).

Zeimal, E.V. 'The Kidarite Kingdom in Central Asia. History of Civilizations of Central Asia, v. 3: The Crossroads of Civilizations, A.D. 250 to 750', vol. 3. UNESCO Publishing, n.d.